Arthur Giles

Across Western Waves and Home in a Royal Capital

Arthur Giles

Across Western Waves and Home in a Royal Capital

ISBN/EAN: 9783744693035

Printed in Europe, USA, Canada, Australia, Japan

Cover: Foto ©Andreas Hilbeck / pixelio.de

More available books at **www.hansebooks.com**

ACROSS WESTERN WAVES

AND

HOME IN A ROYAL CAPITAL

AMERICA FOR MODERN ATHENIANS
MODERN ATHENS FOR AMERICANS
A PERSONAL NARRATIVE
IN TOUR AND TIME

BY

ARTHUR GILES
F.R.S.G.S.

WITH ILLUSTRATIONS

LONDON:
SIMPKIN, MARSHALL, HAMILTON, KENT & CO., LTD.

TO

MY FRIENDS

WHO KNOW MY JOURNEYINGS

AND TO ANY WHO CARE TO DO SO

I INSCRIBE THIS

IN

A JUBILEE YEAR

MAY 13, 1848.

*THROUGH EACH PERPLEXING PATH OF LIFE
OUR WANDERING FOOTSTEPS GUIDE;
GIVE US EACH DAY OUR DAILY BREAD,
AND RAIMENT FIT PROVIDE.*

*O SPREAD THY COVERING WINGS AROUND
TILL ALL OUR WANDERINGS CEASE,
AND AT OUR FATHER'S LOVED ABODE
OUR SOULS ARRIVE IN PEACE.*

MAY 13, 1898.

PREFACE.

THESE glimpses of a vast continent were written for my friends, and have been printed at the request of some who desire to know where I went, and how I was received; what I thought, heard, and saw; and how I liked our trans-Atlantic cousins.

But I hope readers will recognise in the lines a grateful mind desiring to express in tangible form its retrospective gladness, and suggesting the charm and power of Christian union throughout the world when hearts are strung in unison. For such experience I would render unto the Bishops and the leaders of Christian faith, homage; to followers of St. Andrew, under whatever name, brotherly love; to a sister Order, the Daughters of the King, and all ladies, who are the light of homes that are as stars to journeying souls, respectful obeisance; and to everyone, honour.

The appended sections, that touch on home scenes, citizens, and events, are after-thoughts that the narration of pleasant travels in an un-

PREFACE.

familiar country have naturally suggested, traversed as life's journey is through an unknown future from the remembered past.

As I express my gratitude to friends under Columbian skies, I would now add that towards those in whom under Caledonian cloud or sunshine I have been enriched with pleasant memories—very precious these jewelled days at home in the land of St. Andrew.

Nor may I omit the many within Anglian shores, or forget those across lesser waters, the sparkling recollections of whom are still bright amid the jewels of the day.

With chastened thoughts I have seen again a distant home, and traced anew the "grey metropolis of the north," both hallowed with the remembrance of those who have passed to
A BETTER COUNTRY.

*E*DINBURGH   *MDCCCXCVIII.*

CONTENTS.

	PAGE
A BIOGRAPHICAL SKETCH (from *Scottish Standard Bearer*)	1
I.—FROM BROTHERHOOD TO BROTHERHOOD	9
In the *Campania*—Nearing America	10-12
In New York Harbour—Brotherhood Headquarters	13-16
Church Missions House and Churches	18
New York—Brooklyn—Greater New York	19
On the Hudson—Albany—Buffalo	22-23
Niagara—Cleveland—Chicago	31-34
With the Founder of the Brotherhood—Chicago Local Council—About Chicago	35-38
By Night to Canada and Niagara again	39
Toronto—Canadian Brotherhood Headquarters	41-43
Canada in the Fall—Ottawa, the Canadian Capital	45-46
Kingston (Canada)—Through the Thousand Islands	50
Montreal and Quebec	51
Lake George—Lake Champlain—Saratoga—Troy	53-55
With the ex-American Consul	55
Baltimore—A Quiet Hour—The City of Washington	56-60
The Washington Convention—Loyal and Lingering	63-72
The Home of George Washington	74
Good-bye in Washington—Philadelphia	76
Local B.S.A. Assemblies—Philadelphia, Brooklyn, New York—Adieux	80-81
II.—TO THE MISSIONARY COUNCIL	83
Boston—Mount Auburn Cemetery—Cambridge	83-85
Brotherhood Men at Work	85
Hartford—Missionary Council—A Bishop's Blessing	86-91
About Hartford and Connecticut—New York again	92-95
III.—MY LOUISIANA HOME	97
Rejuvenescence—About the Civil War and Civilities	97-98
Interesting Fields	101
Dreamland and Sunnyland—Where the Heart led	103-107
New Orleans—Saturday Night	111
Sunday—Christ Church Cathedral, &c.	114
Fire and Fire Brigade—Old Times and New	119-121
Mardi Gras and "West End"	128
Round the Cemeteries—The Cities of the Dead	129-132
All Saints' Eve	134

CONTENTS.

	PAGE
IV.—HOMEWARD—THROUGH THE ELEMENTS	137
By Fire, Land-and-Water—In Air and Lightning	137-138
Cincinnati, Pittsburg, Harrisburg, to Atlantic	140-145
Aboard the *Lucania*	148
V.—UNVISITED STATES AND TERRITORIES	151
The Unvisited West—United States Cities	152-153
As from the Appalachian Chain	157
British Columbia—American Alaska	163-165
Klondyke and Canadian Cities	166
Awake with Twain in hand	176
"Bon Voyage!"	178
Home again in Royal Edinburgh	180
VI.—HOME IN A ROYAL CAPITAL.	185
A Panorama of the Past	194
The View from Princes Street Sixty Years ago (*A*)	194
A View of the New Town: Same Period (*B*)	200
View of Arthur's Seat and Holyrood (*C*)	212
Battle of Prestonpans	219
View of Edinburgh as seen from the North, 1837 (*D*)	221
View West End of Princes Street, 1837—St. John's (*E*)	223
Princes Street Past and Present	225
Princes Street Firms Fifty Years ago	226
George Street Past and Present	245
Queen Street and transverse streets	255
Terrace and Valley and Bank	264
The Scotsman—Literary Societies	282-287
Book Stores—Stationers, Printers, Monuments	290-324
Presbyterian Scotland	325
Archbishops visit the General Assembly	330
The Church Hymnary, 1898—One in Song and Sorrow	332-334
VII.—IN ANGLICAN CHRISTENDOM	335
The Anglican Scottish Church	335
The Scottish Sees—Trinity College	342-346
Influences External and Internal	348
Two Deans—The Brotherhood	350-352
Basis of Opinion Episcopal, &c.	355
The Daughters of the King—Banner of St. Andrew	358-361
VIII.—AUTUMN LEAVES	365

ILLUSTRATIONS.

	PAGE
The Capitol, Washington	*Frontispiece*
Portrait from *The Scottish Standard Bearer* . . .	1
The Church Congress, Norwich, 1895	6
First International Convention of the Brotherhood of St. Andrew, at Buffalo, 1897	8
Niagara Falls, American and Canadian	32
Parliament Buildings, Ottawa, Canada	48
Highland Piper, and List of Highland Clans . . .	52
Facsimile Signatures of the first American Bishops, &c.	88
State Capitol, Hartford, Connecticut, U.S.A. . . .	92
The Author's Parents (New Orleans, 1838) . . .	97
Canal Street, New Orleans, in 1894	104
Old St. Louis Cemetery, New Orleans, in 1894 . .	136
View of Edinburgh Castle and Old Town, 1838 (*A*) .	192
Scott Monument, and List of Statuettes thereon . .	202
View of New Town of Edinburgh in 1838 (*B*) . . .	208
View of Arthur's Seat, Holyrood, and Burns' Monument (*C*)	216
Battle of Prestonpans, 1745	220
View of Edinburgh from the North (*D*)	222
View of West End Princes Street and St. John's, 1837 (*E*)	224
St. Giles' Cathedral, Edinburgh, and restored City Cross	272
Edinburgh Castle and National Gallery, with Allan Ramsay's House, 1860	288
Linlithgow Palace and Queen Mary	288
Sir Walter Scott and 39 Castle Street	288
Councillor Robert Grant	304
Robert Grant, jun.	306
St. Cuthbert's Church, and List of Parishes . . .	328
St. Mary's Cathedral, Edinburgh	336
York Minster	368

ARTHUR GILES, F.R.S.G.S

A BIOGRAPHICAL SKETCH.

(Reprinted from " The Scottish Standard Bearer.")

ARTHUR GILES, the surviving partner of Robert Grant & Son, is a native of Edinburgh, though five years of his early boyhood were spent in America. He has been longer than any merchant now in Princes Street—this being his jubilee year in connection with the firm of Robert Grant & Son, which is one of the five extant that were doing business in this prominent street of the city in 1834. Messrs. Grant came from the old town, where their business was founded in 1804 by the senior Robert Grant, librarian, bookseller, stationer, and quill manufacturer.

Mr. Giles' grandfather (Arthur Giles) and father (James Park Giles) were burgesses in 1768 and 1807 respectively. They were hereditary Scottish Episcopalians. The grandfather was a vestryman of Old St. Paul's, and also (Non-juror though he was) Treasurer of one of the City Incorporations. He was a son-in-law of a follower of Prince Charlie, and was otherwise related to those who materially befriended his unfortunate adherents. His wife's grandfather was Captain James Park, shipowner, who brought the Chevalier de St. George from Holland, and safely lodged him in his house in Peterhead, where Earl Marischal and other noblemen visited him in private. He was the first Treasurer and Dean of Guild of Peterhead, and one of the officers in command of those ordained to guard the town in 1715.

The Parks, father and son, married Arbuthnots, the Buchan family of that name being related through the noble family in Kincardineshire to the illustrious house of Keith, Earl Marischal, three brothers having in 1560 enlisted under the sway of their kinsman. The father of these brothers was James Arbuthnot of Lentischie (1540). There are now only descendants of one brother, one of whose two sons was the progenitor of many Arbuthnots greatly distinguished as military, diplomatic, and Civil Service officers in various parts of the world. The other, to whom Mr. Giles traces his descent, was Alexander, who went to Denmark in 1589 with the fifth Earl Marischal to settle the marriage of James VI. and Anne of Denmark, and married Janet Stewart, the Queen's Maid of Honour. Other descendants were Bishop Arbuthnot (Killaloe), Abbot Arbuthnot (Ratisbon), Principal Arbuthnot (King's College). Also Dr. John Arbuthnot, physician to Queen Anne, and the friend of Addison, Pope, Swift, Bolingbroke, &c.

At the end of 1837 Mr. Giles' parents went to America, and landed at New Orleans. They found America then in an appalling monetary condition, and the Government grappling with a panic which had begun at New Orleans. Residence in an undeveloped country was unfavourable to a boy's future. There was rightness in the word from home, " not to be carried away with the multitude, but to adhere to your religious duties." After remaining five years in the United States the family returned home.

Mr. Giles' father died in 1848. The sudden event, coupled with early schooling disadvantages of life abroad, told on the son's prospects. Further educational plans were given up, while the death of a relative—an eminent civil engineer—cancelled his training for that profession. Councillor Grant, however, a friend of his father's, made a vacancy for him as an indentured apprentice. In four years, while still an apprentice, he was given a position above other assistants, and in five years later he was offered an interest in the business, becoming a partner in 1861. Mr. Grant, senior, died in 1856, and Mr. Grant, junior, in 1887, since which date Mr. Giles has carried on the business.

Mr. Giles is known for his interest in youth. In his apprenticeship days, he saw the advantage of a knowledge of shorthand, and formed classes of young men, whom he taught gratuitously, as a member of Pitman's Phonographic Society. This fostered a habit of serving those he could touch. While still in his teens, he was a regular Sunday school teacher, influencing the parents and neighbours in the area of his visits by the free circulation of popular religious magazines. When the Guild of St. Alban was formed in London, he offered in 1855 to help as a correspondent, and in the spirit of that guild worked in various ways. He next became secretary of a literary society, and organised in relation to it a Young Men's Christian Union for spiritual life and effort. Of this he was first president, and then secretary.

On the opening of the Young Men's Christian Institute in 1855, his active interest led to his election as general Honorary Secretary. By altering the constitution to that of the London Young Men's Christian Association, he eliminated unwise aggressive sections, and introduced other improvements.

At the same time he brought into touch with the Young Men's Christian Association all the Edinburgh Young Men's Literary and Fellowship Associations, and developed the society in Scotland, uniting the branches, linking them to the English ones, and opening correspondence with Continental and American Associations.

Of British Y.M.C.A. Conferences he was one of three originators who met at Chester in 1857, and co-operated with the Leeds Y.M.C.I. Of the Leeds Conference of 1858 Mr. Giles was joint secretary, and gave a subordinate aid at the London one in 1859. As delegate to British Conferences, and to general ones in England, Germany, and Switzerland, he made the personal acquaintance of the founders and leaders on this side of the Atlantic, as well as of many on the other. At the opening of a new building bought by the Young Men's Christian Association in 1859, he received a handsome testimonial—the Lord Provost presenting it.

Thus for thirty years Mr. Giles had known the religious activity of young men outside Church lines, and had long regretted the lack of it within the Church. When the Young Men's Friendly Society was formed in 1884, he therefore accepted the Secretaryship because the work had the *imprimatur* of the Church. As Central Secretary of the Y.M.F.S. for Scotland and a member of the English Central Council he studied the operations of the two societies, and observed that both required some sustaining active element apart from ordinary guild interest. He then learned about the Brotherhood of St. Andrew, and in 1890 introduced a knowledge of it into Scotland. In the following year he laid the idea before the Church, and the movement took form on St. Andrew's Day, 1891, after which inquiries came from England. Finding Scotland slow to understand it he turned his attention to England. At the time of the Birmingham Church Congress, 1893, he was able to interest several Church dignitaries, and in the autumn an English layman zealously took up the new organisation, and along with Mr. Giles made it widely known. The earlier chapters were formed under their directions, after a public meeting held at the Church House, Westminster, in December of that year.

Mr. Giles being thus publicly committed to the Brotherhood idea, felt it his duty to ascertain for himself its reality and position in the American Church. For this purpose he attended the Washington Convention of the Brotherhood in 1894, where he represented the English and Scottish chapters, and was accorded an enthusiastic welcome as a Scottish Churchman. Having in various ways met most of the American and some of the Canadian Bishops, as also a large number of the clergy, as a Brotherhood man, he was assured of the status and power of the Order, and on coming to England was able to speak with personal convictions of its value. In 1895 he was the appointed reader of a paper on the Brotherhood at the Church Congress, Norwich. This led to a provisional union of the English chapters, and

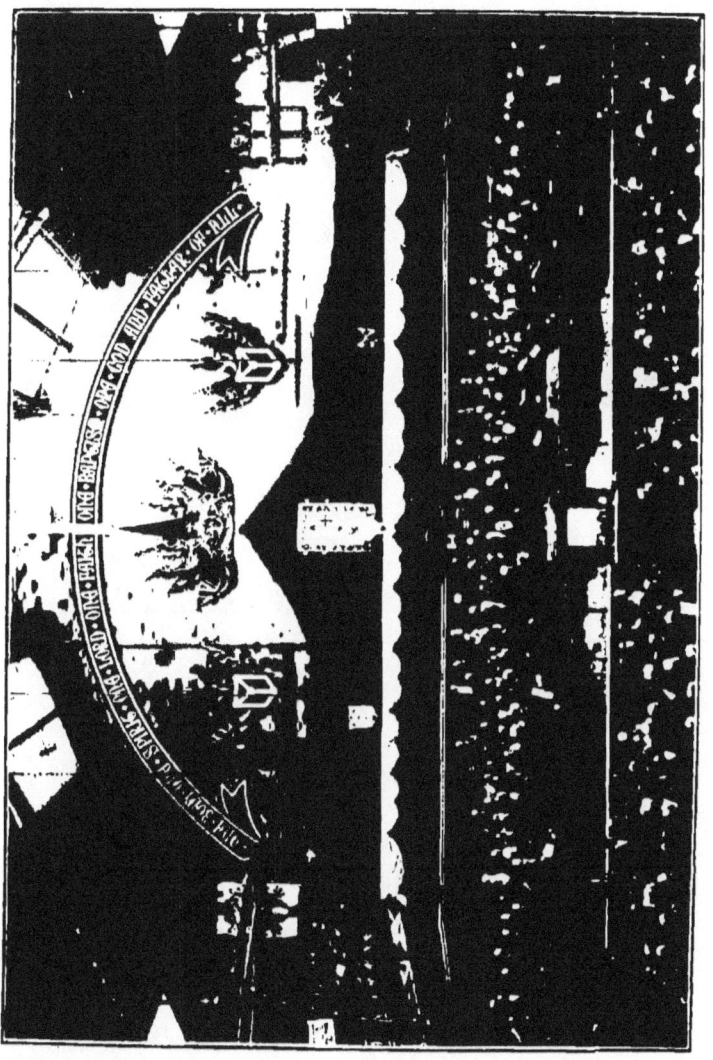

THE CHURCH CONGRESS, NORWICH, 1895

From a Photograph by Albert E. Coe, reproduced by his kind permission

to the election of a duly constituted English Brotherhood Council in June of last year, up to which time Mr. Giles acted in concert with others as provisional secretary. Of the Scottish Brotherhood he was secretary until the end of 1896, and is now vice-president. In other circles Mr. Giles is known as the proprietary editor of *The County Directory of Scotland*, an arduous compilation for which and for other purposes he was the inventor of a Chromatic Sortation Code, a system he patented in 1891.

THE Archbishop of York, speaking at a recent meeting of the Brotherhood of St. Andrew in England, said that the Brotherhood was to him the embodiment of a grand idea rather than the creation of any new machinery. He trusted that those present would aim at getting people to grasp and assimilate it with their Church life and work. The work of the Brotherhood was one of personal service and personal sacrifice. St. Andrew did not ask his brother to go, but said, "I will go and fetch him myself." The idea was not only noble, but very practical. It was, in fact, translating into action those words divinely taught, "Thy kingdom come."
—*Church Newspaper.*

Vide p. 29—Letter from the Archbishop of Canterbury to the International Convention, and cablegram from the Archbishop of York.

". . . The idea of the Brotherhood of St. Andrew is to induce men to follow the Apostle's example and try to bring their comrades and friends to choose the better part. It accepts the principle that every Christian man ought to be a missionary for Christ, not necessarily in outward demonstration in taking services, or open-air preaching, but in quiet, earnest influence on his brethren in the workshop, the fields, the counting-house. It is an American idea, and in the spiritual world perhaps one of the best things that crossed the Atlantic to our shores has been the Brotherhood of St. Andrew. It is not a fussy society; it does not want to sound its trumpet very loudly."—*Church Review.*

*From a Photograph by
Bliss Bros., Buffalo,
by kind permission of
" The Churchman,"
New York*

1. Bishop of Pittsburg
2. Bishop of Niagara
3. Bishop of Western New York
4. Lord Bishop of Rochester
5. James Houghteling *President*
6. Archbp. of Jamaica
7. Canon Gore, Westminster
8. Silas M'Bee, *Vice-President*

(Other Bishops under the respective States)

I.

FROM BROTHERHOOD TO BROTHERHOOD.

"YOU should go to Washington," said a member of the Brotherhood of St. Andrew as we wended our way homeward from a chapter meeting. For days my thoughts fluttered o'er the western waves, and my heart turned towards Washington, and on a summer-like September Sunday evening I bade my chapter good-bye in the beautiful Song School of the Cathedral. The prayer for a person going to sea from the American Prayer Book was added to the chapter office, and some who had thus commended me to the Almighty protection on the great deep, amid various dangers, came to witness my departure as delegate from the Brotherhood in Britain to the American and Canadian brethren. Other friends came also to do me service with specifics for averting, arresting, or sweetening the much-feared adversity, *mal-de-mer*, with kindly smiles like oil on troubled waters ahead.

I crossed the border for Liverpool on the

afternoon of Friday, the 7th September. Scotland's heather was purpler and bonnier than ever, and its burns and braes dearer than before. Between us "seas braid would roar" ere we should meet again, if ever. At Preston, towards evening, a Scottish Brotherhood man was waiting my passing through, and that night I was at Birkenhead, the guest of Mr. Clark, my English colleague in Brotherhood pioneering, and his hospitable wife.

IN THE CAMPANIA.

The *Campania* weighed anchor at sunset of Saturday the 8th, and by morning we were off Queenstown waiting for the mails. It was a lovely Sunday morning. I shall never forget it. All were on deck enjoying the sight of bird life in the bay. Here and there a boat was sailing in the sun, and there was much interest manifested in the arrival of passenger and mail boats —pigmies to our immense vessel. Time was precious. We steamed slowly off before the bags were all transferred, but the mail boat held fast until the last bag was delivered. Then we parted company. Our last words by letter or telegram for England, Scotland, and Ireland were steamed shorewards, and we made for the distant deep. We were soon at full speed passing Fastnet Light straight for the Atlantic.

The day continued fine, with quiet water around; conversation was general on board, and the Sunday was as restful as could well be. Without a service, for some technical reason, hymns with organ accompaniment somewhat supplied that lack.

We had on board Lord Brassey, now Governor of Victoria, and, of the Brotherhood, the Bishop of Wyoming* and five eminent American clergy, two of whom were my cabin fellows. The button soon made us friends; the Bishop, indeed, had learnt in England that I was to be on board, and I had travelled from Scotland with one of the clergy. Monday's sea made some horizontal passengers, and kept many on deck in uneasy chairs, but on Tuesday morning all were on their respective legs or in easy chairs, some in the quietude of the drawing-room, occasionally soothed by song to sleep, or in the yet quieter out of the world library and crescent writing-room, where the bugler intruded last. Five times a day, and in many parts of the ship, the bugle was heard. It sounded to rise, to breakfast, to luncheon, to dress and to dine, and as it divided the day to the passengers the ship bells divided the watch for the crew, and the captain determined the hour of noon for the whole ship. The passengers numbered 1364— being 375 saloon, 319 cabin, and 670 steerage.

* Now Bishop of Central Pennsylvania.

There would be a crew, all told, of 424. Mid-ocean was reached on Wednesday, and in five days we crossed the broad Atlantic, steaming 500 miles a day. Throughout the voyage an unclouded sun shone steadily on us from morn till night, and an effulgent moon from night till morn. Around us, visible even the night through, lay a measureless expanse of restless, but not rough, water, blue to a degree, answering below by day the lighter blue of sky above and around; and the phosphorescent or foam-dappled sea by night, vying with the all but cloudless starry heavens. Fore, by day and by night, we seemed making for some great goal in the wake of Columbus. Aft, we were leaving behind all that were dear to us, the far-stretching tape of foam marking the sea path over which we had steamed.

NEARING AMERICA.

As we neared America we became more earnest in our lookout for other vessels, and the captain's care of us against icebergs was indicated by the hourly registration of the temperature of the air and the water. Friday morning was a glorious one, and we felt sad that our pleasurable voyage was approaching its end. The sea was beautifully blue and smooth beyond description; neither ripple nor crease was visible for miles round. In the distance ahead smoke on the horizon was the evidence that the *Paris* from Southampton would reach port before us. The land grew larger and larger, and all were excited when a pilot appeared and came aboard. The news and newspapers he brought were circulated in every corner of the *Campania*, and we knew the worst and the best from home. The rattle of chains and the noise of blocks attendant on the great anchors and the freeing of the latter proved that we were entering the bay in earnest. The sun was setting in magnificent grandeur. Field-glasses were in full use ; now directed towards the sunset, now resting on the bay, both intertwined in the view. A huge figure appeared in front as we entered the Narrows. It was the colossal statue of Liberty —mighty and imposing—the " Eighth Wonder of the World," so called by De Lesseps, and soon after the far-famed Brooklyn Bridge came into view. These present the more striking features in the approach from the ocean.

IN NEW YORK HARBOUR.

We arrived in New York harbour on Friday evening. The night, pleasantly warm, I spent on deck till past eleven o'clock in converse with the Bishop, and on going ashore for a little I found that two of the Brotherhood had been waiting on the wharf for my appearance since nine o'clock. I was agreeably surprised to see them, one being a stranger who had met the other. It was not until the following morning that passengers could leave with luggage.

Truly the evening scene as we measured our way into the harbour, and slowly crept into the Cunard Company's wharf, was like fairyland. The night was clear and still, and moon and stars were shining at their best. Innumerable lights studded the view, some occupying effective heights, and the brilliantly lit large ferry-boats careered in their transit from point to point with great liveliness and precision, and gave kaleidoscopic variableness of form and colour, to which the *Campania* herself contributed in her stately search wharfwards for her berth. Nor would the picture be all on one side. The loveliness of the night had rivalled the brilliant and luxurious drawing-room to emptiness, and put an end to the evening promenade, for the ladies, no longer left to contemplate the serene tranquillity of the ocean, or bury their thoughts in the fiction of the courtly ship, were now like fish out of water, and the spectators on shore would witness a phalanx of mer-maids lining, if they could not be said to man, the length of the vessel's bulwarks, with head-wraps variously disposed, or hair left to its own girly expression of airy freedom in mermaid fashion.

There was much stir at breakfast on the 15th. Passengers with regret had to part company alike with each other as with their palatial floating edifice which had earned their faith in its sea-worthy framework and foundations. Its relation, however, with monarchy and democracy, and its muchness at sea betwixt both, had fused or confused our eastern and western minds; but having now touched the land of the statue and statutes of Liberty, we had to put aside our English ideas and think in American, with Americans talk and with them walk. We were now New Yorkers—some of us very new ones. Confronted with towering masonry and tall tenements, we had to rise to the occasion and bequit ourselves like large men, and be courteous, as Bædeker says, on a footing of equality, and so avoid any real impoliteness. How to act and what to do was laid down to me by an Edinburgh friend, Dr. Alex. Smith, Professor of Chemistry in the University, Chicago, who knew American ways. After a little instruction in how to get ashore and handle baggage so that one should see it again somewhere, I went with him to locate myself at the Continental Hotel, on Broadway, corner 21st Street, two blocks from Madison Square and the intersection of Broadway and Fifth Avenue (the chief street of wealth and fashion). I was then not far from the Brotherhood headquarters.

X

BROTHERHOOD HEADQUARTERS.

My first call I made under the escort of my friend, Professor Smith, at the Brotherhood headquarters, in Fourth Avenue. There I was at once identified by a coloured member, who told me the secretaries were expecting me upstairs, but the elevator saved climbing here as elsewhere in tall blocks. We were cordially received by the secretaries and other members of Council who happened to be in the office at the time. From that moment I was at home in the States, with many friends to instruct and guide me, particularly Mr. Wood and Mr. Montgomery. Brother Henry, one of those who met me at the ship-side, was assiduous in his attention and profuse in his hospitality. To a member of his chapter I was indebted for the Sunday piloting. At Trinity Church, Dr. Morgan Dix was good enough to express delight at seeing me in America in the interest of the Brotherhood, and looked forward to seeing me at Washington. He recalled his visit to Scotland in the year 1884, on the occasion of the Seabury Centenary, and his enjoyment of Edinburgh. At St. Agnes's Church, Dr. Bradley, with whom I had had long and profitable conversation on board, also cordially received me, introduced me to his father and other clergy, and showed me many kindnesses, taking me over the church buildings. The Brotherhood was strong in his parish, and in the vastness of the parochial buildings there was great scope for its extended usefulness and development. Here I met for the second time Mr. Silas M'Bee, Brotherhood Vice-President, who represented the far south; Mr. Johnson, who represented the extreme west; and Mr. Maynard, the secretary of the New York Assembly. After evening service at Grace Church, Broadway, I met quite a gathering of the Brotherhood from various chapters, and there I found a number well known to me by name, being, as the treasurer (Hon. J. P. Faure, Commissioner of Charities), who sat beside me, said, face to face with many I already knew in heart and was known by.

On the day following, Monday, I became the guest of Brother Henry, who took me to several church interiors, and pointed out many things of interest as far as Harlem. At the site of the Cathedral of St. John we lingered a time, and witnessed the operations that were going on around the foundation stone laid the previous year, where the central tower will likely rise. Grant's Tomb was another object of national interest not far from the Cathedral site, and there we saw the building of the great tomb proceeding—the structure having been since unveiled with imposing State ceremony.

CHURCH MISSIONS HOUSE AND CHURCHES.

The Church Missions House, where the Brotherhood has its headquarters, is the Central Administration building of the Church in the United States. There nearly all the general institutions of the Church have their central offices—Board of Missions and Women's Auxiliary Church Building Fund, the Parochial Mission Society, Church Temperance Society, Girls' Friendly Society, Church Parochial Club, Society for Promoting Christianity among the Jews, the American C.M.S., Daughters of the King, and the Brotherhood of St. Andrew. There also are located the secretaries of the House of Bishops and of the House of Deputies, and the custodian of the Standard Book of Common Prayer.

Trinity Church, a very handsome Gothic edifice, is in the busiest part of Broadway, opposite the beginning of Wall Street. It owns property to the value of at least a million sterling, which produces an annual income of a hundred thousand pounds, used in the support of eight subsidiary churches and numerous charities. In association with it every kind of parochial agency is at work. It is perhaps the richest corporation in New York, if not in America. St. Agnes' Church, which is one of the newest and handsomest in the city, and occupies a commanding position in Columbus Avenue, 92nd Street, is in relation to Trinity, and is governed by its corporation, although Dr. Bradley is practically the directing head of the whole, with perfect parochial machinery. Grace Church is situated in an ideal position in Broadway, just where there is a bend in the busy way. With the adjoining rectory, chantry and church house, it forms perhaps the most attractive group in New York. Zion and St. Timothy Church, which I was also much in, as "Brother Henry" had his office there as a lay helper of an ecclesiastical fraternity, is likewise one of the finest churches in the city, and occupies a splendid position, with a wealthy congregation devoted to good works. It is the union of an impoverished church owning a valuable site and a rich congregation with no building area which found its complement in the other. Other churches I visited I cannot here particularise, but wherever I was taken I had every kindness shown me in the descriptions given me of their leading features. There are 84 Episcopal churches in New York and 55 in Brooklyn.

NEW YORK—BROOKLYN—GREATER NEW YORK.

Two rainy days had to be dealt with as circumstances suggested. Much of the first was spent in Cook's Tourist Office learning the intricacies of railway lines far and near, also in the Exchange, where I was taken by a Brotherhood man I met in Wall Street, who noticed my button. My efforts to reach a chapter of coloured men were unavailing amidst an earnest down-pour of rain. Semi-invalided the second day, I wearily watched from the hotel window the usually busy Broadway all but deserted save by cable cars passing in rapid succession. A blue-skied fine day followed, which enabled me to mingle leisurely with the New Yorkers in their highways, elevated railways, and cars—cable and horse—in one of which I again met a Brotherhood man. The electric cars I had to know later on in Brooklyn. In the evening I was able to pay a surprise visit to Zion and St. Timothy Bible Class, where I was introduced by Brother Henry to the rector's assistant and a number of the Brotherhood. The rector was in England. All were most agreeable, and I said a few words.

New York (by which I do not mean Greater New York, including Brooklyn) is the largest and wealthiest city of the New World, and, among others, inferior only to London in commercial and financial importance. It is mainly an island, strange as it may seem to be so called, the Hudson River and the East River bounding it on the west and east sides, and the narrow Harlem River and a creek completing the circuit ; but its municipal limits lie beyond Harlem, and may be said to be 16 miles long, by 4¼ miles broad. The population was in 1890 1,515,301. There are many narrow and winding streets irregularly laid out at the lower or older part where business concentrates, and these have all along had names assigned ; the numbered streets begin several blocks up, and above 13th Street there is more chessboard regularity. Central Park is one of the finest in the world. It is 2½ miles long and half-a-mile wide. It cost three million pounds to transform it from a swamp and rocky tract. It contains 400 acres of groves, shrubberies, and glades, and 43 acres of ponds. There are 10 miles of drives, 6 of bridle-paths, and 30 miles of footpaths. Although the park is enclosed, and has twenty entrances, there are four concealed transverse roads passing under or over the drives by arches of masonry quite outside the park, although within its area.

Of museums and all sorts of buildings of public importance it would be endless to speak here, although it is necessary I should not pass unnoticed the Statue of Liberty, erected in 1886, on Bedloe Island, at the entrance to New York harbour, and which is the first outstanding object the eye catches on arrival in the bay. Its own height is 151 feet, to the torch top, its pedestal 150 feet high. Forty persons can stand on the head, which is reached by an inside stairway. The torch, lit by electricity, was as a star in the fairy scene I have attempted to describe on our arrival.

A stranger tourist of the later past would have considered Brooklyn a part of New York, separated as it was only by a bridge, but one of great magnitude and unique completeness for all kinds of vehicular as well as for pedestrian traffic. It is only now, however, at the end of 1897, that it is a part of New York included in the temporary term of Greater New York. This new district has until now been the fourth city of the United States in size and industrial interest, with 806,343 inhabitants in 1890. It is the "City of Churches," and the "Dormitory of New York," owing to so many city business men living there. It covers an area of 24 square miles, threaded with electric cars, and has five elevated railways within it, and three railway stations. The beautiful Prospect Park is the chief attraction for strangers. It has 550 acres, the lake being 60 acres in extent.

ON THE HUDSON TO ALBANY.

Rewarded with a fine Friday morning, I found my way to the Hudson River—the American Rhine. Its European sister I had seen, and I was not disappointed. Amid a varied panorama of hill and plain, town, village, and creek, I reached Albany (pop. 94,923), the capital of New York State, in the evening. Here 1 witnessed the American parliamentary ways, a State Convention happening to be sitting. There are many stately buildings in Albany, the Edinburgh of America, particularly the Capitol, the City Hall, and the Cathedral, which is the first regularly organised Anglican Cathedral in the United States, and promises to be one of the most beautiful. Its style is English Gothic.

Next morning I took the day express to Buffalo. Our engine was the celebrated "999" of the World's Exhibition, and said to be the fastest on record. I learnt this from a passenger who recognised the button, and gave me much American information. We traversed many cornfields and orchards, and I saw much of the country, but there were lengths of sameness. We also passed through several important towns and pleasant villages. Among others, Amsterdam, Utica, Rome, Syracuse, Geneva, Rochester, and Batavia, names more like the Eastern Hemisphere.

IN THE EXPRESS TO BUFFALO.

It was an experience to find our express steaming through city streets, although at reduced speed. The engine bells, rung while the trains approach crossings and traverse streets, are much like many church bells in Scotland. In this manner one sees many towns. I reached Buffalo at night, and tried Brotherhood ways by giving a card to a young man, who said he had not gone to a church in the city because he knew nobody belonging to any. The card was to be shown to any one wearing the button at the Cathedral or at any church. An inquiry in a car led to a conversation with another man who did not go to church, and knew nothing about any of them. He had thought of the subject, and found Christians had nothing to offer, although he admitted the other side had nothing either. I tried my best to drop better seed, which he seemed to appreciate. The next was Sunday morning. At the Cathedral porch I looked for my man but found him not; rain might have hindered him—let me hope he eventually implemented his promise. But many Brotherhood men came round me; some showed me the belfry where others were engaged chiming the tunes set for that day's service. The afternoon Chapter Bible Class had not resumed, but the hour was spent witnessing the re-organisation of the very large Sunday school which the rector told me about. My Buffalo correspondent was of another Chapter. We met at Washington. In the evening I obtained a first view of Canadian frontier, which is here to be seen across the river Niagara, a mile out of Buffalo. The International Bridge, built in 1873, at a cost of £300,000, crosses the same river a mile further on.

Buffalo is the third city in New York State, with a population estimated at 390,000, and is at the east end of Lake Erie, which is 290 miles long by 65 miles wide. It has some fine residence streets, imposing public buildings, and pleasant parks. The park system, almost a belt round the city, is very beautiful, there being almost 1000 acres of park land cultivated at an annual cost of £500,000. The principal business thoroughfares are wide, and also beautiful, and the residence streets are wide and shaded, being heavily fringed with luxuriant foliage, and the dwellings well back. The city has received the name of the "Bicyclist's Paradise," because of its miles of asphalt streets, more numerous than in any other city in the world.

Educationally, the city stands high. The University has opened its fifty-second year, and the city supports two large schools and about fifty grammar schools. In September of the present year 45,363 pupils were registered; the attendance increases 3000 a year. The Public Library, opened in September, circulates 2200 books daily, the membership is 20,000, and there are 90,000 volumes on its shelves. Literary, scientific, and art sections are located within it.

In 1797 there were only three white residents, and the city was only incorporated in 1832. Its population now annually increases 20,000. At present it is said to be the fourth commercial city in the world, a gigantic clearing-house between the Eastern and the Western States, growing with the priceless treasures of the West, and increasing in wealth and prosperity with the industries of the East. But the harnessing of Niagara's power has this year given a fresh and far-reaching impulse. To-day there are 150 miles of car lines, and all the cars, threading the area of 42 square miles, are operated by the electric power generated at Niagara, 27 miles distant; and, if I mistake not, the city is, or will soon be, electrically lit from the same source. It is as if Edinburgh were to be electrically lit, and its cars all propelled from the distance of the Falls of the Clyde (our little Scottish Niagara) with the body of water there thousandsfold increased, and the volume maintained through all time. Power is also conveyed from the mighty cataract to the Buffalo Railroad Company.

Twenty-nine railroad lines centre in the city, 450 miles of tracks being within its limit. The largest coal-distributing station in the world, with its mile of coal elevators 200 feet high, it is also the largest flour depot, sheep market, and horse market; 30,000 animals are handled daily. It has forty towering grain elevators of giant size, with a capacity for storage of 20,000,000 bushels. The seven months' season receipts of this year amounted to 200,000,000 bushels, the river of golden grain being almost continuous up and down the huge structures. The output of flour mills is nearly 1,500,000 barrels annually ; and altogether there are from 3000 to 4000 industrial establishments located in Buffalo, giving employment to 100,000 persons. The city water plant is valued at £2,700,000, and there the cheapest water rates in the United States prevail.

It has been suggested by Tesla, the apostle of Niagara power, that Buffalo and Niagara Falls City will one day stretch toward and join each other, and "form the greatest city in the world," the mightiest city on the globe—a great Niagara frontier in the centre of the American Continent. Nearly 6,000,000 cubic miles of water reach the gorge of the Niagara River, and, at a depth of 20 feet, plunge 165 feet over the Horseshoe crest, with a force equal to the latent power of all the coal mined in the world each day—*i.e.*, 7,000,000 horse-power.

Buffalo has 200 churches of all denominations, but St. Paul's perhaps excels all in architectural beauty. Built in 1850, it was made the Cathedral of the diocese of Western New York by the late lamented Bishop Cleveland Coxe. The spire, 268 feet high, was added about 1870. This church and city must now be memorable in the annals of the Brotherhood, alike at home as in America and the Colonies, and indeed wherever the Anglican Communion reaches.

On the afternoon of Wednesday, October 13, of this year (1897), the first International Convention of the Brotherhood met, and was begun in St. Paul's with "Quiet Hours," conducted by Canon Gore, of Westminster (England). The opening service on the following day, held in the same place, was also taken part in by him and by the lord Bishop of Rochester (England). On the Friday morning it was the scene of the corporate celebration of the Holy Communion, lasting from half-past six till nine, when about twelve hundred Brotherhood men communicated—the lord Bishop of Rochester being the celebrant, assisted by American, Canadian, and West Indian clergy.

In the Music Hall 1335 delegates met for conference and business for three days. There were represented the United States and Canada in large numbers, and also England, by the Bishop and Canon above mentioned, along with a Fellow of All Souls', Oxford; the West Indies, by the Archbishop; the Scottish Brotherhood, by a letter from its Council; Australia and New Zealand, by cablegram; the English Council, by a letter from its president, Mr. George A. Spottiswoode, vice-chairman of the House of Laymen; and a cablegram from Earl Nelson, vice-president of the English Brotherhood; and myself, as vice-president of the Scottish Brotherhood, by a cablegram, while deeply regretting my inability to be at the Convention. Ireland, China, and Japan were also represented, and there was a delegation of American Indians. 14,660 members in 1545 Chapters within the Anglican Communion were thus represented.

But perhaps the unofficial messages of the two English Primates were those that most delighted Brotherhood hearts.

The Archbishop of York sent a cablegram—

"Heart-felt good wishes and prayers."

The letter of the Archbishop of Canterbury was the news of the day, and "brought down the house." His Grace thus wrote :—

"LAMBETH PALACE, S.E., *August* 16, 1897.

"MY DEAR BISHOP OF ROCHESTER,—I was very glad to hear from you last February that you were going this autumn to the Convention of the Brotherhood of St. Andrew. I have been watching the proceedings of the Brotherhood with much interest for some time, and I am more and more inclined to believe that it will prove a very real and very great help to the Church as a body, and to many Christian souls. I do not think it wise to be hasty in recognising such Brotherhoods, and I have kept somewhat aloof that I might have some experience of their actions before I took any step which I should afterwards have to retrace. But their aim is unquestionably high; their methods are simple; there is no extravagance in their requirements or in their practice; their perseverance is steady; and I think they have now justified the position which they have assumed.

"I believe your presence among them will be a help to them, and your report of their proceedings when you return will be of great value to us. I shall be rejoiced if your visit to them, as bearing with you the hearty good will of a Bishop of the Church in England, may end in drawing them into closer relations with us, creating at once a clearer understanding and a warmer affection and respect from each towards the other.

"The Blessing of our Heavenly Father be with you.
"Yours faithfully,

"F. CANTUAR."

To myself the Bishop of Rochester was kind enough to write from Buffalo the day after the Convention:—

"I have given your remembrances to the leaders of the Brotherhood here.

"The Convention has been a wonderful one—most inspiriting; there seems to be a really great work doing, and in prospect, in the Brotherhood."

The proceedings continued over Sunday, when the Bishop of Albany preached the Convention sermon, and a mass meeting was held in the afternoon. Twenty Bishops took part in the proceedings, and a standing International Committee* was determined.

* Of this I am now a member.

NIAGARA.

Now near Niagara, I resolved to spend Monday there. An hour's rail brought me to Niagara city early in the day. Before doing the falls I ascended the elevator to view the surroundings from a height. Looking down on these amid so much matter of fact world, I could hardly realise what I had come four thousand miles to behold. The impression would have been the same had I seen the great river Niagara flowing from the clouds. Trollhättan falls, the European Niagara, I had seen, and I was not quite ready to give my Swedish waters a secondary place. When I descended from my elevated point of vision to true terrestrial relations, and reduced my mind's high ideal, I then discerned the beauties of the scenery, and drank in the magnificent grandeur and glory of the American cataract. My fancy roamed around it. The immensity of breadth and height and volume of the everlasting waters seemed an emblem to me of living unity. They had gathered drop by drop from above, and had grown into a form of overpowering force. In their flow they would permeate every nook and crevice. Their life in their unity had entered my soul. I lingered beside them, walked among them, stood shoulder to them, hid within them, heard their voices, encompassed them, and companioned with the round rainbow that dwells there as nowhere else. I duly did the falls, following the directions given me before I left home by a Scottish nobleman, and omitting nothing appertaining thereto, including Canadian and American descents in oilskins behind the huge water curtains and the attack in front on board the *Maid of the Mist* in storm costume. In crossing the Suspension Bridge from the Canadian side I met a distinguished lay-representative on his way to the Aberdeen Church Council, from which I was myself perforce a truant, being due in the same week in Washington. After a brief explanation how we had so met suspended in neutral space, we parted north and south to our respective engagements.

CLEVELAND.

Next day I was at Cleveland, where I found many buildings and monuments of great interest, and a splendid electric car service. Here I saw several of the Brotherhood, and returned a visit of the Rev. Mr. Mann, the deaf-mute pastor, who has twice called on me at home. On the journey a loquacious old negro, who could only find a standing at my seat, lectured me as if I were to be the next or a coming President. His topics were varied, Fred Douglas, the relations of the negroes, their wages and work, yellow

fever, the millennium, and the world's improvement when Christ comes, &c. My efforts to interpose remarks or correct his ideas were vain, but the passengers were much amused. Cleveland in 1830 had only a population of 1000. In 1890 it had 261,353, having increased 60 per cent. in the last decade. Its manufactures employ 50,000 hands, and are of the annual value of £21,100,000, while its iron and steel works are valued at £5,000,000. It is one of the chief ship-building cities. The streets are broad and well paved, with green lawns and squares and numerous trees, by which it has acquired the name of the "Forest City." Its chief business blocks are substantial, and the public buildings handsome. The Garfield Memorial, which cost £26,000, and is 165 feet high, is perhaps the most beautiful monument of the kind. It is in Lake View Cemetery, at the further end of Euclid Avenue, one of the extremely beautiful residence streets in America, with handsome houses surrounded by pleasant grounds and trees.

My first experience in a sleeper was in my continued journey to Chicago. With a lower berth, which gave me the advantage of the window, I turned the early morning hours to account in studying the character of the country. Lengthy freight trains and lines of streets indicated the arrival at our destination.

CHICAGO.

"Fixed" at a hotel in Dearborn Street, my wandering footsteps led me to the World's Exhibition grounds. Much remained to indicate the extent of the grounds and the disposition of several important buildings still standing intact or wrecked by recent incendiarism. Here I fell among thieves, from whose machinations, however, I adroitly escaped with life and purse, somewhat with the aid of my protecting button, a monitor to avoid even the appearance of evil. This incident might well have settled in me the wickedness of the place to the exclusion of every redeeming feature, but I endeavoured to read the ways of the world fairly. If I could detect badness I could also see much goodness, much to surprise and something to admire. That night I dreamt the dream of the button, that which had attracted me across the Atlantic, the study of the power of which I had declared at Inverness to be my last Church work on earth, was conceived in the city in which I now slept and in the street where I dreamt. But a few doors up were the first head-quarters, and James Houghteling, the banker, and founder of the Brotherhood, there pursued his vocation in Dearborn Street. That which brought me over the great deep through dangers had protected me. There was a God of Bethel, and He alone knew where my pillow was that night, far from home.

WITH THE FOUNDER OF THE BROTHERHOOD AND THE CHICAGO LOCAL COUNCIL.

I awoke to joy and gladness, and the day had not long passed ere Brother James Houghteling and I grasped each other's hand. I, who yesterday was at the mercy of miscreants, was to-day safe in the bond of Brotherhood, and securely surrounded by Christians from morn till night. Mr. Houghteling, who had that morning returned from a long holiday, laid letters aside to show me every kindness, and as I was not quite well, he was most thoughtful and considerate in what he proposed.

Fraternal attentions of all kinds were shown me, and I had an open sesame power at my command. Places, buildings, public, private, and wonderful, were explained and explored. I received a welcome from such numbers the freedom of the city itself could hardly have enhanced. In an hour or two I knew numerous leading and earnest men to whom the button had bound me, and great was my joy in meeting them. Mr. W. R. Stirling, of the well-known Perthshire family of Kippendavie, to whom I had an introduction, was among the first we called on. He recognised me at once in a truly brotherly manner. He is one of the original Brotherhood men, and is chairman of resolutions at all conventions, taking a leading part in the whole business of the Brotherhood. When in Scotland this year he met the Edinburgh Brotherhood men, and others of our Scottish clergy and laymen.

Mrs. Houghteling extended a very true and hearty welcome, the children even were happy to see me. They knew some live Scotchmen in Chicago, but I was the freshest from the Atlantic. For the time being I felt I was one of the Houghteling family, as I was indeed so in the Brotherhood. Bidding farewell to Mrs. Houghteling, and good-bye to the little ones, my fraternal host led me to the Local Council, where I recognised many I had already seen. There might be nearly forty present. All rose as we entered. The business proceeded, but was interrupted after a while to introduce me and to exchange addresses. The chairman, in whom I recognised a correspondent, gave me the greetings of the Local Council, and after I had addressed the meeting in reply, Mr. Houghteling spoke of my visit as no ordinary one, because of the unique relation of the American and Scottish Churches in their historical connection. Under these references I had again to speak. Mr. Houghteling had dwelt strongly on the circumstances although it had in no way been introduced into our conversation. It was evident that the subject was as much a matter of American Church History as anything else. Again and again throughout America had Bishops, clergy, and laymen spoken of it. Occasionally even in Canada there was a reference to the neighbouring Church's early Episcopate. It was of interest to the meeting to know that I had perhaps the only relic left of the "Upper Room" where their first Bishop was consecrated. It formed part of the altar rail of St. Andrew's Chapel in 1784. Since my visit fragments of it have found their way into the Seabury Museum, Minnesota, the pastoral staff of Delaware, and the Chapel of Sewanee University, Tennessee, the Bishops of the two first mentioned dioceses and Mr. M'Bee, now the Editor of *The New York Churchman*, having severally laid me under contribution. Upon our leaving all stood while the chairman bade me good-bye in their name. Mr. Houghteling then accompanied me to the station for the midnight express to Detroit on the borders of the States and Canada, and rendered me most important brotherly service in threading the way by car service in the great city, and in little, but invaluable, attentions. His kindness in driving me round in the early part of the day to various points I regard as one of the most pleasurable incidents of my tour. To find myself listening to plans being discussed at a Chicago meeting and regarded as interested in the question was sufficient to Americanise me, while the Seabury link self-constituted me, for the nonce, an American Churchman within the Catholic chain.

ABOUT CHICAGO.

Chicago is, as all the world knows, the second city in the United States, with a population, in 1890, of 1,099,850. It has a water front on Lake Michigan of 22 miles. Its streets are wide and straight, and its buildings in the business quarter so lofty as to be famous. To name the various public halls, art, educational, literary, and other institutes, municipal and commercial buildings, and state edifices, is to enumerate every kind of structure in any city except a Cathedral, although it has a Bishop. 600 students entered its University in 1892.

Its public parks, embracing 1795 acres, form a green band round the city, and afford a continuous drive of 37 miles. Lake Shore Drive, Michigan Boulevard, and Drexel Boulevard, are fine residence streets, with tasteful houses and ornamental gardens. I must not omit to mention the Pullman car works, which constitute a model little town of 11,000 inhabitants, there being five or six thousand operatives in the works. The famous stock yards had no interest for me. Instead, I paid a visit to the University, where my friend Professor Smith was, and I also left my card of introduction at the Bishop of Chicago's City rooms.

The trade of Chicago is second only to New York, and in 1892 was of 308 millions sterling value, its manufactures being 117 millions. 21,123 vessels entered or cleared Chicago in 1892, being 25 per cent. above New York. The Illinois Steel Co., of which Mr. W. R. Stirling, of the Brotherhood Council, was the vice-president, employs twelve thousand men, and the M'Cormick Company produces 120,000 harvesting machines annually. The many enormously tall edifices are really steel-framed buildings veneered with stone and brick, the lower ornamental walls being often filled in last. Their height is now limited to 150 feet. The rapid running elevators make the upper stories as accessible as the ground ones. I found it quite easy to have my hair cut twenty stories up without finding it standing on end. The airiness of the position was refreshing. Like New York, Chicago is not its own State capital, that being Springfield, Illinois, a town of only 25,000 inhabitants.

BY NIGHT TO CANADA AND NIAGARA AGAIN.

Travelling by night, I passed the town of

Michigan and other important places, on the north side of Lake Erie, in darkness. Detroit was reached in early morning. There I had a couple of hours which I spent to the best advantage in cars and around the central public buildings. Leaving Detroit the train of eight long cars was run on to a ferry-boat and so transported across the river. On the further shore its three portions were adroitly drawn up by the train engine, and I was on my way to Canada—Toronto being my first point there. I had, however, to sleep at Niagara Falls city. Late in the afternoon we were in sight of Niagara, travelling on the Canadian side. Very soon the train drew up at Falls View, and the passengers were allowed to leave the carriages for five minutes and feast eyes on the splendid sight obtained from that point. The trees are cut down to give an uninterrupted view. Further up we crossed to the States by the railway suspension bridge, and so round to the town of Niagara Falls. This afforded me an opportunity of revisiting the falls before dark. I loitered about Prospect Park till after nightfall, listening the while to the rush of waters with which I was now so familiar.

I was early up next morning, and before breakfast had been at the Niagara Co. Power House, a mile distant, and to the largest paper mill in the world, as I was told by one of the employees lately from Mid-Lothian. Another run down to the falls, and I was in the ten o'clock train for Toronto *via* Lake Ontario. The rail track lies on the American side of the river to the point of embarkation, and the rapids and whirlpool are seen far below the river cliffs. Having on the Monday been as far down the river on its north bank, I had now seen it and the falls from every point of view, and every height and depth. In crossing the lake the steamer loses sight of the shores, and occupies about three hours in the passage. The day was beautifully bright, and the lake calm and clear. The luxuriously upholstered cabin was deserted for the deck. Again my button led at once to a few hours' pleasant companionship on board with a friend of a Brotherhood man.

TORONTO.

Landing at Toronto on a Saturday afternoon, my introductions were too late for offices. I therefore again resorted to street car tours, and a stroll in the leading thoroughfares. Here I witnessed a singular semi-military funeral of a Scotchman who had fallen in battle an age before. His body had just been discovered in course of excavation in the neighbourhood, and was to be buried in the old country. In a strange way I met in the dusk the son of the

Scottish rector for whose congregation I was the lay representative at the Church Council. A remark led to conversation, and a reference to Scotland to our identification of one another. This episode and the observation of so much that was British led me to feel myself more at home. Throughout the whole day's experience of place and people I felt I was no longer in the United States, but in a British colony, the visible representations of home relations being the postman, the police, and the Queen Victoria coinage. Shops and places of business are also in their style more English. The ladies are less American in caste and manner, and seem just those we meet in London or Edinburgh thoroughfares.

The Queen City, as Toronto is called, is the second in Canada, the population being 181,220. It extends eight miles along the lake, the buildings being substantial and sometimes handsome. The spire of St. James's Cathedral is 316 feet high, and was once the highest in America. At the Queen's Park, a wooded area of 40 acres, stands the massive buildings of the Provincial Parliament, costing £300,000, and the University of Toronto, the finest composition of college architecture in the Western Hemisphere. The main building, designed by Cumberland & Storm, costing £100,000, was burnt in 1890, but has been rebuilt, the architect of the restored building being Mr. Dick, once of Edinburgh, who hospitably entertained me as a friend of Mr. Hippolyte Blanc, R.S.A., and drove me round a good part of the city. 1300 students attend the University and College, and 300 that of Trinity College, an Anglican University.

CANADIAN BROTHERHOOD HEADQUARTERS.

I awoke on Sunday morning as if I were in Scotland. The sun was shining, and the streets quiet. A milk van now and then, or an occasional vehicle, broke the stillness. There were no cars plying. St. James's Cathedral was not far, and there I made myself known to such of my Canadian brothers as I came into touch with. I was in due course introduced to Canon Du Moulin (now Bishop of Niagara) and other clergy. My Scotch friend was also taken in hand by the chapter. After dining with Mr. Dick, who called for me at my hotel with his carriage, I was taken to St. Thomas', where Bishop Hall was giving an address to men under Brotherhood auspices. To him and the Bishop of Toronto I was introduced. The latter in announcing Bishop Hall also spoke in praise of the Brotherhood. The church was crowded, and there were within it many men from various Toronto chapters, including Mr. Davidson the President, and Mr. Waugh the

Secretary, of the Canadian Brotherhood. As soon as the service was over, Mr. Davidson informed me that I was due at his and his mother's house to tea, and to Canon Du Moulin's house to supper. I met some friends at Mrs. Davidson's, and was made at home in the family circle, one of which had just returned from visiting her aged aunt, who turned out to be a near neighbour and an acquaintance of my own in Edinburgh. There was much more to make Toronto seem within measurable distance of home. For evening service we went to a church where it was at once evident the Brotherhood was strong and energetic. It was no surprise to find a crowded congregation and a hearty service, and it was a pleasure to the President and myself to be obliged to take a back seat, and a still greater to have a youth by my side to turn up the places. The Prayer Book was that of the Church of England; I therefore had to lay aside that of the Protestant Episcopal Church of America. Soon after we were seated I observed a whisper travelling round the aisles, which was no doubt the word for assembly in the parochial room, for there after service I found a large chapter to welcome me and show me through the buildings and explain the chapter's work. The rector mingled with the members in a brotherly manner, and we conversed so pleasantly that we had to hasten our steps to Canon Du Moulin's. Canon and Mrs. Du Moulin and family were most cordial in their hospitality. Had I apprised them in time they said I should not have been allowed to go to a hotel. The Rev. F. Du Moulin is a son of the Canon, and was the first Secretary of the Canadian Brotherhood. The Church, the Brotherhood, Home and Colonial questions, general and local, were the topics at the supper table till a late hour. I was sorry to leave, but I had to be up betimes, and I had a considerable distance to walk, the tortuous part of which Mr. Davidson convoyed me.

I was to meet the Canon at Washington, and there was also in store a happiness in seeing him in Edinburgh in 1895, along with Mrs. Du Moulin and the Rev. Frank Du Moulin; the startling sermon and sympathetic addresses he then delivered being still remembered by Churchmen in Edinburgh.

IN CANADA IN THE FALL.

At midnight the silence of the city was broken; and with the morning the streets resumed their wonted din. A sharp walk in the chief thoroughfare before breakfast impressed upon me the fact that I was on the edge of a Canadian autumn, and window displays of furs were premonitory of winter. The early express by the Grand Trunk found me "aboard" for Ottawa. Glimpses of the lake were obtained from the car, and the autumnal tinted trees, gloriously golden, and studded with scarlet and crimson foliage, were a continuous panorama of delight. At Kingston I obtained reliable information respecting the Montreal boat, and continued on to Brockville, where I was night bound through a break in the train relation. I made a good supper, as I was to go breakfastless next morning by a very early train. I rose at five and made my way to the station in the morning dawn. At the station I watched the lovely sunrise at six. As the train moved off the sky became a sea of variegated crimson.

IN OTTAWA, THE CANADIAN CAPITAL.

Ottawa, the capital, was reached about the breakfast hour, and Canadian air had insured an appetite. Mr. Dick, the architect, who had shown me much kindness in Toronto, had honoured me with an introduction which secured admission to the Parliament buildings, and to these I at once directed my steps. The gentleman to whom I had been introduced explained not only all about the various chambers, but much about the capital, the Canadians, and the country. The Government buildings, forming a magnificent group, with fine tower 220 feet high, and commandingly situated, cover an area of four acres on the bluff overlooking the Ottawa river. Erected in 1859-65, they cost £1,000,000. The material of which they are built is very beautiful, being a cream-coloured sandstone with arches of warm red Potsdam sandstone and dressings of Ohio freestone, age freshening the beauty of their colour. Their style is based on the Gothic of the 12th century. The library behind the Central Houses of Parliament building (which contains Senate Chamber and House of Parliament) has 160,000 volumes, and is open as a free reference library. Upon it adornment has been lavished, and it is one of the most beautiful and convenient structures for its purpose in America. The book cases and panelling of Canadian pine are ornamented with excellent carving, and the arms of the Dominion and provinces. There is also a statue of Queen Victoria—the mother country's Queen—and busts of the Prince and Princess of Wales.

Ottawa was only incorporated as a city in 1854, when it had but 10,000 inhabitants. It was made the capital by the Queen's selection of it as the official capital, in order to end the conflicting claims of Montreal, Quebec, Kingston, and Toronto. Like Washington it has thus had the opportunity to make itself worthy of the position to which it had been raised, and is already one of the handsomest and best kept cities of the Dominion. Like its States sister, too, it is the scientific centre of the country, with the headquarters of the chief scientific societies and collections, while the presence of the Governor-General constitutes it a natural focus of cultivated and fashionable society.

The first settler established himself in 1800 on the opposite side of the river—the district now called Hull, with 11,265 inhabitants. Twenty years after he transferred his claim on the subsequently called "Bytown" side—the original name of Ottawa until it became a city. The inhabitants of Ottawa numbered 44,154 in 1891, and must now have risen to 50,000. They are nearly equally divided between French and British and Protestants and Roman Catholics.

The Rideau and Chaudière Falls close to the city are very picturesque. The Rideau descends by six locks into the Ottawa River, picturesquely situated beside two bridges at acute angles. As the car to Rideau Falls put me down at Rideau Hall, the residence of the Governor-General, who is the Earl of Aberdeen, I regret I did not learn till too late that I might have been within court etiquette as a tourist Scotchman in leaving a card for his Excellency. The Chaudière Falls (Hull district) supply waterpower for countless saw mills, and generate electricity for lighting, heating, and propelling

PARLIAMENT BUILDINGS, OTTAWA, CANADA

Reproduced from "America, Scenic and Descriptive," by express permission of the Publisher, James Clarke, New York

tramcars through the chief streets of Ottawa and to Rideau Hall. There are usually 120,000,000 feet of lumber at the falls, and the value of the produce of the saw mills is about £1,000,000, equal to 350,000,000 feet of timber.

Among other objects of interest I visited the great lucifer match, pulp, and paper mills in the district, which seemed a little town of timber hills, and my attention was much taken up with the timber yards and saw mills. In the evening I called on my Brotherhood men, and remained till late with Mr. Orde, one of the Council, and Mrs. Orde. In the morning I was introduced to Archdeacon Lauder. I was impressed with the Archdeacon's faith in the Brotherhood, and I noticed he wore the button conspicuously, as he himself observed.

Amid a downpour of rain I made my way by car to the station. The main street was stirred into a mud-way in a short time, and was only properly fordable at certain intervals. More golden and scarlet trees lined the journey back to Kingston, on arrival at which place we were told the boat due at 4 p.m. was storm-stayed on the lake, and could not be down till 3 a.m. This disappointment, however, only enhanced the pleasure of seeing Kingston, and of spending a pleasant evening with Mr. Vashton Rogers, Q.C., one of the Canadian Brotherhood Council, and a leading lawyer of the town, and his wife.

KINGSTON (CANADA).

Kingston, the key of the upper St. Lawrence, was the seat of Government from 1841 to 1844, and in 1812 the naval arsenal for Lake Ontario. Its name originated with the loyalists after the American Revolution. Prior to that it was Fort Frontenac from 1683. Its Royal Military College has 80 cadets, and its University of Queen's College, attended by 450 students, some of whom are women, is one of the leading universities of Canada.

THROUGH THE THOUSAND ISLANDS.

Bedded in a hotel in sight of the pier, at midnight, I kept the lamp in to aid my knowledge of the early hour I was to be astir. I rose at two, and listened for sounds on the lake. I heard none, but presently the waiter came to tell me that the boat was in. I hastened dressing, avoiding unnecessary exactness, and joined two other storm-stayed passengers on the way to the steamer. The crew were still coaling. During the operation, I wandered through the ship examining the immense cargo of fruit, flour, spirits, and preserves, with which it was laden. In pitch darkness we sailed at 4 a.m., and steered our course by the lake beacons. The morning was chilly. Light dawned towards five o'clock, and we then began to thread the Thousand Islands, the picturesque part of the lake for which I returned to Kingston. The islands, which number about 1700, big and little, were passed through in about an hour. After that we entered the river St. Lawrence, eventually proceeding for a while by the canal which enables vessels to pass up and down the river reach where the rapids are dangerous. In the canal there are many locks to retard progress.

MONTREAL AND QUEBEC.

Late in the afternoon we landed at Montreal Leaving my valise at the station, I saw as much of the town as I could before nightfall, attended a lecture on Sir Walter Scott by Mr. Wallace Bruce of New York, and then proceeded by boat to Quebec. Mr. Wallace Bruce's lecture was given in the Windsor Rooms, a capacious hall, and was under the auspices of the St. Andrew's Society, to the President and Secretary of which I had the honour of being introduced. Before the lecturer entered, a piper in Highland garb paraded the platform for some minutes, and delighted the audience with hill and heather music. The opening words of the lecture were about Edinburgh's Princes Street and the Scott Monument. The latter I had seen inaugurated in my boyhood on the Scott Anniversary in 1846, and I had lived to be the oldest merchant in Princes Street, with now fifty summers' reminiscences of its pavement and outlook, its stores and stories, old-fashioned and up-to-date, and the people—home, foreign, and colonial, past and present—who have constituted the living stream that passes along it in varying weather and season.

In booking for Quebec a change of carriages at an early hour in the morning prevented me taking a sleeper, and but for some vociferous athletic spirits on their way to a lacrosse match—Ottawa *versus* Quebec—I should have slept well in the ordinary carriage. As it was, however, I arrived at Quebec in good form, and rejoined my river-boat friends on their landing from Montreal. All the interesting points and historical places in Quebec were included in our carriage tour of the town, and from Point Lèvis we obtained a splendid view of Quebec rock. The view from Dufferin Terrace is one of the finest in Canada, stretching out to the gulf of St. Lawrence. Of the 63,090 inhabitants, five-sixths are French Roman Catholics.

Before the sun set we were on board the steamer to Montreal, watching the dying day as we ascended the river. We had a comfortable Canadian supper on board, and soon retired to our snug berths. In early morning Montreal was again reached, and, being Sunday, I made

THE SCOTTISH CLANS

Copied by permission from the Scottish Clans and their Tartans, with historical account of each clan, &c. W. & A. K. JOHNSTON, Edinburgh.

CLANS.		
Brodie of Brodie.	MacBean or MacVean.	MacIntosh.
Bruce, King Robert.	MacBeth.	MacIntosh, Chief.
Buchanan.	MacDonald.	MacInnes.
	MacDonald of Clan-	MacIntyre.
Cameron, Erracht.	ranald.	MacKay.
Cameron, Lochiel.	MacDonell of Glengarry.	MacKenzie.
Campbell, Argyll, Chief.	MacDonald of Sleat.	MacKinlay.
Campbell, Breadalbane.	MacDonald of Staffa.	MacKinnon.
Campbell, Cawdor.	MacDougal.	MacLachlan.
Campbell, Loudoun.		MacLaren.
Chisholm.		MacLean of Duart.
Clergy.		MacLaine of Lochbuie.
Colquhoun.		MacLeod, Dress.
Cumin.		MacMillan.
		MacNab.
Davidson.		MacNaughton.
Douglas.		MacNeil.
Drummond.		MacPherson, Dress.
Dundas.		MacPherson, Hunting.
		MacQuarrie.
Elliot.		MacQueen.
Erskine.		MacRae.
Farquharson.		Malcolm.
Fergusson.		Matheson.
Forbes.		Maxwell.
Forty - Second, "Black		Menzies.
Watch" and Campbell.		Munro.
Fraser.		Murray, Athole.
		Murray, Tullibardine.
Gordon.		
Graham.		Ogilvie.
Grant.		
Gunn.		Robertson.
		Rob Roy.
Jacobite.		Rose.
Johnston.		Ross.
Kerr.		Scott.
		Sinclair.
Lamond.		Skene.
Leslie.	A HIGHLAND PIPER.	Stewart, Old.
Lindsay.		Stewart, Royal.
Logan or Maclennan.		Stewart, Hunting.
	Macduff.	Stewart, Dress.
MacAlister.	MacFarlane.	Stewart, Prince Charles.
MacAlphine.	MacFie.	Sutherland.
MacArthur.	MacGillivray.	
MacAulay.	MacGregor.	Urquhart.

A HIGHLAND PIPER.

arrangements for service. I found one of the Brotherhood at Christ Church Cathedral, and met with great kindness from him, while the rector was delightfully frank, as he knew many people and places in Britain, he having himself held an important living in England. He was much interested in my mission across the Atlantic. General Booth was in the town, and, being near the hall of assembly, I took the opportunity of hearing him for a short time, and seeing a Salvation Army gathering. My chief interest was in the General, and the way in which he pinned his text to the daily life and conversation of his followers appeared to me to be successful and very practical. A search in the suburbs proved that my Brotherhood correspondent had just entered upon a course for the ministry at Lennoxville College. I afterwards heard from him on my return to Scotland.

Montreal is the largest city in Canada, and the chief commercial centre. More than half the population (270,000) are French, while about three-fourths are Roman Catholic. It occupies a series of terraces culminating in Mont Réal. The Church of Notre Dame (Roman Catholic) contains 10,000 to 15,000 worshippers.

LAKE GEORGE—LAKE CHAMPLAIN.

There were 600 miles betwixt Montreal and

Washington, where I was due by nine o'clock on Wednesday morning. The night mail was therefore necessary to cover the ground and give a day in New York for packing and despatch of baggage, and one for Baltimore. I missed the boats by Lake George and Lake Champlain, which had been taken off that day.

Lake George (New York State), called the Loch Lomond or Windermere of America, is south-east of the celebrated Adirondack Mountains, an area of pleasure resorts stretching 120 miles north and south, and 80 miles east and west. It is 33 miles long, and from ¼ to 3 miles wide, dotted with 222 pretty islands. Its position made it the scene of conflicts between the French and English in the 17th and 18th centuries, and is associated with the romances of Fenimore Cooper.

Lake Champlain receives the waters of Lake George at its north end, and discharges itself into a Canadian river which flows into the St. Lawrence. Its length is 120 miles, and its width varies from ¼ to 12 miles. It extends a short distance into Canada. There are 50 islands in it, the largest of which is 30 square miles. The Adirondacks are on its west side, and, like its neighbour lake, it was the scene of battles until England obtained possession in 1759. General Abercrombie, Lord Howe, Lord Amherst, and General Burgoyne were prominently engaged in actions along its shores.

SARATOGA.

Saratoga is the most noted inland watering place in the States—180 miles from New York, 36 from Albany, and 12 from the Hudson. Its normal population, which is 12,000, is doubled in July and August, when the wealth of the United States is there displayed. Political, legal, and banking conventions are popular. At the battle of Saratoga, in 1777, Sir John Burgoyne surrendered to the Americans. The hotels accommodate 20,000 visitors. One has a dining-room 275 feet long. Broadway, the finest street, shaded by fine elms, is three miles long. A band plays thrice daily in the prettily laid out Congress Spring Park.

TROY.

Troy, which we passed in early morning dark, I had seen on a bright sunny day by electric car from Albany. It is an important railway centre, and a busy industrial city of 60,956 inhabitants, with handsome charitable and other buildings.

WITH THE EX-AMERICAN CONSUL.

On meeting Mr. Wallace Bruce in alighting from the train in New York in early morning, he kindly invited me to dinner at his house in Brooklyn. I received the most complete directions respecting points and conveyances, which I was to reach by specified times, and superadded a liberal latitude for unavoidable lateness. It was a busy day, and I was truly delighted to find myself at last, I might almost say, at home at the family table of the ex-American Consul lately at Edinburgh. His consular residence had been only a stone-throw from my one. The loving cup I had seen presented in the civic room by the Lord Provost and Town Council of Edinburgh was before me, amidst much that was Scottish, particularly in works of Scottish writers, rare editions of Sir Walter Scott, Burns, &c., and a treasured Shakespeare which had a history. I had to reach a distant part of New York by midnight, and left my generous host's dwelling at eleven. The care he had taken to instruct me in the morning was manifested till midnight. Accompanying me to the proper car, the conductor was given precise injunctions what he was to do with me at the terminus in reference to the night ferry-boats.

BALTIMORE.

I was at Baltimore, the monumental city, about breakfast time, and found a hotel conveniently located for departing early trains. My distance from Washington was that of Glasgow from Edinburgh, the relative character and importance of which Scottish cities are much the same as Baltimore and Washington. I knew there were many Brotherhood men in the city, but in the absence of their addresses it was not easy to apportion any of my very limited time to looking them up, and I was sure to meet a number at Washington. As it happened, I made the acquaintance of sundry afterwards, and one eminent Baltimore clergyman was one of those who devotedly kept by me both at Washington and Hartford. As a special preacher at one of the Washington churches, he made special reference to my presence at the Convention as a Scottish Churchman, and dwelt on the relation of the American and Scottish Churches.

Druid Hill Park, with its half-mile-long lake, is its pride, and contains 700 acres of pleasure grounds. It was a private park for 100 years, and its hills afford beautiful views. It is under bicycle police surveillance, a sergeant of which rode up to me, dismounted, and entered into a lengthy conversation. In return for much he explained to me, I had to attempt enlightening him on Presbyterianism in Scotland, about which he was most curious to learn something, as he had heard so much about the difficulties of comprehending the niceties of their differences. It was apparently the outstanding peculiarity of Scotland, about which kingdom he knew only that it was a part of England! I did not make out his own ecclesiastical proclivities, but I may here note that the Roman Catholic Archbishop of Baltimore (Cardinal Gibbons) is Primate in the United States. There are numerous charitable institutions of great interest, and some noted educational ones. John Hopkins' University has 600 students.

Coming from the north one is struck with the large proportion of negroes in Baltimore. The coloured maids sweeping at the respective doorsteps in the morning was a new experience to me. Here and further south a stranger white feels a degree out of place, and an apology is suggested for being white. The Washington monument is an object of much interest, and from it a splendid view of the whole city and surroundings is obtained. That the name of Washington should be worshipped and reverenced near his home is not to be wondered at, but such is the estimation in which the nation holds him that the name permeates the older States in one way or other. In the case of monuments either to Washington or to the other generals or presidents there is a striking simplicity in the inscriptions that tell the greatness of the men, and add much to the solidarity of the memorials. At nightfall a deluge of rain commenced, and fell throughout the whole night. Often up to see the progress of the hours by the glimmer of a lamp, it was a terrible lookout for me through the drenching rainfall with the prospect of an early morning journey to the American capital, and the anticipated brightness of the Convention became woefully dimmed. It was, however, the dark cloud with a silver lining, and when after five o'clock the darkness and the cloud sped away, the silver grey of the morning appeared, and the sun rose on Washington, the district of Columbia, and the diocese of Maryland, with resplendent power. It was the long-looked-forward-to 10th of October, warm, bright, and beautiful, and I was approaching in course the far-off spot of which in my childhood I had so often dreamt, but which through all my manhood I had never dared to think I should ever behold.

A QUIET HOUR.

I had attended important Y.M.C.A. Conferences at home and abroad. Abroad in Germany and Switzerland I had arrived at my destination accompanied with many members on their way. But when I left Baltimore with the early morning through special, it was to enter Washington alone, unaccompanied by friend or stranger, in a long otherwise empty car. Preceding the Convention proper, this was the Quiet Day for all. It was but fitting that for me there should be a quiet hour to trim my thoughts. It is impossible to recall the crowded memories of that quiet hour, some hovering near but stretching back beyond the forties, some far homewards to country and kin, and thinking deepest of those that were no more. I was a representative of others. Of these others I thought too. To them I had to return with good things for their own good and the good of others.

IN THE CITY OF WASHINGTON.

About eight o'clock, after an hour-and-a-half's run, I was roused from my reverie by a consciousness that I was in the vicinity of Washington, when there burst upon the view a vista of trees lining a magnificent street, with the Capitol and its soaring dome dominant over all else. The train made its way round a section of the city, and in crossing fine avenues brought the Capitol again and again into sight. As the train entered the city the sensation of a triumphant entry possessed me, Washington was *un fait accompli.*

On alighting from the train I caught sight of Brotherhood men and Brotherhood boys. One

THE QUIET DAY.

stepped forward, at once shook hands with me, inquired what he could do, and what were my arrangements. He offered any kind of service I wanted. In due course one of the Brotherhood boys was given car tickets for two, and despatched with me to Georgetown (or West Washington), where I desired to be taken before the Quiet Day service began. The boy became my attendant for sundry matters for fully an hour, and I cabled home where I had anchored. On the way to Georgetown I was recognised in the car, and at once named on saying I was from Scotland. At the Church porch several introduced me to many local or known men of the Brotherhood arriving simultaneously with myself. The Church was nearly full and the service had just commenced. Here and there I recognised some from New York and some from Chicago. There were altogether about 250 members, and the occasion was my first contact with large numbers. As I looked around, after awhile, I felt not that I was a stranger to all, but that ere the day closed we should all know one another and be overpowered with the same Spirit resting on the placid waters of our souls. There was the quietude of the neighbourhood, and the solemn hush of the Church to frame our spiritual emotion, and the deep and dear lessons so lovingly and brotherly laid before us by the Bishop of Vermont. How engraven on the memories of many must be the hours of that solemn day filled with manly, inspiring, and ennobling thought, robust and genuine and spiritual, binding all to the world as not of it, in imitation of our Lord and Saviour in His childhood, boyhood, and manhood. There was an absence of physical strain by the intermissions for quiet exercise among the shade tree avenues, or the river side, and the repose of the devotional luncheon hour, during which I sat beside a coloured man. I watched with deep regret the falling darkness as the stained window pictures, which I had gazed upon all day, faded away from my physical sight. But if the light of the earth had departed, there came at eventide the Light of the world to shine into the soul.

During the intervals my personal acquaintances grew apace, and at the end of the Quiet Day there was hardly a Brotherhood man in Washington I seemed not to know. On registering at the reception hall in the evening I received my white silk delegate's badge, and I was shown my rooms at Ebbit House, where I was to be the guest of the Brotherhood Council during the Convention week. My trunk had arrived a day before, as Mr. Houghteling, the President, informed me in the course of the day, and I found it located in an airy sleeping apartment, with every accompaniment of elegance, ease, and comfort. There were perhaps 300 or more rooms, the occupants of which, nearly all Brotherhood men, filled the dining-room, hall, and writing-room, whenever the Convention was not sitting. Besides these, however, the house being the Brotherhood headquarters, flying the flag of the Order, there were constant visitors from other hotels and boarding-houses, whose interest was more concentrated on " Brother Scotland " than on any other single delegate. My geographical knowledge of Scotland and some parts of England pleased many, whose forefathers had come from places I knew of.

THE WASHINGTON CONVENTION.

The Convention of the Brotherhood of the United States formally opened on Thursday morning, by which time 1000 delegates had registered. It was a genial typical October day, for which Washington is famed, with blue sky and a flood of sunlight. Added to the thousand of the Brotherhood rank were many visitors who crowded the Church of the Epiphany in every part, numbers being unable to obtain admission. The Brotherhood occupied the entire floor of the Church. The Venerable Bishop of Alabama was among the Bishops in the procession, there being sixteen altogether at the Convention. The choir was partly composed of surpliced ladies, whose voices, to my mind, lent uniqueness to all the services of the week. The charge to the Brotherhood was delivered by the Bishop of Maryland, who dealt out straight and serious questions for every chapter to consider. It was in a measure unexpected, because faithfully exacting, and caused considerable heart-searching and anxious endeavour to grasp the truest ideas of Brotherhood duty.

The business sessions and conferences were held in Metzerott's Music Hall, a capacious building with a large gallery and accommodating probably 2000. There were many strangers present at the meetings besides the now registered 1300 delegates. The delegates from the respective States were massed together as arranged beforehand. The front centre seat was labelled "Scotland," on the right of which were four indicated for "Canada." For want of room on the floor the Virginia delegates, of whom there were a great number, were seated in the gallery. On the Convention being called to order, the Rev. Dr. Morgan Dix, of Trinity Church, New York, led the devotions, and an address of welcome was given on behalf of the city by the Hon. John N. Ross, Chairman of the Board of Commissioners, who ranks as corresponding to a Lord Provost inasmuch as the district of Columbia, an area of 6510 miles, is ruled directly by the President of the United States, and Congress through the board of which Mr. Ross is the chairman. The inhabitants belong to no State, and have no national and no local vote. A similar address was given on behalf of the Churchmen of Washington, by the Rev. Dr. Randolph H. M'Kim, the host of the Convention, as the rector of Epiphany Church.* Next came the hymn, "For all the Saints who from their labours rest," followed by the solemn minutes, when all stood until the death roll of 42 who had "entered into rest" since the previous Convention was ended. Some formal business was then transacted, including the reception of delegates representing certain distant fields, who addressed the Convention. It fell to my lot to speak for Scotland, and Britain generally, as I was also the formal representative of English chapters. I cannot refer to the ovation I received as other than one accorded specially to the Brotherhood in England and Scotland. What the character of that was the Washington papers noted, and others repeated. Never for myself or others was I the recipient of such honour, and no higher distinction than to have been so received in the city of Washington can by any possibility await me again. Three countries were represented—the United States, Canada, and Scotland. The various States numbered 37, the chapters

* Now Dean of Virginia Theological Seminary.

487. Bishops and clergy were from all parts, and of the 1300 delegates six were coloured men and four were Red Indians, two of whom had to speak through an interpreter. In respect of profession they were thoroughly representative, and they were men of all ages, wide-awake, business-like, progressive—the average age being about thirty. Strong words on prayer and service were given a primal place in the proceedings. Then came the 8 p.m. service, preparatory to early morning Holy Communion, held in the Church of the Epiphany; the choir going silently to the chancel, and Dr. Morgan Dix proceeding to the pulpit and speaking earnest and heart-searching words into the faces and souls of a thousand men. Of these 900 returned in the morning to renew their vows in the body corporate. It was a mighty company of men assembled in the grey morning of the Cross and Passion, a scene not soon to be repeated anywhere, never in that great church with its dear and noble chancel, separated from the nave by its beautiful rood screen. Hearty choral responses and a reverent service were the framing and front of the picture of united souls.

In the business session following, four places, if not five, contended for the privilege of entertaining the next Convention. The Bishop of Kentucky, in an eloquent presentation for Louisville, carried the vote in favour of that city.

The others were to continue their claims for another year. The Conference on boys' work, to which we had all become more or less indebted on our arrival in the city, was full of interest, and its value in parish work was forcibly presented. At the hour of noon, according to established custom, the proceedings were interrupted, and the whole Convention joined in the Collect for St. Andrew's Day, and the Prayer for Missions. In the afternoon the Bishop of New York's address on the City and the Nation drew hundreds of Washington people to the Convention, the galleries and aisles of the hall being completely crowded. Later on, the Convention broke up into sectional conferences on important subjects, and the Church of the Epiphany, again crowded, became once more the scene of the Convention proceedings. "The Church and the Brotherhood" was introduced by the Bishop of New York, who presided. Mr. Davis, vice-president, in an address on the "Past and its Lessons," showed the necessity there had been for simplicity in organisation, a rigid adherence to the two rules, and unswerving loyalty to the Church, as also the regard to be paid to quality rather than quantity, and to the individual life of members. Mr. Houghteling, the president, in his "Present, and its Opportunities," spoke of the golden opportunity men who bore the Gospel message now had amid so much discontent, which meant that men were waking up—their eyes opening, their hearts warming, and their fetters dropping—which all pointed to an uprising and betterment, and to men being drawn together, as never before, in the spirit of fraternity on the basis of sympathy, with righteous discontent purifying discontent that it may not work mischief and destruction, but emancipation and the coming of the kingdom of God.

The next day messages were read from Charles H. Evans, the Brotherhood Missionary in Japan, and Bishop Groves of China. The self-denial week in Advent for missionary work was arranged, and practical suggestions for Brotherhood meetings followed along with the sectional Conferences. The speech of special interest was that by Mr. Mott, one of the leaders of the Students' Volunteer Movement for Missions, whose eloquence and vivid picture of the darkness of heathendom burned into the hearts of all present. In the evening one of the most vital questions before Christendom was discussed by a most representative quartette—a Bishop, a learned divine, a large employer of labour, and a labour leader who disclaimed membership in any religious body, and yet was found next day in church among the Brotherhood, whither he had not gone for years. How attachedly to him, and he to them, were seen the group of members after the four addresses ; he and they all earnestly, in a spirit of Brotherhood, continuing the solution of labour questions in the light of Christianity.

Among the resolutions passed during the business sessions none were of more general importance than that which provided for a basis of union for all the Brotherhoods, styled the "Washington Basis," which was duly adopted by the various Brotherhoods of America, Canada, Scotland, England, Australia, and Jamaica.

On the Sunday morning there was early Communion in all the city churches, and at half-past nine. Epiphany Church was filled for the anniversary sermon by the Bishop of Louisiana, on "The Kingdom of God." Perhaps it had been inspired by the previous evening's wonderful meeting when the Bishop was one of the speakers. In it was woven, however, the deepest philosophy of a lifetime. Its theme was the kingdom as for this world and the call to the Brotherhood to establish it, and justify to men the kingdom of Christ. It was spread out with glowing eloquence to a spell-bound congregation.

The Music Hall, an immense building, more like a railway station than a hall, was filled with a concourse of people variously computed, but not less than four or perhaps five thousand, a large proportion of which must have been non-Churchmen. The addresses delivered to this mass meeting were, "Why we have Bishops," by Mr. M'Bee, vice-president of the Brotherhood; "Why we use the Prayer Book," by the Rev. Dr. Barrett; and "Why we build Cathedrals," by the Bishop of Albany. The answers were spoken with dignity and convincing power, and yet the Church teaching was set forth without offence. The Apostles' Creed was rehearsed by the multitude, and the hymn, "The Church's One Foundation," magnificently rendered by hundreds of voices.

The final service was held at half-past seven. The aisles of the church and the adjoining schoolroom were required to accommodate the numbers present to hear, if they could not all see. The Bishop of Maryland presided, and the subject was "The Kingdom in the World." The speakers were the Rev. F. W. Tomkins, jun., Bishop Gilbert, Bishop-Coadjutor of Minnesota, and Bishop Dudley of Kentucky. Shelley's anthem, "The King of Love my Shepherd is," was beautifully sung by the choir while the alms were being collected for the only time during the whole of the Convention. Then the Bishop affectionately bade the delegates good-bye. After the service followed the farewell meeting, the Rev. Mr. Tomkins conducting it, vested in cassock. Final messages were said by others. *Gloria in Excelsis* rang out; and all joined in the General Thanksgiving, followed by the prayer for the Missionary Council meeting at Hartford the following Sunday, and where I was then due. Then the Bishop of Maryland dismissed the delegates to their homes with his blessing, and the largest and best of the Brotherhood Conventions ever held was over.* I was no stranger to young men's Conventions, many were sacredly stored in memory's records, but my highest joys culminated in this one. To me it was the best, the noblest, the most heart-binding. I could hardly pray to be spared to see another like it. I should certainly never again experience a Washington one, and none will nestle nearer my heart all the days of my remaining life, than that one bearing the name of my earliest learnt hero in the capital of the country with which my earliest religious impressions are associated in Church, school, and family. At it too it was my delight to meet again—alas that it was for the last time !—the Rev. Dr. Chauncy Langdon, Secretary of the League of Christian Unity, who was my official guest in 1857, when he put me in correspondence with two Churchmen in England with whom I acted in the promotion of British Y.M.C.A. Conferences. Notices at the time of his death have shown the important position he held for the Church both in Italy and America. He was buried on St. Andrew's Day, 1895.

* This was penned before the Buffalo one (v. p. 28).

LOYAL AND LINGERING.

Perhaps no out-town delegate stirred a step from the Convention during all the meetings. Monday was the day appropriated to seeing the city, and all the local men that were available placed themselves at the service of Brotherhood men to guide them in parties round the respective sights. The day was brilliantly fine, and the full forenoon was devoted to the Government and other buildings. Unexpectedly, and to my own surprise, I found I had become a wonder by walking up the Monument to join my party, for whose ascent in the free elevator I had not arrived in time, and walking down again to rejoin them. It seemed to be the opinion of some that none but a Scotchman could do it. When I arrived at the top, a climb of 900 steps, a burst of applause for Brother Scotland greeted my ears ere I quite knew where I had landed.

The obelisk is a worthy memorial of Washington. It is 555 feet high, and is constructed of white Maryland marble, with walls 15 feet thick at the base, and 18 inches at the top. The elevator takes 8 minutes to ascend, but walking requires 20 or 25 minutes, in which way, however, one sees all the stone tablets presented by States and Corporations. It is said to be the highest structure of masonry in the world.

Washington, which has a population of about 190,000, or 203,000 with Georgetown, covers an area of about 12 square miles, and is one of the most beautiful cities in the United States, of which it has been the seat of Government since 1800. Its wide, finely laid out, asphalted streets, leafy squares and circles (some adorned with statues) and its shade tree avenues bearing names of different states, presents a system which deserves the name of city gardening. Pennsylvania Avenue, stretching a distance of a mile and a third, runs from the Capitol to the White House.

The Capitol is one of the most beautiful buildings in the world, 751 feet in length, and from 121 to 324 feet wide. The main edifice is sandstone, painted white, but the two wings are white marble. It occupies an area of 3½ acres. The park in which it stands is about 50 acres in extent. Its style is Classic, with Corinthian details. Opposite the central portico on the east side is a colossal statue of George Washington, and on the broad steps in front of the main doorway the inauguration of the Presidents of the United States takes place. The west side, upon which the city has extended, is approached by broad flights of steps, with a fine marble terrace. Sculpture and painting has contributed to perpetuate at the Capitol the political and historical events of the nation. The Hall of

Representatives measures 139 feet by 93 feet, and is 36 feet high. There are desks for 352 members and 4 delegates. The size of the Senate Chamber is only 113 feet by 80 feet, the height being the same as the other chamber. It is more ornate than the Hall of Representatives.

There are, of course, many Government buildings which were open to us, but the Bureau of Engraving and Printing, for the manufacture of paper money and bonds, and the Treasury Building, with its hundreds of millions of dollars in coin, appealed to the common interest of everyone.

THE HOME OF GEORGE WASHINGTON.

In the afternoon a party of 250 remained to visit Mount Vernon, 15 miles distant, by steamer. There was a religious feeling mingled with this pilgrimage to the home and tomb of Washington. At the latter, in full sight of the sarcophagi containing George Washington's and Mrs. Washington's remains, the doxology was devoutly sung with all heads uncovered. In the grounds miniature axes made of cherry tree wood planted by Washington were for sale, one of which some reminded me I must buy. Along with it I also brought away a gavel made of maple wood for my Brotherhood chapter. The house was called by Washington's brother after an Admiral of the British Navy. Among the relics is the notable key of the Bastille. The piazza tiles came from the Isle of Wight, and the garden contains trees planted by Washington.

Our return Brotherhood boat touched at Alexandria, where several chapters were waiting us at the pier. A brief service was held on our arrival in Christ Church, of which General Washington was for many years a vestryman. The rector explained the associations of the Church, and, the pew of Washington being particularised, everyone in turn desired to occupy it in succession to the First President of the United States. The ladies of Alexandria were indefatigable in their preparation for this Brotherhood contingent, and provided a supper sumptuous and happy. After supper one half of the party said good-bye, and sailed with the Norfolk boat, while the other returned to Washington by the Brotherhood boat. Both on approaching Mount Vernon and in returning, several Brotherhood hymns were sung by the company on board, the effect of which in the quiet autumnal sunset on the wide Potomac river was most inspiring.

It was said at the time that the effect of the Convention upon the Washington community was a subject of comment. A deep impression had been produced by the insignia, although it was no uncommon sight for the city to have various orders displaying such through the streets, but there was believed to be an impression of manliness, thoroughness, and devotion, that the red cross worn only could represent.

GOOD-BYE IN WASHINGTON.

A late reception at Professor Cable's on our return to the city wound up my engagements in the capital of the United States. The Rev. J. Thompson Cole, now secretary of one of the missionary societies, who showed me unbounded kindness from the beginning to the end of the Washington Convention, was with me, and as the evening wore on he held his watch in hand to keep me right in respect of the moment of departure for the north midnight mail, which he eventually saw me safely seated in, and off to Philadelphia.

PHILADELPHIA.

It would be about three in the morning when I found myself in a huge dimly-lighted, although excellent and well-warmed, depôt at Philadelphia. In the solitude of the station I renewed acquaintance with my trunk, which had preceded me by several hours, and would be checked further on, when I should resume my journey in a day or two. With many hundred feet of forms their partitions denied me room to go to sleep in, and if any marble tops were of the prescribed length, their warm piping underneath warned me off. Having wandered through all the wide corridors and broad steps upstairs and downstairs, and made myself familiar with through-the-night station life, I adapted my limbs to the furniture of the place and slept thinly till seven or eight, at which hour I was able to get a revolving seat at the counter of the restaurant, and a much relished breakfast. It is the City of Brotherly Love, and, as it happened, I was to share the hospitality of a Brotherhood family, who entertained me for two or three days. I was also hospitably treated by the Brotherhood's second vice-president, from whom, and from other Philadelphia leading Brotherhood men, I received great kindness. It was with sincere regret I could not include a visit to the Rev. Dr. Stone, who had so cordially invited me to see his home at Philadelphia. He is now rector of St. James's, Chicago, where the Brotherhood originated. The Brotherhood, I note, variously aids "right earnestly" the Episcopal City Mission, whose field covers sixty hospitals, homes, &c., with an income in 1894 of £8000 (one half for the Consumption Department).

Philadelphia is the third city of the United

States, but although it covers 130 square miles, and is 22 miles long by 5 to 10 wide, it has only 1,046,964 inhabitants, a large proportion of its houses being small; they are usually two storied structures of bright red brick, with white marble steps. It has 30 miles of water front on its two rivers, and is the headquarters of two great railway systems. Its steamers ply to various ports in the world. The names of William Penn and Benjamin Franklin are bound up with its history, and it is the scene of most important official steps, such as the Assembly of the first Continental (American) Congress, in 1774; the Declaration of Independence, July 4, 1776; the promulgation of the Constitution in 1787; and the place of assembly for Congress up till 1797. I saw in the Market Place the huge statue of Penn, 37 feet in height, which has now been raised to the tower of the New City Hall, 510 feet high. The huge pile covers a greater area than any other American building, being 4½ acres, compared with Washington Capitol, with 3½ acres. It has a granite basement story and white marble superstructure, and has taken twenty years to build. Its style is modified French Renaissance, and the building contains 750 rooms. The Council Chamber and municipal offices are on the first floor. The Supreme Court of Pennsylvania occupies the third floor. Opposite the City Hall is the most handsome

Broad Street Station of the Pennsylvania Railroad, and in the same square stands the Masonic Temple, a great granite structure in the Norman style, costing £300,000, with tower 250 feet high. The lodge rooms are in seven different styles—Egyptian, Ionic, Corinthian, Norman, Gothic, Renaissance, and Oriental. The universally known Wanamaker's Store—the *Bon Marché*, Whiteley's, Jenner's, or Cranston's of Philadelphia—with 4500 employees, is quite near. Through this I had the privilege of being taken, dining there. The United States Mint, in Chestnut Street (which is the Princes Street of the City), is a white marble building of immense internal interest. The officials were magnanimously courteous, and some bestowed great attention upon me as a Great Britainer by pointing out things they knew would specially interest me. I was able from a very limited numismatic knowledge to correct a misplacement of a British coin in the unique collection, a hint they received with courtly deference. The Post Office is a large granite building in the Renaissance style, and cost £1,000,000. It contains other Federal offices, and the United States Courts.

Independence Hall, the old State House, is only a brick edifice, erected 1729-34, but is perhaps the most interesting building in the States. It contains the famous Liberty Bell, the first rung in the United States after the

Declaration of Independence, adopted in that Hall. It cracked in 1835, and has been silent half a century (since 1843). Originally cast in England, it was recast in Philadelphia. The first American flag—thirteen stars and thirteen stripes—was made at No. 239 Arch Street.

The University is attended by about 1800 students. Fairmount Park is the largest city park in the world, covering 2800 acres, and extending four miles along both banks of the Schuylkill, 11 miles of a narrow strip along the Wissahickon Creek being included. The Zoological Garden is thought to have the best collection in the country. The great Centennial Exhibition of 1876 was held in the Park.

LOCAL B.S.A. ASSEMBLIES—PHILADELPHIA.
BROOKLYN. NEW YORK.

At Germantown, a large suburb of Philadelphia, the local Assembly of the Brotherhood met. It consisted of a service, with addresses by Rev. S. C. Hill, Mr. Houghteling, and Mr. M'Bee. As the members assembled I was introduced by several of the Washington Convention men, and by the local leaders. In the procession were 250 of the Brotherhood, who followed the choir into the church. I was ranked in front along with the vice-president, after the president and secretary. At the conclusion of a hearty service many of the Brotherhood and congregation lingered for a while in the pews, a habit it seemed to me of Americans.

I was due the next evening at Brooklyn Local Assembly, but having mislaid the address, I had on my arrival at New York but the faintest clue to where information could be had, and less than an hour to reach the church. By strange chance, however, I found a Brotherhood man near a closed church, who told me his chapter was going. On his taking me to the rector's house in an adjoining street, I found myself known to two of the Brethren from Washington. The place of assembly was two or perhaps three miles distant, and there we found a crowded congregation, which was addressed by the Bishop of Louisiana, Mr. M'Bee, and Mr. Wood, the secretary of the American Brotherhood, all as representing the Washington Convention and its message to the Brotherhood. In the car I sat beside the rector of the church where Rev. W. M. Tuke, the Scottish Brotherhood Commissioner in 1891, was *locum tenens*.

ADIEUX.

My Brotherhood programme yet included a third Local Assembly at Grace Church, Broadway, New York, where were gathered the next evening the leading officers of the New York chapters, and a church-full Brotherhood congregation. Mr. Houghteling, Mr. M'Bee, the Rev. Dr. Huntington, and the Bishop of New York, after an impressive service, addressed the congregation. Here also after service many lingered in church to exchange inquiries. A former member of the Edinburgh Young Men's Friendly Society, and some members of a clergyman's family I should not otherwise have seen since my acquaintance with them in Scotland, were here able to see me. In the vestry I met the rector and half-a-dozen of the leading Brotherhood men. Coffee and cake were handed us, and we discussed the Brotherhood for a little while. There I bade good-bye to Mr. Houghteling, the father of the Order. At Washington I had answered his question as to what I thought of the Brotherhood, by reference to the Queen of Sheba's words, "The half had not been told me." "Are you still the Queen of Sheba?" he said as we parted, upon which I assured him most earnestly that I was still of her mind in respect to what I had learned, and with that recital of my faith in the Brotherhood of St. Andrew we parted.

1 KINGS x. 6, 7.

II.
FROM THE BROTHERHOOD
TO THE
MISSIONARY COUNCIL OF THE AMERICAN CHURCH.

NORTH BY NIGHT TO BOSTON.

ANOTHER through-the-night journey was before me, and my Y.M.F.S. friend, who was a member of Brother Henry's chapter, became my pilot to the depôt. I was in my sleeper berth by midnight, seeing nothing, and knowing little of the journey until nearing Boston, which I reached about the breakfast hour. I chose my hotel in convenient proximity to my depôt of departure, but found it to be in the most charming centre of the city. I soon met in the street Father Frisby, one of my cabin fellows. Three Brotherhood men, on their way home from Washington to Portland, and known to both of us, came up as I was inquiring about them. We all met again at the Church of the Advent the following morning.

Albany may be the Edinburgh of the United
States because of its political influence and
relations to the State of New York, but Boston
has the nearer resemblance to it in the eye of
the tourist and visitor of taste and culture. Although not possessing the commanding dignity
of a castle upon a picturesque eminence, it has
a beautifully laid out park in the very heart of
the city somewhat relative as Princes Street is to
the rest of the town. Boston Common, as the
park is called, occupies 48 acres, shaded by fine
elms and other trees, and, on account of its position near historic buildings and ground, it is en-
twined with the interests and affections of the
surrounding population. There are also other
parks of some importance. The city is perhaps
the wealthiest in America in proportion to population. Its valuation in 1892 was £188,200,000.
There are some public buildings of great interest
and importance, and scientific, literary, and educational institutes, that indicate the higher culture of the residenters. Among a group of fine
structures in a well-exposed area is the new
Public Library, a dignified and imposing edifice,
vis-à-vis to the noble Trinity Church, of which
the late Bishop Phillips Brooks was rector, and
where he preached the opening charge to the
Brotherhood on the occasion of the Brotherhood
Convention of 1892. Faneuil Hall, styled "the
Cradle of American Liberty," was the place of

assembly of that Convention. Boston Public Library is known to be the largest of its kind in the world. It had 600,000 volumes in 1891, the circulation being 1,812,106 books in the year. Doubtless higher numbers can be quoted in its newer habitation.

MOUNT AUBURN CEMETERY AND CAMBRIDGE.

The graves of the Poet Longfellow, Bishop Phillips Brooks, and Lowell, in Mount Auburn Cemetery, Cambridge, were visited at a period of the day in harmony with the picturesque and peaceful surroundings. It was Saturday, late afternoon, when the sun was beginning to cast its long shadows amid the many trees and tombs. Longfellow's house from 1837 till his death in 1882, which was also that occupied by Washington in 1775-76, was to me one of much interest, as was also the elm where the latter took command of the American army on July 4, 1775. Harvard University, the oldest, richest, and most famous of American seats of learning, is the characteristic attraction of Cambridge (a suburb of Boston).

BROTHERHOOD MEN AT WORK.

Coming out of the breakfast room on Sunday morning, my eye fell upon a card, "Bureau of Church Information," and beside it I recognised two Brotherhood men who at once gave me information about how to reach the church I desired to go to. While in conversation with them others sought similar information, and one left to visit the coffee-room. I found they were two of a band who visited every hotel in the city on Sunday, and were under the direction of the local assembly of Boston. In my way through the city I witnessed the funeral of one of the army veterans. The church I went to was my cabin friend's, Father Frisby.

HARTFORD—THE MISSIONARY COUNCIL.

To be at Hartford (Conn.) for the opening service of the American Missionary Council, at 7 or 8 p.m., I had to leave Boston about 4. I regarded myself as an outsider and a perfect stranger, but, to my surprise, when I alighted on the Hartford platform, I was at once offered, by a gentleman, a seat in a cab to convey me to my hotel, and on to the church. When I found that my Brotherhood relations were included in the intentions of such courtesies, I was only too glad to be so accommodated, and accordingly soon found myself at church, and not as a stranger there, but afterwards recognised by many American Churchmen, Bishops, clergy, and laity. I thought I had parted company with all my friends when I got outside the

Brotherhood gatherings. I was totally and surprisingly mistaken, and even at Hartford, three hundred and thirty miles from Washington, the Brotherhood reigned. The status spontaneously and generously accorded to me was founded on my Scottish Churchmanship, my Brotherhood delegation, and my personal historical and individual relations, and no more welcome and fatherly embrace was it ever mine to experience than that of the venerable Bishop Williams, of Connecticut, Presiding Bishop of the American Church (the President of the Council), when he so joyously received me that evening, recognising me as a familiar friend, and desiring that I should "forgather much" with him. Then there were Bishops and clergy I had known in Scotland, and had conferred with at Washington, and elsewhere in America, as well as laymen I had already met in The States. Beside these there were more Brotherhood Bishops, clergy, and laymen, to superadd their welcome. At the Council there were about forty Bishops, and the roll was a representative one of clergy and laity. Among the latter was Mr. G. C. Thomas, a prominent banker of Philadelphia and a member of the Brotherhood Council. He it was that conducted the preliminary mass meeting of 1500 children in connection with the Council, at which addresses on missionary work were given by Mr. Thomas, Rev. Yung Kung

Yen, of China, and Rev. J. G. Prevost, of Alaska.

The Services and Conferences were held in Christ Church, Hartford. In the opening address reference was made to the Washington Brotherhood Convention, which was frequently alluded to by Bishops and clergy in the course of the proceedings. A formal resolution was also passed recognising the Brotherhood as an auxiliary of the Church. To all the advantages of membership I was admitted, and asked to seat myself anywhere. Most anxious were several of the Bishops and officials that I should understand I was included in the invitation to the receptions—one at Trinity College, and another at the suburban mansion of a wealthy layman of the Church, who personally expressed his gratification that I was among his guests. I was also invited to be a guest at the Connecticut Church Club dinner, after the Council, which I regretted much not to be able to stay for. There were many things at Trinity College interesting to everyone. Bishop Seabury's mitre was to me exceptionally so, and likewise the original document of the Concordat between the first of America's Bishops and his Scottish consecrators, Primus Kilgour and Bishops Petrie and Skinner (to the first-mentioned of whom my forebears were related by marriage). Professor Hart, who visited

Top of Altar rail St. Andrew's Chapel (The 'Upper Room)', Aberdeen, where Bishop Seabury was Consecrated, Nov. 14, 1784. See page 37.

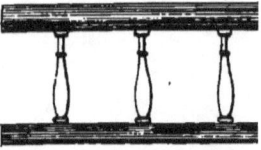

FAC

Robertus Kilgour Episcopus

Arthurus Petrie Episcopus.

Joannes Skinner Episcop

Scottish Consecration Deed of First Bishop of the American Chu

Samuel ▭ Bp. Ep. Ch Ch Connect.

Robert Kilg

Arthur

John

Samuel

Signature and Seal of Bishop Seabury, First Bishop of Connecticut.

Concordat between the Scottish Seabury re Communion Offi

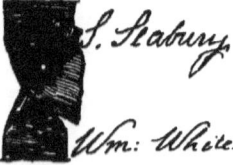
S. Seabury
Wm: White.

* Bishop T. J. Claga was re-interr

FROM CHURCH DOCUMENTS.

English Consecration Deed of First American Bishop consecrated at Lambeth Palace, England, Feb. 4, 1787.

We William Lord Archbishop of York, Charles Lord Bishop of Bath & Wells and John Lord Bishop of Peterborough were present and assisting at the Consecration within mentioned.

W. Ebor
C. Bath & Wells
J. Peterborough

Signature of Bishop White (First Bishop of Pensylvania).

Wm. White

American Consecration Deed of First Bishop consecrated on American Soil by all the previous Bishops, 1792.

Provoost   J Madison

1 Bishop of Maryland), buried at Croom 1816, dral (near the Iona Peace Cross) Nov. 2, 1898.

Scotland on the occasion of the Seabury Centenary in 1884, knew me at once before I recognised him, and remembered very well our former opportunities of meeting. The Rev. Dr. Williamson Smith, the President, was most kind. A few of us remained for Evensong with the students.

The proceedings at Hartford extended from Sunday the 20th to Wednesday the 24th October, and embraced a variety of arrangements. There was an interesting and soul-stirring meeting of the Women's Auxiliary, the speakers at which were ladies of evident energy of life and thought, the organisation being for missionary purposes and able to command the most liberal subscriptions and unfeared pledges. I conversed with the secretary, whom I also met this year in Scotland, and other lady office-bearers, and was struck with their undaunted courage in their work. At the meeting a sum of £500 was raised in fifteen minutes for a training home at Shanghai.

The subjects discussed by the Council were the "Anglican Missionary Conference," held that year in London, of which some reported an adoption of many ideas of mission work from the American Board; "Domestic (Home) Missions and Missions to the Coloured People"; "Associate Missions" (Clergy living in community); "Lay Helpers and Missions"; "Missions to the Heathen and to the Indians";

"Missions in the Cities," and reports from recognised auxiliary Church organisations, in which relation the Rev. Dr. Lindsay, Rectory of St. Paul's, Boston, spoke of the Brotherhood and its mission to Japan. Twenty Bishops took leading parts in the discussion, being those more conversant with the respective subjects. That of "Lay Helpers" was handled by the Bishop of Western Texas, whose interest in the Brotherhood is manifested by the visit he paid to me in Edinburgh during the present year.

I received much kindness from the Bishops of Cairo and Wyoming, and from the Rev. Dr. Lines, who was, I believe, high in the ballot for a coadjutor to the Bishop of Connecticut; also the secretary of the Missionary Council, the late greatly lamented Rev. Dr. Wm. Spaight Langford, who, to quote from the sermon preached before this year's Missionary Council, "was a man of most winning personality, of noble heart, and supreme consecration to the interests of the Kingdom of Christ upon earth. Faith, enthusiasm, consecration, were his guiding words, and being dead, he yet speaketh."

The vicar of Stratford-on-Avon, the Rev. George Arbuthnot, and Mrs. Arbuthnot, were not a little surprised to hear on their arrival that I was at Hartford. I was able to carry home tidings of them in their extended tour across

America, the first lady I met on reaching home being the vicar's mother. They had begun a six months' round trip across America, and the vicar was receiving great honour, and meeting with much enthusiasm, because of his reputation and Shakespearian knowledge.

A BISHOP'S BLESSING.

The one more sacred association with Hartford must ever be that of the venerable Presiding Bishop's blessing, pronounced over me in the vestry of Christ Church on the afternoon of the last session, when he had to rest for an interval in retirement. The good Bishop had that morning arranged that I should follow him when he vacated the chair, and had watchfully observed where I sat in the Church. By indication he reminded me of the agreement to follow. We remained alone for a while, the Bishop earnestly speaking with much solicitude of the Scottish Church, and pointing out some things I would have noticed as praiseworthy in the American Church, and the absence of some irritations. With deepest regret, he said how he should like to cross again to Scotland, and charged me to do what I could through the Brotherhood and other ways to secure unity of feeling, which was the more to be striven for in a small body, differences in which were often accentuated in the eyes of the outside public, and grieved the whole Church.

The closing service was in the evening of the same day. At the conclusion there were a good many to say good-bye to, but the one commanding figure which before all others claimed my parting respect was the venerated Bishop of Connecticut. To find him I had, after the recessional, to enter the robing hall of the Bishops, and pass to the upper end. There the Bishop added his good-bye words, and I kissed the hand that had that day rested on my head and blessed me. As I retired, I was the subject of much American hearty hand-shaking by the other Bishops and Chaplains, the final of which was that of the Bishop of Wyoming,* whom I had first met on board the *Campania* at Liverpool. I was about to disappear when he caught sight of me, and called me back with " Good-bye, my Scotch friend." One or two other good-byes, and I was on the way to the station.

ABOUT HARTFORD AND CONNECTICUT.

Hartford, which is the capital of Connecticut, is finely situated on the river of the State name, and is a pretty town with 53,230 inhabitants, and noted for its powerful insurance companies. A conspicuous object is the Capitol, a building

* Now Bishop of Central Pennsylvania.

STATE CAPITOL, HARTFORD, CONNECTICUT

Reproduced from "America, Scenic and Descriptive," by express permission of the Publisher, James Clarke, New York

of white marble erected in Bushnell Park beside the Park River. There are many pleasant drives in the vicinity. It is the residence place of Mr. Clemens ("Mark Twain"), and was that of the late Mrs. Beecher Stowe, of "Uncle Tom's Cabin" fame. But of those associated with Connecticut our interest lies in the reflection that among the pioneer laymen of Christian America was Samuel Gunn, born in the State in 1763, baptized by one of the S.P.G. missionaries, and confirmed by Bishop Seabury. He became a devout and devoted lay reader, and continued for ten or twelve years to be the binding link to the church of his parish, near Hartford. After that he exercised the same office in the then wilds of New York State, and, later still, in the further West once solitary banks of Ohio, where his own family were at first the sole congregation, until a parish was organised and he became senior warden, a clergyman being sent to it, after three years of the simple service conducted by Gunn. Dr. Chase, the friend of Gunn, was also born on the banks of Connecticut River, and became a devout, active, and self-sacrificing missionary, rector, and Bishop in the North, South, and West, being successively on the outskirts of civilised life in the diocese of New York, a fellow-labourer of the founder of the Church in Oswego, and the first rector of the earliest settlers' congregation in the Southern

States—that of Christ Church, New Orleans, then the rector of one of the Hartford churches, where he was greatly beloved; after which he returned to the scene of his missionary labours, to find the once dreary salt marsh and uncomfortable cabin transformed into busy villages with lofty warehouses. Passing on to struggling villages in the unbroken forest of the State of Ohio, he organised parishes, and in 1819 was elected Bishop by the votes of clergy and laity. He appointed lay readers where he could not give much help or supply clergy, and Samuel Gunn was one of the most pious. His circuit was 1279 miles on horseback, often under burning sun and pelting rain, through mud and swollen streams. The necessity of founding a college to prepare proper instruments for uncivilised districts weighed on his soul. He came to England, collected £6000, purchased 8000 acres, and built a college and village, and around all was changed. How beautiful even in the forest are the feet of him that bringeth good tidings.

But the outstanding ecclesiastical event of the diocese was the election of Dr. Samuel Seabury to be Bishop of Connecticut, and his subsequent consecration at Aberdeen in 1784 as the first Bishop of the American Church—acts that required great courage, but which have cemented the never-to-be-broken friendship of the American and Scottish Churches. Samuel Gunn, Philander Chase, and Samuel Seabury, were all Christian leaders in their land.

BACK AGAIN TO NEW YORK.

It was a rainy, rainy night, and a cold look-out for the midnight boat at New Haven. At the station, however, I found quite a number of the Council members, and among them many of the Brotherhood. The latter on seeing me questioned me about my goings, and leagued together to take me in charge to the boat's side. In the course of the journey I learned they had telegraphed for a carriage to await the arrival of my train at New Haven, on reaching which Dr. Lines and another friend accompanied me in the drive, truly brightened by their attention and conversation, which, but for them, would have been dreary enough, through dismal streets, lanes, and cargo sheds to the river side.

New York was reached about six in the morning, at which hour the streets presented a very different appearance to what I had known of them in other hours. When I left the boat after breakfast it was to tackle a variety of desires, intentions and obligations. Some of these I dealt with at the post office. My wanderings were erratic, as it was my last day in New York with any time fragments. Much pressed, I was hastening to an overhead station when observed by a Brotherhood man, a stranger to myself, but not to the button. We were going in the same direction, and I had flitted past him in front. Somehow he had sighted the button and hurried after me. We exchanged cards, and I told him my concern for the address of a rector who with his family had visited Edinburgh, and whose son, Mr. H. A. Sill (then at Oxford), had been the chairman of the Brotherhood Executive, and a factor in its Scottish development. In a moment I had it from his pocketbook, and had just time to reach the house, four or five miles distant. To have gone *via* a mutual friend's, as I was doing, would have certainly found me "left" after my train for the south had departed—that is to say, after the ferry-boat timed to take passengers across had gone—but I caught the boat, and consequently the express train for New Orleans.

III.

MY LOUISIANA HOME.

A RE-VISIT.

REJUVENESCENCE.

THE purpose of my visit to America was now accomplished. By individual desire and personal endeavour, I had sought to render to the Brotherhood my quota of duty, not mechanically, but with earnest love of the espoused idea. That done, according to my opportunities, there was now to be added to me memories precious as pearls. As I crossed the Hudson River, and entered the train for New Orleans at one of the Jersey City stations, my thoughts glided from the Brotherhood to the days of earlier years—those of a little life in a strange land—albeit that of my childhood home, where the seed sown and watered and tended, growing within Church borders, had been grafted into institutions and made me a St. Andrew's Brotherhood man, and so brought me back to the hallowed scenes of innocent joys.

It was a continuous journey of 1377 miles, and occupied nearly two days and two nights, but that was much longer than tabled owing to a breakdown of a freight train ahead during the second night—an occurrence which interrupted our progress, but which, causing our cars to be shunted into a rural siding, enabled us to slumber in peace until day-dawn, and we awoke in a fairy grove. The chief stopping points were Bristol, Atlanta, Montgomery, Mobile, and Ocean Springs, but in the fairy region the stoppage was perforce four or five hours, which seemed in that latitude to be in mid-summer night dreamland, where, no one being within reach, I was puzzled in wakeful interstices to comprehend how the fastest express should be timed to tarry anywhere the night through. But all was well, and ended well. As we passed through fagot fires in the woods, where the mishap to the freight wagons had happened, the dawn not yet having broken over the pine-tree tops, I understood from the window of my wheeled dormitory somewhat of the cause of our detention.

ABOUT THE CIVIL WAR, AND CIVILITIES.

In the previous day's journey I had made the acquaintance of a gentleman who desired that we should sit together in the saloon car. From him I learned much about the American past, and a great deal about the Civil War and its effects. He particularly interested me in the narrative of his father's and his own service on the staff of the Confederate Army, and his hardships and poverty when the conflict ended with his side defeated. He told me how he and a friend had to begin life again at the bottom of the ladder, drive a cart to the hills, and there do anything for anybody for food and shelter ; put his hand to shoemaking, painting, carpentering, and any kind of work for daily bread ; how he had at last been fortunate, and had risen, through his adapting himself to various conditions, and picking up different crafts, to be the railway engineer of the line. I believe his hardships were only what many officers engaged in the war were compelled to undergo. When we reached Atlanta I lost his companionship.

We were due at New Orleans in early morning, where we should have breakfasted, but we had still some hours to run, and as the dining car had disappeared it was necessary to have déjeûner at some stopping-place. This was an agreeable change, as it enabled passengers to mingle more with one another, and the courtesies over the passage of pepper and salt had a pleasing effect, so that tongues that had stiffened in the train were pliant for the remainder of the journey. Having thus gained the confidence of

two fair ones who sat on my right, I found
their reserve disappear upon our re-entering the
cars, and they eventually confessed that they
knew who I was, as they had heard my speech
at the Brotherhood Convention, and had seen
me at the Brotherhood service and supper at
Alexandria, as well as observed my button when
they entered at Washington. Through them I
got into conversation with other ladies, and was
also invited to sit with a family in another car,
so that, tardy as the train had been, the termination of the journey was reached amid sincere
regrets. It goes without saying that the domestic information of the ladies was an agreeable complement to a Civil War report of an
ex-officer. Much of it was supplementary to
what I had learned about New Orleans on
board the *Campania*, and as I now neared the
Crescent City I was able to fill in, on the spot,
what I had not fully comprehended, or had forgotten, of what had been told me by a Crescent
City maiden and her sister, and at whose church
there was a chapter of the Brotherhood. I was
looking forward to thanking these in their own
city for their kindly interest and never-to-be-forgotten guidance. In my more particular
informant I had seen in the crossing of the
ocean the pole-star of my purpose peradventure
I should find myself where I now was. The
confidence with which she inspired me of finding

undisturbed landmarks of my earlier years, and the consequent longing she had generated, had much to do with a greater determination that I should not return home until I had found the object of my quest.

INTERESTING FIELDS.

Running by Philadelphia and Washington, the cars had traversed the States of New Jersey, Delaware, Maryland, Pennsylvania, Virginia, North and South Carolina, Georgia, Florida, Alabama, Mississippi, and Louisiana. Tobacco and cotton, sugar-cane, rice, and orange districts had come successively into view as we trained south in an almost direct line. Of the tobacco plant and the sugar-cane we had seen little, it being the very end of October, and the first mentioned being so sensitive to frost that it has to be gathered before the possibility of an early freeze, and must be packed in barrels when stored. In the cotton fields, however, we had observed both negroes and whites at work from sunrise—men, women, and boys deftly picking the fleecy cotton from the bursting bolls into their large wickerwork baskets either in groups or dispersed through the field. Here and there we had also passed wagons of cotton on their way to the gins to be converted into bales. Whether we saw any rice fields I cannot say, but I had no doubt about the orange trees, heavily laden with their golden fruit, some of which was still in the green state. As we fringed the State of Florida, its wealth of orange groves, magnificent palms, and gorgeous flowers and dense foliage extended as far as the eye could reach.

The semi-tropical day was now a contrast to that of the more northern latitudes I had known, and the sensation produced upon returning to those southern scenes magically awakened memories which had long lain dormant, and so impressed my mind and heart as to make me feel a child again amidst those scenes of early boyhood which can never be effaced from my memory.

Sometime after noon the train slackened pace, and we steamed into and along a street with a number of houses of ancient appearance and primitive pattern, just as I could have remembered leaving them. We halted on the Levee at Esplanade Street, the place of transference to the Texas Pacific Railroad across the Mississippi and also, as it happened, the point of departure of all my kind feminine friends. There was a train mile further to go, and the cars crept that distance along the Levee, through freight wagons, bales, and barrels, past the French Market, and historical Jackson Square, until it reached a wayside terminus.

DREAMLAND AND SUNNYLAND.

Leaving my "hold-all"—which "all" was little and hardly worth calling an "all" at all—with the clerk at the dépôt, whose courtesy, like the initial ones of the ladies I had left, was number one of full many I experienced from first to last in New Orleans, I instinctively, like a carrier pigeon set free to find its home, gyrated on the Levee until I realised my bearings and could take in long-lost landmarks of an early home. If I had passed through night the mid-summer dreamland, I now stood at noontide, rejuvenescent, amid the sun-blaze of boyhood's summer days where so long ago I gleaned among the empty sugar barrels and scrambled over cotton bales, or watched the Mississippi steamboats loading or discharging their cargoes of figs, rice, and raisins, sugar and molasses, melons, pine-apples, bananas, and Indian corn, or whatever I could remember of juvenile interest and *taste*. It could not then have been all work and no play; rather it seemed all play and little work, if work there was any other than the task of early lessons at a French school, where English and American were taught to Creoles, Americans, and British subjects of any faith but white features. Family anxieties were then father's and mother's. It was mine then to feel, as now to remember, in affectionate gratitude, the protection from concern as well as from the wide way. But the ocular camera that had received the past picture of the Levee and the leaving for home had sharply defined a farewell hour, and now there hung betwixt heaven and earth on the screen of memory the cinematograph vision of all that were dear going home, and I was with them, happy. It was all as I had known it ever so long ago. I stood again in the same scene, but alone and sad, for they who were dear had all GONE HOME. They were sleeping in Scottish mould, and I had come again to trace and to tend, for a short hour, the turf of her they had laid to sleep in a foreign land—her little crescent life resting in the memories of the Crescent City, and her little soul in the gracious keeping of a Father of All.

Peering again into the periscope of the past, I saw myself a little American boy, lively and light-hearted, basking in the sun, which seemed to be the source of all my smiling days in life and the light and heat of human existence. Since then, what had come and what had gone? —what had changed, what had remained? We had taken ten weeks to sail home. I had returned in half that number of days. Steam had supplanted sail; the locomotive the wagon.

Letters with shillings to pay, and weeks of wearying were no longer, while a wire would bring me in an hour knowledge of home. I had

New American Part *Old French or Creole Part*

CANAL STREET, NEW ORLEANS

not this time sailed from the Canal Basin,
Lothian Road, nor got out of course into the
Bay of Biscay, nor would I return to a little
Haymarket terminus in an uncovered wagon—
a railway "carriage"—with engine-ashes in a
bandaged eye. I would not again be driven
along a dusty Princes Street in a minibus
past the rubbish shoot of the East Gardens,
nor pass an unfinished Scott Monument with
a tenemental background—the tall flat-domed
Bank of Scotland, moneyed monarch of all it sur-
veyed, and more, asserting its sovereignty over
the City Gardens and viewing an unbridged
Forth. Since then "Auld Reekie" had become
the Queen City of Britain, and New Orleans
had experienced "a sudden and swift descent"
from the zenith to the nadir. Its commercial
ascendancy and renown, represented by some
£65,000,000 of trade before the war, had nigh
stood still, but the golden horn of the crescent
had again attained the altitude of yore, with all
those of the coloured race I now saw around me
freed for ever from slavery.

After thus musing, and taking a survey of life
on the Levee in black and white, all so unnew,
I turned to the city and walked meditatively,
where long before I had run merrily, to the
main street, a spacious avenue three miles long,
with two streets, one on either side of a neutral
grassy strip and shade trees, and which once

upon a time formed a moat outside the city ramparts or fortifications, and next an irrigation canal which gave it the name of Canal Street. The strip is given up to car tracks from which radiate lines all over the city. There are about thirty different lines with very clean cars drawn each by a single mule, the driver seeing that each passenger deposits his fare in a box. The street is the dividing line between the French, or Creoles, and Americans; the older, or Creole, side having French names—the titles of the Royal Family of France.

When I reached the neutral strip, its frizzled dried condition, and the dusty sunburnt trees after seven weeks' exposure to rainless and almost tropical heat, presented a sorrowful reminiscence of the green ground and green leaves of juvenile play-times, and I could fervently join in the whole city's rejoicings when on the following day the heavens burst with heavy rain showers, and I lived myself anew. My immediate pursuit was that of a hotel, and the first on my list led me to the Creole portion, which I therefore prospected with a defined interest. I could observe the French quaintness of the houses and the narrowness of the streets, necessary for shade in a hot climate. From their foreign façades and unfamiliar un-British names I turned to the American portion, where English live and English is spoken, and there I found the Grunewald Hotel in Baronne Street, an excellent new house (in buff brick, red stone, and marble) just a few doors from Canal Street, and not far from the Christ Church site of former days. To it I transferred my all of the day, and, after so doing, was not a little surprised to meet so early my *Campania* ladies, to whom I communicated my Sunday arrangements, which I found to be correctly planned.

WHERE THE HEART LED.

It was now afternoon and too late for introductions. Ready, therefore, to go where the spirit dictated and the heart led, I strolled into Canal Street and took the down direction, which would be called *up* elsewhere if the water ran down to, instead of up from, the river as it does not do in this city below banks, the streets being several feet below the river level. Excepting on the roadway and the surface-open gutters and bayous or creeks my eye fell upon nothing remembered ; but having one night been rescued from drowning in the latter, I had reason to recall their existence ; the changes, however, were far short of my calculations. Gradually there stole over me a feeling of homeness, and what was new resembled the past. I continued down some blocks, conscious that I was nearing the area of early days, but with no idea of finding any trace of former dwellings. I read names of cross streets with semi-familiar or hazy recollection until I reached a fully remembered one which bounded the swampy land of long ago, the scene of many a boyish ramble through cypress trees and among the blackberries and palmettoes. At this I stood, surprised to find again the old one-storied brick street no longer verging a marsh but forming part of a middle district. But I was more amazed when I discovered that my old home at that corner on Canal Street was still visible from the gate as a discarded residence of one whose newer mansion had been built in front with garden in line with the street. Here was truly a joyous discovery, and, introducing myself to the occupant, whose family as she explained had owned the property from before my father's tenancy, I was admitted to the ground and allowed to ascend the balcony stair and enter the rooms of sacred memories. There as I stood by the window that caught the setting sunlight, I remembered the morning in shadow when I was carried in a father's arms to look for the last time upon my little playmate, white veiled in the calm sleep of death.

Could I forget a solemn and sad hour when I beheld the innocent of Earth winged for Heaven? It was to me alike the ideal of the angels, the bright revelation and hope of an after life, the thought-seed of belief in and love for the kingdom of spirits. In that realm mine was an angel there, alive in the fulness of joy.

> "Dear dead! they have become
> Like guardian angels to us;
> And distant Heaven, like home,
> Through them begins to woo us;
> Love, that was earthly, wings
> Its flight to holier places,
> The dead are sacred things
> That multiply our graces."

But it was also the birth home of her—my companion of maturer years. While a father stood by the little form whose life had lapsed here, a mother was bending over another little one left to console her in sorrow and to continue her love, and to be the guardian to me of thought and action after her.

> "They whom we loved on earth
> Attract us now to Heaven;
> Who shared our grief and mirth
> Back to us now are given.
> They move with noiseless foot
> Gravely and sweetly round us;
> And their soft touch hath cut
> Full many a chain that bound us."

As I closed the gate and thought again of the workshop once within it, I felt Frank too had gone. Frank, my affectionate negro, for whose memory I esteem my coloured brethren!

Frank, whose smile I remember! Was I not the better of his companionship, and of that of those others who liked to call me "the boss"? How sorrowfully a little further on had I witnessed the gang of incarcerated slaves in chains on their way to work in the woods.

Passing down Villerè Street to the Old Canal, I recalled the building of the bridge there and the many play-hours among its timbers, and the fishing for crayfish, a species of lobster, in the canal and bayous. Soon the sight of the old cemeteries, unexpectedly reached, prompted a visit. It was past sundown, but the whitening and garnishing of the tombs preparatory to All Saints' Day, which was the following Thursday, had kept them open till nightfall, and enabled me to go around them all.

When I came to the old St. Louis Cemetery and found its location relative to the house I had re-visited, I verily believed I had found the only place fitting my memory of my little sister's funeral day, but I was told the registers of all the cemeteries had been destroyed or lost to the authorities, two being then in the private possession of a Frenchwoman, to whose address I obtained a clue. The aged sexton was sympathetically kind, and promised me some place where I might lay my All Saints' Day flowers, in accordance with the custom of the citizens, if I determined that the grave I sought was within the walls. In the meantime I had threaded a way among the tombs (which are erections above ground like little houses) that followed the dictates of my memory, but without seeing any English names, nor, as far as one could judge, those of any Protestants. Answering in every respect the location of the spot I sought, it was difficult to account for the absence of English burials; but I had no doubt that Christ Church register would determine the point, and the Bishop had promised at Washington to be home that week to help me. Proceeding to the deanery at Christ Church, I learned there that the Bishop had arrived, and would preach at the following morning service.

NEW ORLEANS—SATURDAY NIGHT.

Returning to the hotel, I found an invitation to dinner awaiting me from the son of an eminent Scottish lawyer, a pleasure my arrangements obliged me to forego. In the reading-room were plenty of papers with elephantine and communicative headings of sensational and startling events from racial riots and negro shooting on the Levee that day, down to the citizens' meeting about the "dirtiest city in The States," which, as it happened, nature had not washed for seven weeks, and where the arid mud was content to remain at rest in the channels and elsewhere. The elasticity of the American editorial and reporting pen is the better of more or less salt—generally more—for British acceptance, to reduce its ideas to the proportion of others to which we are accustomed and of enterprises and possibilities that we can only attempt. The usual pyramidal array of attractive railway folders describing the beauty, speed, or convenience of their respective routes, or the elegance and comfort of their cars, were before me as instructive and useful lessons in transatlantic geography, allowance being made for the American faculty. The respective systems are mapped with rail tracks so wide and straight as to make each appear the backbone of the continental transport service—a range of wide mountainous highway over the land. Cities, rivers, and lakes, from New York, Niagara, and Superior downward, are packed and pegged in at the forks and bends as best to suit a fast age in the iron grasp of railway kings.

My room (being one of 250) was lofty and comfortable, and electrically lit. It would have vied with any in the St. Charles Hotel, a building in ashes when I arrived, but that week again to begin to rise, phœnix-like, and by this time, I suppose, as fine a house as any in The States. It was designed for coolness—two sides were all windows at figure height that swung full open into corridors, so much so as to make incomprehensible the warning to lock the door. The bed, with mosquito bar, was not, however, the honest full-sized one that provided amusement for little souls, as well as athletic feats for larger bodies, in their escape from the terrors of the swampy insect tribe after big game. These enemies in the summer nights were now out of town, and I feared no such stinging intruders. Notwithstanding, for the novelty of imagining the pleasure of defying the gnats and knowing the nights of old, I dropped the bar about me. But after my first sleep, my facial prominences were irritated by a blue-bottle which buzzed and danced and bumped down upon me with annoying pertinacity. Its expulsion beyond the network of my defences brought relief.

Not all the events and journeyings of the week, from Boston to Hartford, through New York and past Washington again, till I rested foot in the city that morning, followed me to sleep as did those between noon and night of that day. To awake 4700 miles from home where I awoke in boyhood's days was like arousing from a delectable dream. It was Sunday morning, and the dream continued. I went my accustomed way to the Sunday School across Congo Square, where beautiful kites were flying, though never any of mine on that day. The sun was shining and the day was hot, and I sat on a little form in a large hall with the wide windows in front full open to the pleasant breeze. It was above the fire station I knew best, and perhaps it was the morning when the engine went off with flying speed. It couldn't have been that when the station itself was on fire, and we had our lessons within charred window frames. I shall find the spot. The lesson is the 13th chapter of St. Matthew —*The same day went Jesus out of the house, and sat by the sea side. . . . Behold a sower went forth to sow;* and that leaf in the family Bible is thumbed and worn and torn, the page over which I had pored, because *he that received seed into the good ground is he that heareth the word and understandeth it.* The better to understand it, then, my own hands had sown in all places. Had I, in life, received the good seed, and had I grown it again from good ground? Then I came away for the last time with the TEACHER'S PARTING GIFT, that treasured little book at home which told me of GEORGE WASHINGTON, and taught me how to keep the commandments and write them all upon my heart.

SUNDAY—CHRIST CHURCH CATHEDRAL, ETC.

But it was now the hour to rise to reach Christ Church Cathedral for the early Communion Service. There I found a large number of communicants, and, when I reflected that the Office was that received from the Scottish Church, I regarded my Communion as possessing a double appropriateness. Only in New Orleans could I find links to the past, both national and personal, while Aberdeen and New Orleans linked ecclesiastically one could hardly imagine.

The pioneer Protestant congregation of the South-West, Christ Church, was organised in 1805, when the population of the city was 10,000, nearly all French or Spanish Catholics, or coloured, 45 votes out of a ballot of 53 determining it as an Episcopalian Church attached to the diocese of New York. The original site of the church was on Canal Street, where it was rebuilt in 1847; but in 1886 a new edifice was erected up town, whither the congregation had gone, and on the former site a row of handsome and attractive stores was erected, where will always be found the *élite* in search of the elegant and fashionable, after the habit of the *élite* in Edinburgh on Princes Street. The new church, chapel, and guild house, with the Bishop of Louisiana's see residence, form a fine Gothic group beautifully situated in the finest residential street in the city, St. Charles Avenue. The interior is rich with stained-glass memorial windows, jewelled in the chancel, where the furnishings are of the finest in carved oak (reredos), mural paintings (the Church Militant and Triumphant with two adoring angels), mosaics (the evangelistic symbols, wheat and grapes), fine metal work (altar cross, eagle lectern, and pulpit), and elaborate embroidery (altar cloth), while the baptismal font is of white marble in the form of a cross and exquisitely designed. The church is lighted by electricity and is seated for 800, and the chapel alongside perhaps for 200. It has 500 communicants. There are ten other Episcopal churches, their aggregate communicants numbering 3500, giving a total of 4000 for the city, where there are also ten Roman Catholic churches, eight Presbyterian, six Methodist, and ten of other denominations—45 in all. Trinity Church, which alone has 1100 communicants, is the best attended Episcopal Church, and of the Protestant churches has reputedly the best choir and the finest music. Its memorial window to General Polk, the fighting Bishop, is noted for its secret of colouring.

As a city founded by the French and Spanish Catholics, special interest attaches to the Roman Catholic element. It is the residence of the Archbishop of the Province of New Orleans and Arch-diocese of Louisiana, who receives all who call with visiting card. The palace was once the State Capitol. St. Louis Cathedral is the third building of the name called after the patron saint of France; the second was burnt on Good Friday, 1788, when the whole city was nearly destroyed and the colony crippled. A wealthy Spaniard spent £10,000 on the rebuilt edifice, completed a hundred years ago. Former Archbishops are buried in a vault beneath the altar. Early mass is usually attended by market-goers, who take their baskets into church. The beadle shows strangers to seats and keeps order. He wears a cocked hat, red coat, sword, and halbert, and circulates through church "a terror to small boys and stray dogs." At the Jesuits' church the compositions of Mozart, Weber, and Gounod are most artistically rendered by the trained voices of the opera and by Creoles. Brother Ignatius was "the polite sexton." New St. Joseph's is the second largest church in The States. It seats 1600, and visitors are impressed with the lofty nave and beautiful gigantic columns of polished red granite. St. Alphonsus' has a seating capacity of 2500, and of it, as of several others, it may be said that on the interior has been lavished every kind of art, sometimes giving an air of great richness. More than one has had its foundation impaired and threatened. The churches of other denominations do not call for special remark.

After breakfast I returned to Christ Church, to enjoy the morning service, at which the Bishop preached with his usual *empressement*. He had only returned the day before, and the

Daily Picayune had reported his Brotherhood addresses at Washington and elsewhere. Many remained to see him after the service, myself among the number. His impression then was that the registers, with other books, had been destroyed by the Federal Government, and the rector displaced because he refused to acknowledge it. He was glad to know that I possessed an extract of my younger sister's baptism. The tower, however, was to be searched by the following morning for any papers relating to burials. In reply to my inquiry what he thought of the Brotherhood, he said that it was the only thing by which the earnestness and enthusiasm of men had been called out, and that to be saved is to be a saviour of others.

In the afternoon I sought for and found the Roman Catholic Church, where one of my lady travellers had said I should see the pews of the older Christ Church edifice. The sexton alone was within, and was most communicative. He corroborated what I had been told, the truth of which was supported by the adjustment of old panels to pillars and corners. I entered one positioned as near to that in my life's picture of worship in my early days as I could determine, and, imagining myself back into the old pews of the old church in Canal Street, I daydreamed the pealing of the organ, operated as I

then fancied by the touch of angels in Heaven
—no human operator being visible to my
little eyes. The evening found me in the
Church of the Annunciation. It was the Harvest Festival, and I heartily enjoyed the sermon
by the rector, Archdeacon Percival, who, along
with his daughters and niece, had been a passenger in the *Campania*. Running through
thanksgiving thoughts for the world's reapings,
there were in my case special ones for the spiritual harvest gleaned that day in the Crescent
City, and they who on the Atlantic had lent a
tow rope were fellow-worshippers. After service I had the happiness of shaking hands
with Archdeacon and the Misses Percival, and
renewing my grateful thanks to them, my
presence and doings in the city being the
evidence of the services rendered. I was there
first introduced to Mr. Zacherie, to whom, later
on, I was under a debt of gratitude.

FIRE AND FIRE BRIGADE.

My peregrinations from point to point had
taken me by many fire-stations, and at several I
had stood in admiration of their equipments and
readiness for the rapid rescue from flame of a
largely wooden city. Fire-engines have a fascination on me. In my boyhood I had a make-believe honour of belonging to a New Orleans

Boys' Fire Brigade which had a wooden engine, and doubtless as inefficient hose and helmets, but we turned out at the alarm of the fire-bells and proved to each other, and perhaps to some citizens, of what stuff we were made. Through the remembrance of youthful enthusiastic fire attacks, I have a sympathy with the modern Boys' Brigade, because it implants in the impressionable heart a knowledge of virtues that in after life may have to be practised. The tombs of firemen, some of which are very fine, were then as representative to me of heroes as those of officers in any army can be now. The chats I had with the real firemen, and the views I got of the up-to-date engines, were fuel to my ardour to see a genuine fire at midnight. The elevator professedly taking me to repose carried me instead to the garden roof, from which a fire on the Levee was attractively visible. It was an altitude of excitement. I had but to follow the crowd and keep the fire glare ahead to avoid walking into the Mississippi or falling over timber logs, or finding myself shot into a molasses barrel, the remembrance of which, sweet in the past, might not have been so in the present.

When I reached the fire scene I found myself among rail tracks, and locomotives puffing and shunting about wagons as actively as the fire-engines were snorting and playing on the flames stationary or processional. A whole long freight train was ablaze from end to end, and a freight shed and contents formed a long fire mass bar separating the immense crowd on the city side from that along the river. Already another freight train had caught fire in several parts, and hose were plentifully directed to save it, as the locomotives hauled it and others to a place safe for themselves and for all. The hose ran all over the rail track, and the river engines did splendid service. The conflagration was caused by the spontaneous combustion of an unprotected lime load exposed to the unexpectedly heavy rain that day. 346 fires occurred in 1893.

The fire brigade is well organised. It has 150 alarm stations, and, to cope at the earliest moment with an outbreak, the alarm boxes are automatic and electrically connected with the central station. Fire bells in church or city towers respond at once, and indicate the district by taps corresponding to its number, each figure being represented by a succession of taps with a pause before the next. Twenty taps call out the entire brigade (320 men and 35 engines), which has sometimes to fight fierce and extensive flames. One tap signifies that the fire is out.

OLD TIMES AND NEW.

The problem to be solved on Monday was how the position of St. Louis's Cemetery should coincide with the location so fixedly in my memory, and that there should be no trace of the site. Added thereto was the task of obtaining negative testimony respecting other cemeteries widely scattered, but neither too new nor too far afield to be rightly overlooked. Through Mr. Clark, Liverpool, I had received from Mr. Westfeldt (then in Europe), a vestryman of Christ Church, a letter of introduction to his brother. His and the Bishop's further information was my hope. Mr. Westfeldt gave me every assistance, and took much trouble while I worked out his ideas. The city registers did not go far enough back, and the Bishop's impression respecting the destruction of the church registers was confirmed. The Bishop knew, however, that there had been an old cemetery related to the church, and he introduced me to a lady who was one of the oldest Churchwomen in the city. From her I learned that previous to the blocking out of certain streets the church burying ground was outside the Roman Catholic part of the Old St. Louis one, but it was not within her knowledge to explain more, or whether any of the houses around now occupied the area. Her reminiscences of the city and Christ Church of fifty and sixty years back riveted my attention, as they fell partly within my own, and I could not resist the idea that we were speaking about times nobody else could remember, and were not improbably the two oldest inhabitants, if my short juvenile residence entitled me to that appellation. Such a supposition may be fairly based on the normal mortality of cities, and the changes incidental to the development of the commerce of a country, alongside of the observed youthhood of the American nation, partly owing to the immigration from Europe, but not unaffected by climatic influences on advanced lives. Then, in the case of New Orleans, depopulation caused by fever epidemics in the past, the Civil War, and the consequent decadence of commercial prosperity would account for an increased ratio of absent lives.

I left the ancient citizen with a degree of satisfaction to work out much data I had acquired to an affirmative or negative conclusion on the respective points, but I had by this time a settled opinion that the quarter I had fixed on was the right one, and I therefore mapped out my research to include all the haunts of my boyhood. Jackson, Camp, Rampart, Esplanade and Magazine Streets, having a military ring, had been early fixed upon my mind, and, with Franklin, Gravier, Lafayette, and Villerè, had charms to make them remembered. The last had its dark stretch where ghosts abounded, but did not frighten me. I had not attempted Tchoupitoulas and such like names. Next there was the Carondelet Canal, into which the sailors had dipped me to terrorise the captain whose ward I was on my way "across the lake," the Calaboose, or prison, with fire-bell tower, the fire station where above it was the Sunday School. Congo Square modernised by telegraph poles and wires, kite-tails suspended from which reminded me of my American kite days as those did the story of Franklin, the origin of that which had given the posts a *locus standi* as well as the wires a world to girdle. The trees were now half-a-century higher, and underneath one rested an old man who recited his earliest reminiscences of the place and I mine. The nine o'clock at night cannon would not fire again to warn slaves home. It was silent for ever. Then there was the street where I once slept to guard a companion from ghosts, while he was prepared with pistol under the pillow to keep live ones (white or black) at bay during a period of so-called repose in a phantom erection.

A short line of railway took me to Lake Pontchartrain one day, and another, by a different route, the next day. There I could recall my sail across from one pier and my return to another from the hermitage in the woods at Gum Creek, a little paradise where clear brooks rippled and the birds were always singing, and the air was fragrant with aroma from the iris, the honeysuckle, and the jasmine, and I lived amid nature undisturbed.

I have no weakness for fruits or sweets, but those tropical ones, water melons, sugar-cane, and sweet potatoes, which I am barred having at home, had charms above their edible properties. The first and last I found in New York, and a timely tropical downpour of rain in a suburban part afforded sufficient excuse for my enjoying in a provision store the other of the trio. There I bought a whole stalk of sugar-cane, and, after having it sawn into convenient bits, I sat down upon a barrel, where, between the inspiration of both cane and barrel, I believed myself a boy. I was doubtless a novelty of the hour to the lads taking the shelter of the awning, who all wore American smiles.

New Orleans is the twelfth city of the States. In my "citizen" days it was the fourth, ranking after New York, Philadelphia, and Baltimore. It is the chief city of Louisiana, and the most southern metropolis. After Liverpool, it is the largest cotton market in the world, handling 2,000,000 bales annually, and is the third of American seaports. The population is about the same as Edinburgh, 242,039 (winter, 260,000), the percentage of nationalities being—Anglo-American, 18 per cent.; French, 17; German, 15; Irish, 14; Italian, 8; Spanish, 2.3; and 25 per cent. coloured, or 177,376 white and 14,663 coloured. Baton Rouge, a quaint old place 89 miles up the river, with a population of 10,478, is the State capital. In latitude 29.56 and longitude 90.4 W., New Orleans is 106 to 108 miles from the Delta of the Mississippi, in the Gulf of Mexico, and is one of the most picturesque and interesting cities in America owing to the survival of the buildings, manners, and customs of the original French and Spanish. G. W. Cable describes it as "a city of villas and cottages, of umbrageous gardens intersected by 470 miles of unpaved streets shaded by forest trees, haunted by song-birds, fragrant with a wealth of flowers that never fails a day in the year, and abundant in season with fruit—the fig, plum, pomegranate, and orange." The Creoles are "a handsome, graceful, and intelligent race, of a decidedly Gallic type." Its history begins with the mention of the Mississippi being traversed by white men (Spaniards) in 1536, then in 1539-41-42-43; with the settlement of French in 1699, the city being founded by Bienville in 1718, and passing under Spanish domination 1764-1801. It was then Americanised by purchase, 1803; besieged in 1812 by the British, being the scene of battle in 1815, and taken in the Civil War in 1862. Its State was admitted to the Union in 1812.

There are five parks, four libraries, four theatres, eighty public or private schools, fifty institutions (of which eleven are charitable), twelve insurance companies, ten railroads, twelve steamboat lines, thirty-four sea-going. Its exports are £248,000,000 ; imports, £50,000,000 ; bank capital, £2,000,000 ; and its valuation in 1894, £28,000,000 ; manufactures, £12,000,000 ; commerce, £88,000,000 ; revenue, £600,000 ; debt, £3,100,000 (steadily if slowly disappearing). There are twelve miles of water front.

Since the '30's, when the city bade fair to reach if not outshine New York, there has not been such a spirit of emulation and enterprise as there is now. Public and private improvements are being carried out on a liberal scale. The conversion of 186 miles of streets into beautiful avenues, and transforming the car service from horse to electric, is costing £1,000,000, —(one system was the first in the States)—and all around the least changeable is all change.

The Chamber of Commerce Book asserts that the city has resumed its place among the world's ascendant cities in spite of war, war debts, "scallawaggery" of various kinds, degrees and complexions, epidemics, and bad crop seasons, and is itself again. It claims that at last it is awakening to follow the sun to the zenith even to the bridging of the Mississippi, the Father of Waters, one of the engineering enterprises of the age, that river being from a quarter to half a mile wide as it passes round the crescent after its flow of above four thousand miles from its sources in far distant States. It does not claim to be the foremost or finest city, but it is studying architectural adornments, fashions, and graces of the day; or the best situated, most healthful, or best governed; or the richest, with the most extensive factories, office buildings, luxurious hotels, and palatial mansions, though it has warrant for some measure of boast that its ladies may be lovely and the most charming, its society the most cultured, and its people generally the gayest and most content in the land. It has a night side : on its bright side, however, are industrious people, enterprising houses, men of wealth, cultivation, honour, good morals, and home pride ; above all, it is a CITY OF HOMES.

MARDI GRAS AND "WEST END."

After the winter gaieties the great Carnival of Mardi Gras precedes Lent and winds up all festivities. There are night and day processions of moving tableaux with a wealth of artistic details, all prepared by clubs and individuals, sometimes costing £6000. The show is said to be unsurpassed the world over. Then follows the lake side excursions to "West End," the popular resort of the citizens, an open-air concert platform built out upon Lake Pontchartrain, with shade-tree and flower-bed promenades. There boating and yachting are enjoyed and restaurants abound, including some famed for fish cookery. The lake is 30 miles long and 24 wide.

ROUND THE CEMETERIES.

My excursions were subordinate to my main purpose, and some cemeteries were visited only to find them too new to be taken any account of. One of the St. Louis blocks was for coloured people, and there I witnessed a long funeral procession of coloured people accompanied with banners and a band of music. The two next blocks were those of which I traced the registers to a Creole Frenchwoman. She reported on my return that two of my surname were buried there, but not a Grace Fraser Giles.

On visiting the Girod Cemetery (that of Christ Church) I found the register contained entries dating as far back as the period of inquiry, but no record such as I sought, which I, however, did not expect to find, as the ground lay in an opposite direction to my idea of it.

In the Métairie Cemetery, the largest and handsomest in the city, and beautifully laid out with exquisite flowers, were many fine tombs of notable families and armies. In one beside it I noticed the ground of the St. Andrew's Society, which I thought had a forlorn aspect that day, compared with other looked-after parts, and I wondered if I was the only Scotsman near, or if its wild homeliness was meant to be symbolic of the land from which some laid there had travelled, on their way to the "Land o' the Leal." In my pocket I had the certificate of my father's brother's membership of the St. Andrew's Society of New Orleans of 1837, but it afforded no clue to the whereabouts or offices of any such body after the lapse of sixty years.

Having explored every cemetery not obviously new, I returned on Tuesday to the old St. Louis one, and found the same impulse lead me as before. I then narrated to the sexton all my investigations, and my deepened conviction that I was near the spot I sought, whereupon he suddenly rose, took his staff, and, going out of his office, bade me follow. His confident step gladdened my heart, but when I observed that he went the same winding way among the tombs my fear of renewed failure grew and reached a point of resignation as we faced the last alley, apparently lining the wall. There, however, he took his stand, and, pointing over the tombs I looked upon for the third time, exclaimed, "It is there, you will require a ladder." It was clear, however, as we talked on our way to the gate that no ladder was at hand, and with the necessary permission I returned and climbed the little houses. By this means I attained the wall-top, and, descending a rubbish heap on the further side, I found myself at last within the area I had travelled so far to find. All doubts dispelled, as, like a modern Old Mortality, I cleared the tomb tablets of débris and disclosed English inscriptions. On one I read the Scottish name of Robert Sinclair. Notwithstanding the custom of the place to bury above ground as a matter of necessity, my remembrance of the little coffin being let down "earth to earth" was absolutely correct, as the vaults were built in the ground beneath the surface and so resembled British graves. This fact was clearly established by the open grave vaults that rendered treading the ground, concealed by accumulated vegetable matter, dangerous.

In the course of the same evening, my last in New Orleans, I received a letter from Mr. Westfeldt urgently enjoining me not to leave the city until I had seen Mr. Zacherie, both having, however, concluded that the Girod ground was the cemetery I sought. Although of a decidedly different opinion by that time, I deferred my early morning return to St. Louis ; and, after morning service at Christ Church and a visit to the Bishop to thank him and Dean Paradise for their kind help, I saw both Mr. Westfeldt and Mr. Zacherie, the conclusion to which we all came being as I myself had on the previous day determined. But this conclusion was confirmed by printed and official papers in the hands of Mr. Zacherie, who was the convener of a committee that had issued a report on the same old burying ground to the Diocesan Synod, with a view to its being put in order and cared for, there being graves within it of some people notable in their day, among others the first Governor of the State of Louisiana. The report noted the difficulty in finding the spot, which had no access, also that no one could be heard of who had attended a funeral there. It surprised my friends to learn that I had, and as it is even possible that I was at the last burial there, probably no one alive now is the immediate relation of any interred within it.

My departure on the Wednesday compelled me, deeply to my regret, to give up the honour of dining with the Bishop, who had twice invited me to do so. "Now that is too bad," he said; "you have not given me the opportunity of showing you hospitality."

THE CITIES OF THE DEAD.

The cemeteries of New Orleans are termed the Cities of the Dead, as they mostly consist of the little white houses which serve as tombs, with two or more vaults. There are larger structures with a number of vaults for the burial of members of societies which own them. Around the walls are also built rows of vaults called ovens. All are well cemented after burials, and vigorous laws prevent them being re-opened too soon. The tombs are usually brick or marble, and cost from £20 to £200 and upwards. The old St. Louis Cemetery (No. 1) is the oldest in the city, and it is difficult to find one's way through its tortuous alleys, the tombs mostly bearing French and Spanish inscriptions. Within it are buried the ancient Creole families, many of which figured in colonial history. The handsomest tomb is that of the Italian Society, commandingly high with white marble statue of Religion supporting a cross ; the loftiest is that of the Société Française, and other large erections are the tomb of the *Artillerie d'Orléans*, surrounded by cannon, and the Portuguese tomb. There is also a vault of the Chinese Society. Noted tombs are those of Daniel Clark, American Consul in Spanish times, and Stephen Zacharie, the founder of the Mississippi Valley Bank. Paul Morphy, the famous chess player, a native of New Orleans, is also buried here. (The City Chess Club leads the van with 700 members, but the champion is a Scotchman.)

At the end of an alley one enters a quiet nook, the private ground of the Layton family, and containing also a private chapel for the burial of the Jesuit priests. When I wandered into this beautifully kept precinct I thought no corner in the city could be more desired by me within which to rest my floral thoughts, and I little dreamt that at the moment I was within a few yards of the spot to which I should return after all my wanderings in the city were over and at an end, and my efforts to discover the lost precinct successfully crowned.

It is remarkable that I should have arrived in the city with no preconceived plan, and, going about promiscuously, should have been thought-led first to one place, and then in an hour or two so near to another which I had hoped to find, that I was practically at it, or really indeed within it, as the same ground had before been within that of the Christ Church graveyard.

The enclosure measures only about 60 feet by 45 feet, but that of the Laytons belonged to it until the family, joining the Roman Catholics, were allowed an entrance from the Cemetery. There is even yet only a high wooden paling between the two portions. Prior to this the whole ground would be nearly double the length, when a brick wall was built to separate the Christ Church part from that retained by St. Louis Cathedral, where only those of the Roman Catholic faith could be interred. The wall was built about 1838 or 1840 to settle the disputes that arose between the clergy of the two Churches, and its erection was probably subsequent to my earliest knowledge of the graveyard.

ALL SAINTS' EVE.

On All Saints' Day, November 1, all the cemeteries are visited by thousands, when the tombs are ornamented with natural and artificial flowers, statuary, china vases, draperies, and lighted candles, the trees being whitened several feet from the ground. "We cover the coffins of our beloved with flowers as a token of affection," says a reverend father; and it is said of man, "He cometh up like a flower, and is cut down." It is not strange, as Mr. Zacherie says in his New Orleans Guide, that we should repeat so beautiful a ceremony and cover their tombs on one day set apart for the purpose each recurring year. On All Saints' Eve, therefore, the larger florists in Royal and Canal Streets, and every such store throughout the city, were filled with floral devices — wreaths, crosses, stars, crescents, or other designs, constructed of dried immortelles or fresh cut flowers, beautiful and costly—which would require hundreds of wagons to convey them at dawn, to distant or nearer cemeteries, in advance of the moving mass of the people of all faiths and colour, who would desert the city that day to fill with life and animation the aisles of the sleeping cities of the dead. Already some were being conveyed to the various cemeteries. It was that day when I concluded all my inquiries, and had deferred my visit to St. Louis until I should see Mr. Zacherie. At Christ Church I had been left alone, and there I remained a little to view the whole interior—the walls, pulpit, and windows; the altar and the beautiful font—after which I closed the door with thankful thoughts. To leave the city without another and final sight of the old home would have been a regret, and I had just time to accomplish its distance and have a last look at it from the gateway.

In ten days I had to be in Scotland, and I was only at the Gulf of Mexico, but one thing still remained to be accomplished. Finding at the florist's the St. Andrew's Cross of heather I had brought from Scotland, and had had brightened with local immortelles, I repaired with it and some added flowers of Louisiana land to the now known enclosure. There, clearing a little space as well as hands could do without implements, I laid my tribute from far as well as near in unison with the sentiments of the Crescent City on that day. Then, as I gave a last look at the untended, deserted, and forgotten plot, lovely and sacred in its still loneliness, where the sun alone may enter by day and the stars shine by night, I remembered the lines o'er a little grave by the sweet Norwegian Fiord:—

"Fred med dit stov,
Kjœrt er os dit minde."
"Peace with thy dust,
Dear to us is thy memory."

As I passed out of the old St. Louis Cemetery gate, I bade the sexton a grateful good-bye, and turned towards Scotland. ✠

Protestant THE OLD ST. LOUIS CEMETERY, NEW ORLEANS *Roman Catholic*

IV.

HOMEWARD—THROUGH THE ELEMENTS.

BY FIRE, LAND-AND-WATER.

 WAS *en route* for home by half-past three, *viâ* the Queen and Crescent line, because I wished once more to go across the lake, though now an a-bridged passage by car and wheel, not by schooner and sail.

Immediately after leaving New Orleans the train traverses five miles of marshy ground and crosses the longest bridge in the world, a trestle one, 26 miles long, seven of which span the narrow part of the lake, with two drawbridges for vessels to pass through, the lake being really an arm of the Gulf of Mexico by which vessels get behind the city. It then enters a forest land destitute of novelty to tourist or traveller. The region, however, was full of interest to me, for there somewhere my little legs had had many a run and ramble, "where the mocking bird has no sorrow in his song, no winter in his year." As swamp, creek, and bayou were passed, and the cars rumbled along by burning tree stumps, I lived anew my boyish days and delights, and for far on the way I sat ruminating over the long past. Thus, in train of thought immersed, I trained through tree lanes and vales recalling scenes of the wood and the way, and in particular, the night when, somewhere in the same far-stretching forest, fatigued and sleepy, I fell from a laden ox wagon beneath which I might have lost my life, or have been a "Babe-in-the-Wood" among the alligators, had my calls in the dark distance not surpassed the noise of the creaking wheels.

IN AIR AND LIGHTNING.

In American parlance I was in a "lightning express" and "air line." The one idea assured me that no time would be lost as the cars rattled and the train thundered along 40 or more miles an hour for 50 hours on end, and the other inspired me with confidence that I should swoop down upon the deck of the *Lucania* before it left the dock at nine o'clock on Saturday morning. Obliged to fast, because I had a fast train to catch, I had bought "crackers," an orange, and a peach pie for the journey through air in lightning. The first went off at once, the second

I had placed on the carriage window-sill to await its verdict of ripe or over ripe, and consequent absorption or freedom, and, while my mind was wool-gathering where only forget-me-nots grew, it toppled over and was lost in the woods perhaps not far from its native grove. The peach-pie survived to cross the Atlantic as a stowaway, and found a watery bed in the Mersey at the hands of the steward, of pie-ous memory, and a man of Mersey.

Travelling within only a few hours of November with windows open to catch as much breeze as the momentum of the train could generate out of a tropical day was a pleasant experience on the "air line." The country, however, lacked interest. On the authority of the guide book the first 200 miles had only unimportant stations. After that, until 300 more are traversed, only progressive places on the way to importance are by the wayside; then several battlefields, one historical as the bloodiest in modern days, at Chickamauga, near Chattanooga, in 1863, where 30,000 were killed or wounded out of 112,000 engaged. Burlington, founded by the author of "Tom Brown's School Days," is a hundred miles further on.

Ten hours of the journey would be in the sleeper with the crescent moon to the west. After that the country would have been delightful had we been walking through and about it instead of "lightning" and "airing" over it, for there are natural bridges, a cantilever one with big spans, tunnels long and wonderful, great rivers with splendid views, rail tracks on cliffs, falls of great height (!), picturesque districts, high points, mountains, and, above all, below our feet, blue grass occupying a region of 10,000 square miles of correct pasture for high bred horses with reputed pedigrees.

CINCINNATI, PITTSBURG, HARRISBURG.

Having crossed the States of Tennessee and Kentucky, and touched the Alleghanies, we entered the State of Ohio at Cincinnati, its chief city, and the ninth in the United States. It was the terminus of the air line from the south, and we arrived as darkness had fallen. We were transferred across the city in the night air in a 'bus to the system in correspondence for New York—a well arranged change of air. Not feeling well all day I had high tea at the station, and was comforted to find that my sleeper had been booked by telegram from New Orleans.

Cincinnati, the Queen City, is finely situated on two terraces rising from the Ohio river along an amphitheatre of hills. It has ten to twelve miles river frontage. The best residences are on the surrounding highlands. It has about 300,000 inhabitants, one third being of German origin. The cities of Covington and Newport, with an additional population of 62,289, are connected by five fine bridges, one a suspension bridge costing £360,000, 2250 ft. long and 36 wide. Relics indicate occupation of the site in historic times. Its trade by river and rail is very important, and it has some fine Government and public buildings, and a most successfully designed fountain in a square, which forms the business centre from which radiate many tramway lines.

Although I had a comfortable sleep I awoke wearied and unwell, somewhat indifferent perhaps to where I was or how I should get home. My only desire was a cup of tea, if I could get it where I lay, but I was told I must go to the buffet car and sit down to breakfast. As that was impossible, and I had no appetite, I lay still, resolved to be the last to rise, a privilege the coloured porter sympathetically accorded me, not making up my berth until the morning was well on. That, however, was not his chief kindness. With a sympathy I will always remember, he kept the conductor from troubling me, and of his own motion got me a cup of tea from the buffet, for which no charge could be or was made, and yet it was more the manner and the tone of my friend that penetrated my heart and cheered me, sick and lonely as I was, far away from home, with the cold Atlantic to face on the morrow—*and he was a negro.* I found all the attendants on the sleepers, who are coloured men, willingly attentive, and wonderfully agile in all their movements.

Between Cincinnati and Philadelphia the railway systems traverse important regions and pass many large towns, or cities, to use a correct term. On this, my last day's run from Cincinnati to Pittsburg, which was passed in early morning, and Philadelphia, only Pittsburg and Harrisburg stand pre-eminently requiring notice by a traveller kept much in the dark half of the way and out of reach of all the whole way.

The most beautiful part is between Pittsburg and Philadelphia traversed by the Vestibule Limited train by daylight, and as on the first morning of my journey south, so in the last of my return, I had the good fortune to have the companionship of a gentleman to point out all the features and beauties of an interesting stretch of country with many varied associations. He had travelled much in America. The course of conversation, instructive and entertaining, embraced no end of subjects, which only the leisure and comfort of a saloon carriage could make as highly enjoyable. It is one of the pleasures of American travel that one who is willing to respond agreeably to the words of another finds a thrill of delight in rightly estimating the true proportion of things around him, Americans being good conversationalists.

Pittsburg, the Iron City, is not the capital of its State, nor is it one of the great cities of the United States, but it is one of the chief industrial ones. In Scotland, Carnegie libraries have increased our knowledge of Pittsburg, but although literary light and light literature are the outcome of many such munificent gifts, the idea of the city is but iron and smoke; perfectly true in respect of the lower lying parts, but not altogether the character of its residential districts, which are on the high lands above the Monongahela and Alleghany rivers and the Ohio river, when we include the sister city of Alleghany, which has a separate government, but is related to Pittsburg. A Greater New York may some day be followed by a Greater Pittsburg that would represent, but in increased ratio, 344,000 inhabitants instead of only 238,617, Alleghany having 105,387.

Harrisburg is the capital of Pennsylvania, although Philadelphia is the third city in The States, and the largest in area. The population is about 40,000, as compared with a million more in Philadelphia. It is finely situated on the river Susquehanna, where it is a mile wide. The conspicuous Capitol contains a good library. There is a war monument 110 feet high. Four bridges cross the river, one being the quaint one described in Dickens' "American Notes."

After Harrisburg there was a delightful run

of 105 miles to Philadelphia, occupying about three hours of a sunny afternoon in the fall, the tropics being left behind. The railway crosses streams of all kinds, narrow or wide, deep or shallow, rocky around or rocky in mid-stream; summer resorts ; fields of wheat, maize, and tobacco in the Piquea valley; the picturesque defiles of the South Mountain ; the beautiful valleys of the Susquehanna and Juniata, and the peaceful Chester valley, of which a splendid view is obtained as the train crosses the Alleghany mountains and enters the "Garden of Pennsylvania," one of the most carefully cultivated farm districts in America. It then reaches the region of suburban homes, and it is difficult to determine whether one is in rural or urban ground, the distance from Philadelphia Station being about 20 miles. Here there is a monument commemorating the British defeat of the Americans in 1777, and as the train progresses it passes Villa Nova, a Roman Catholic College, monastery and farm. Bryn Mawr College, a college for women (130 students), and Haverford Quaker College, situated in a finely wooded park, and a most important institution. Various suburban stations—tasteful buildings with flower gardens—are passed at West Philadelphia, by which the handsome Broad Street Station is reached. In these hundred miles iron works and limekilns appear ; and Lancaster, a prosperous manufacturing town of 32,000 inhabitants, and an important tobacco market, is passed about 36 miles from Harrisburg.

On reaching Philadelphia I had traversed a loop line to New Orleans of 3146 miles, including the further distance to New York by a different line. That occupied four-and-a-half days and four nights, which, with four days in the Crescent City, added eight days to my Brotherhood visit—ever to be memorable.

TO THE ATLANTIC.

Continuing the journey, I reached New York about seven or eight o'clock in the evening, but without my "hold all," which having strayed on the way, I had nothing at all to hold. With my brass "baggage check," I had no fear of its being lost, although we had parted company nearly 1583 miles away, only it would have been better had I known a new patent label of a dean who lost his speech on the way to a Church Congress, to "stick to it one's-self." To discover the baggage store where my trunk lay, book at the hotel, and see there if anybody in the world wanted me, and get my last supper in America somewhere, occupied the evening until the hold-all that had held on its way all alone was espied surmounting a heap of baggage trundled into the depôt from the ferry-boat. Sometime before 11 I found the Cunard shed and threw my then little belongings amid a mélange of goods of all sorts, which I could hardly imagine a vessel of any tonnage able to stow away.

When I reached the hotel again, two friends were waiting me—one, Mr. Perry Worden, a student of Columbia College, now in Germany, where Mr. H. A. Sill, ex-editor of *St. Andrew's Cross*, is now distinguishing himself, and Mr. Duff, a former member of the Edinburgh Y.M.F.S. Mr. Perry Worden, having been my guest in 1892; was proxy for the Scottish Brotherhood at the Boston Convention. Sandwich-wise between a long railroad run and an Atlantic voyage, the night was passed till 1 a.m. with Mr. Worden in the chair, and I myself *on* bed longing to be there *in*, and after four hours' sleep obliged to be there *out* again at 5 a.m. In Broadway by half-past five, both of us under umbrellas that never before or since weathered such meteorological forces, I cabled home, and was heard of again in Scotland, to which I felt myself, though only by wire, re-attached. Then we had breakfast at a restaurant on the way. At the baggage depôt the trunk was redeemed, storage paid, and a cab obtained for a dollar and a half, my friend demurring to two dollars for a fifteen minutes' drive along the wharf.

We were soon at the Cunard Co.'s shed, an

immense station-like yard, stretching out into the harbour, along one side of which the R.M.S. *Lucania* was moored, with steam up and ready to sail, a thousand passengers pouring in while the rain was pouring down. On alighting I left the trunk to look after itself, while I laid hold of my little hold-all, which had held its position where I had laid it over night like a Jack in office. Mr. Duff had also come to see me depart, and very soon every passenger was aboard, severed from their friends' farewell, save by the waves of handkerchiefs and umbrellas. At nine o'clock preparations to get under way were begun. It then rained whales rather than cats and dogs, and amid that we were out of the dock and off, leaving our companions under a plateau of umbrellas, symbolically signalling adieux, as weather permitted.

America is a land of spiritual, intellectual, material, meteorological, and topographical contrast, from pole to equator, and through every latitude and longitude of thought, from demoniacal rhapsody to celestial theme, peopled, too, from every nation and clime. And so our last morning, not even fair, contrasted with the fairy scene that greeted our coming, and which we prefer should live in our memories for ever more and more than ever.

The deluge of rain, however, suddenly ceased as we moved out into the bay, and we saw our assemblage of speed-bidding friends dwindle to a point and become a speck in the panorama of proud edifices and floating palaces. We passed the great gateway of the western world under the fair but imperious colossal "Janitress of the Land of Liberty," enlightening the world as the sun shone out upon our rippled realm to rule our course for the kingdom upon which it never sets.

ABOARD THE "LUCANIA."

Luncheon was heartily enjoyed by all, after which we found our voyage home well begun, and our ship in the Atlantic again, beyond the pilot's range, although the increasing wave curls made us credulous as to consequences. Towards evening I felt my liberty would be much better circumscribed. I therefore made the practical acquaintance with my state-room, being one correspondingly the same as in the *Campania*, but with the sole possession of two berths and the sofa. A sudden lurch, which brought my trunk right into the middle of the floor, and a bundle from the upper berth, simultaneously rolled myself from the sofa on to the trunk and other articles about my feet. This prepared me for possibilities of a voyage in November, but, fortunately, it was the last lurch as well as the first; and, but for the cold, which limited our deck exercise, and a somewhat cloudy sky, the passage, being devoid of storm, was an excellent one. Although I rested on Sunday, the *mal-de-mer* was not a disturber of my peace nor of my sleep, and I did every justice to the sumptuous meals. We had 178 saloon passengers, 114 second cabin, and 720 steerage—total, 1012. When not reading in the library or drawing-room Mr. G. W. Cable, Mark Twain, or other American literary lights, I found delightful passengers to occupy the days and evenings in any quarter of the ship, with occasional excursions to the lower regions, where the giant engines worked restlessly in an unvisited region of scrupulously polished steel framing.

The library, 29 by 24 feet, was a paragon of solace for the mind and comfort for the body, suggesting the French Renaissance. Light and elegant as befitted a sphere meant to illumine the intellect with brain sparks from intellectual anvils, it was in shape like a crescent, and might not inaptly have had a motto around *Crescetur culta*, for it is true of the mind as of an acorn, *it is increased by cultivation* at sea as well as the other is on land. The glazed book-cases were beautifully carved, with Amboyna panelled doors below, the books being bound in green morocco, numbered in accord with the printed reference catalogue, and admirably arranged for the convenience of "members." Passengers got them from the librarian "to take home," which might be anywhere in the ship, a progressive fire-and-water parish esteemed in the Atlantic. If lost amid the slumbers of the deep they generally turned up below a sofa in the drawing room, and took a course to their mother crescent, where they were all safe, while their beau-peeps had fallen asleep and left their tales behind them.

The room was richly carved, like the bookcases, with highly ornate ceiling, oak parquetry floor with Turkey carpet, and upholstered profusely in Mecca (which superinduced many a pilgrimage there), and blue velvet with window curtains of rich brocade. This is but a sample of the palatial magnificence of the whole ship, and of its sister the *Campania*, in both of which life at sea in fine weather is Elysian, but there are ups and downs on water as well as on earth. There were about a dozen windows in the library with sea views ahead and on either side. Like the whole ship the room was electrically lit. By the windows were sixteen desks, which supplied a scratch orchestra the end days of the voyage—*scribere scientes*, men skilled in writing. In the outward voyage we had a vocal concert at the end, with Lord Brassey in the chair, a large collection being taken for Sailors' Orphans' Homes (British and United States).

V.
UNVISITED STATES AND TERRITORIES.

WAS a constant "subscriber" to this globe circulating library, having nothing on mind to occupy my thoughts (as in the sister ship), and when I was done Cable-ing and Mark-ing Twain in the latter's Life on the Mississippi, I naturally and frequently fell asleep and thought myself back in the Crescent City. I also sought out other Americana in print or picture, and felt quite at home amidst it.

Travellers may record what they intelligently learn as well as what they observe, and they are sometimes justified in their observations with only sampling places. In regard to America I was more at sea on the *Campania* than on the *Lucania*, but in my home voyage I had the advantage of having sampled Columbia and the Dominion, so that I may imagine myself sunk in the isolated cosiness of the crescent—a kind of man in the moon both at home and at sea —in a reference here to the unvisited parts.

THE UNVISITED WEST.

Although the area of the States that I may be said to have touched or circumscribed is, speaking roundly, about 885,865 square miles, that of those I may call west of the Mississippi is 2,615,545 square miles, and—as between New York and San Francisco— Chicago, my farthest point west, is less than a third of the distance across, or 720 miles compared with 1860. The total area of The States is nearly thirty times that of Great Britain and Ireland, being 3,501,410 square miles, while the latter is only 120,928 square miles. In the vast West there are 23 States and Territories, containing 24 principal cities with over 33,000 inhabitants, the total of which last (2,280,122), added to the total population of the other 66 principal cities in the 27 eastern States (10,730,673), is 13,010,795. The full population (1890) of the fifty States, including the Indian and other Territories, the district of Columbia and Alaska, is 62,654,045, compared with 37,880,764 in the British Isles; the eastern ones having 46,160,075, and the western 16,493,970. It is estimated that the present population is divided—25 millions in cities out of a present total of 72 millions, there being 30 cities with over 100,000 inhabitants—that of Greater New York now numbering the total of the United States at the time of the Declaration of Independence, 3,200,000.

Canada in the west is as yet a great comparatively unoccupied region, yet gradually attracting inhabitants in the less trying climate, and it remains to be seen how the Yukon River gold field may influence the development to the extreme north-west, lying, as Klondyke does, sixty miles within the Canadian boundary.

The area of the Canadian Dominion, or British North America, including Newfoundland, is 3,617,000 square miles—less than that of Europe, but somewhat greater than the area already given for the United States, with Alaska. The population is said to be about 5,000,000 (1,300,000 of French descent, and 120,000 Red men).

So much for the light that a man in the moon may throw upon the United States and Canada, their areas and inhabitants. In order to get at the spirit of places, a dose of Mark Twain's mes-mer-ic mixture, with his swampy 'ssippi, is necessary to take the reader along and make another twain. He will be wideawake enough to mark when he is soaring, and when dreaming.

UNITED STATES CITIES.

There are ten American western cities of over 100,000 inhabitants, and in order to take them in by covering the imaginary ground, the reader will accompany me in the crescent lunar fly. We return at once by the flash-air-line, with nap-shot, 100 miles past Cincinatti to Louisville (161,129), "The Falls City"—because of the Ohio River rapids. It was visited in 1890 by a terrific tornado, which destroyed £600,000 worth of property, killing 76 persons. It is the largest city in Kentucky, and handles a third of the tobacco raised in America. Natural gas is used here to some extent. From Glasgow Junction, 100 miles off, a short line leads to the Mammoth Cave, extending 9 to 10 miles below ground, the avenues totalling 175 miles, and the area beneath containing about 100,000 miles of open caverns. Some have distinctive names—*e.g.*, "Giant's Coffin," "Corkscrew," &c. There are also rivers and lakes within them, where eyeless fish and crayfish are seen by fireworks, and a "city" 500 × 200 × 120 feet.

Nashville (76,168) is 100 miles south, where the Confederate army of 40,000 was defeated, and 16,500 soldiers' graves are near. Turning north we find Indianapolis (105,436), the centre, capital, and largest city of Indiana, in a wide plain, its manufactures amounting to £1,320,000. The Capitol cost £400,000.

Beyond Chicago, on the western shore of Lake Michigan, Milwaukee (204,468) occupies a pleasant undulating site at the mouths of the river Milwaukee and two tributaries. Half of the inhabitants are Germans, and thus music and art is successfully cultivated. Its lager beer is known all over The States (2¼ million barrels were produced in 1892). It is the largest city in Wisconsin, but Madison (13,426) is the capital, and is situated further west between the beautiful lakes of Mendota and Monona. There the Historical Society has 150,000 volumes, also an art gallery, and a valuable museum ; 1000 to 1200 students attend the University. Its Washburn Observatory is one of the best in America.

Keeping eyes on the rail track, the twin cities of St. Paul (133,156) and Minneapolis (164,738) are reached —270 miles N.W. The former is the capital of Minnesota, the "North Star State," and the latter is the argest city in the State, and chief flour-making place in the world. St. Paul is at the head of the Mississippi navigation, and is finely situated, mainly on terraces. A great railway centre, its industrial products are £6,520,000. Summit Avenue gives the sense of an expenditure liberal, without ostentation, directed by skill and restrained by taste. Minneapolis is only 10 miles above St. Paul. It lies on both banks of the Missouri at the river's Falls of St. Anthony. Its 25 flour mills produce 7,000,000 barrels of flour annually by the Holla or "Hungarian" system (appropriate for the purpose). The value of its manufactures is £16,000,000. The falls have all been utilised for power. The lumber mills are most interesting; one cuts 25 to 30 million feet of timber annually, the logs being sawn into planks before they are quite out of the water. The university has 1000 students (both sexes). The graceful Falls of Minnehaha, immortalised by Longfellow, are in a pretty glen, 5 miles by car or rail. Lake Minnetouka, 12 to 15 miles long, is a most delightful resort, 10 miles S.W. The State has 7000 to 10,000 lakes.

About 150 miles north, over a partly uninteresting and partly unreclaimed forest land, Duluth (33,115) is finely situated on Lake Superior, its superior name being the "Zenith City of Unsalted Seas." From this we return to St. Paul and proceed down the Mississippi, past La Crosse (25,090), through its expanse into Lake Pepin (30 x 3 to 5 miles), Dubuque (3030), Davenport (26,872), and Quincey (31,494), all in the State of Iowa, and reach St. Louis, which has a population of 451,770 (150,000 Germans). It is the fifth city in The States, and the largest of the State of Iowa. Its frontage on the Mississippi is nearly 20 miles. A valley, spanned by seven bridges, divides it into north and south. This was once called Mill Creek. What if Edinburgh had had the "Nor' Loch" made into Canal Creek? as was one idea for the Union Canal basin (Auld Creekie, instead of Auld Reekie)! From St. Louis down to New Orleans, 700 miles, once stretched the territory of Louisiana, called after Louis XV., and of French origin in 1764 as a fur trading station. There were only 1000 inhabitants in the city in 1804, when that whole territory west of the Mississippi passed to the United States, the Spanish having acquired it from the French by secret treaty in 1764, when Louis XV. had just ceded the territory east of the river to "England" [Britain]. There is a procession and fair in October, after the style of the Mardi Gras of New Orleans. St. Louis is the fourth manufacturing city in The States, and the chief tobacco-making in the world, and produces quantities of all sorts of things from railway cars to "crackers," live stock to packed meat, stoves to drugs, hard ware to soft shoes for wear. The street plan and nomenclature follows Philadelphia, and we can walk along Broadway, Market Street, and Tree Streets—Chestnut, Olive, Spruce, &c. The parks (2100 acres) are among the finest in the United States, Philadelphia alone exceeding them in area. Forest Park has 1370 acres. One of the lions is the great St. Louis Bridge. Its construction cost two million pounds, and it consists of three steel spans, one 520 feet and two 502 feet, on massive limestone piers. Its length is 2070 feet. The railway occupies the lower story, and vehicles and pedestrians use the upper. Christ Church Cathedral (Anglican) is one of the important buildings. Cairo, 150 miles down, is a manufacturing town of 10,324 inhabitants at the confluence of the Mississippi and Ohio. A fine bridge crosses the latter. Memphis, 180 miles further down, the second city in Tennessee, is one of the most progressive cities. Between 1880 and 1890 its population all but doubled (in 1890 it was 64,495). There is no bridge over the Mississippi below the city—550 miles or more from the delta.

AS FROM THE APPALACHIAN CHAIN.

At Memphis we touch the further south, from which we came by the "air" and "lightning" line. Though easier to retrace that in an even higher flight of imagination, the Appalachian chain of mountains affords an altitude from which a sweeping view of wide latitude may be better fancied. They are the sky-scrapers of the Atlantic slope, the two principal ridges averaging an elevation of 3000 feet and the chain being 1500 miles long and 150 broad, from Maine to the edge of Alabama, 100 miles from the coast in the north and 300 in the south. Their elevated position and commanding influence over the raining powers have constituted them the parents of the Atlantic rivers, particularly of Father Mississippi and his family in the sunny south and that of St. Lawrence, so far as her stately daughters flow from the south to mingle their fortunes with the North Canadians. There is a wind and water relation between the St. Lawrence and the Mississippi, both having sprung from a point in the north-west where the watershed is but a few yards, and within 200 yards of the sources of two other great rivers flowing to the Arctic and the Pacific. The highest Appalachian ridges are respectively 4636, 6634, 3924, 3804, 3718, 4200, and 6470 feet. (Ben Nevis in Scotland is 4406.)

Three hundred miles straight east from Memphis the Cumberland range takes us 5520 ft. above the sea. From that point the Valley of the Mississippi stretches to the west a thousand or more miles, and contains the largest tract of exuberantly rich soil in the world, a forest region of 1000 miles by 300 on the left bank of the river, and prairies on the right bank. The winter of the river is Norwegian at the source and Spanish at its delta. Two tributaries, the Arkansas and Red River, are received from the Rocky Mountains.

The Rockies opposite, which we shall pass over, extend from the Arctic Ocean to Mexico; thence the chain is continued by the Cordilleras in Mexico and by the Andes in South America, a distance of 9000 miles—the highest of the respective ranges being 17,800 feet, 17,000 feet, and 22,296 feet (more than four miles high, and fully five times the height of Ben Nevis).

As we shorten our view from the Cordilleras, San Antonio (37,673), Dallas (38,067), and Galveston (29,084), respectively the chief, largest, and third cities in Texas, are in a line of sight. The first is the "Cradle of Texas Liberty," and an important military post. An interesting Spanish coast city, Americans, Mexicans, and Germans in equal proportions constitute the inhabitants, with a few coloured people. The second is an important railway centre, with a trade and manufacture value of £5,800,000. The third is the first of commercial importance, and third cotton shipping port in The States (700,000 bales). The resident quarter abounds in luxuriant gardens, shaded with oleanders, magnolias, &c. The Beach is an unrivalled walk, 30 miles long. Vicksburg (13,373), the oldest city in the Mississippi State, was prominent in the Civil War as the key to the Mississippi.

Atlanta (65,533), the capital of Georgia (which I passed through going south), was also famous in the Civil War, as may be said of all these parts more or less. Savannah (43,189), "the Forest City," the second in Georgia, near the coast, suffered in the war, its ports being closed for four years. It is second only to New Orleans in the cotton trade. From it sailed the first steamboat that crossed the Atlantic in 1819. The Wesleys and Whitfield visited the city in their day. Charleston (54,955), the largest city in S. Carolina, and a chief seaport, is an old-fashioned town, with more than half its inhabitants coloured. At it the Civil War began, and it was more than once attacked. St. Michael's Church was struck six times by the Federal bombs. A statue of William Pitt, erected in 1770, is in front of City Hall. The first shot in the Civil War was fired by the Citadel cadets. Norfolk (34,871), the second city of Virginia, was founded as far back as 1682. Its chief exports are cotton, coal, oysters, and early fruits and vegetables. Its large *Cotton Compresses* reduce by hydraulic pressure the bales of cotton for transport to one-fourth their original size.

Of Richmond (81,388) there is more to be said than can be here noted, the city and surroundings being very much mixed up with the Civil War. I regret much that the civilities with which I was bombarded at Washington by Richmondites, who pressed me hard to be their guest, were unavailing. I am sorry I did not surrender and allow myself to be taken. The city was founded 1737. Important Conventions have met at it, and it became the seat of government of the seceding States in 1861, and had to be defended with great obstinacy. A large part of the city was destroyed when the tobacco was fired by the evacuating Confederate troops on 2nd April, 1865. For three years (1862-65), battles raged all round. Richmond fell in the seven-days' battle in 1862. General Ulysses S. Grant lost 15,000 in attacking the Confederates, while thirteen pitched battles were fought near Petersburg, 23 miles from Richmond, the siege of that place lasting from June 16th, 1864, to April 2nd, 1865. One of the most beautiful monuments in the States is the equestrian statue of General Lee, erected in Richmond, and situated in Capitol Square, a tree-shaded area of 12 acres, where wonderfully tame grey squirrels are interesting. The Senate Chamber was the Confederate House of Representatives during the Civil War. There is also the House of Delegates. The State Library has 50,000 volumes and numerous relics. A statue of Washington occupies the central hall, and there is another of that hero on his horse—one in Capitol Square surrounded by figures of six famous men. The same square contains other statues. About half the inhabitants are negroes. 600,000,000 cigarettes are made by the brand of the American Tobacco Co. Trade and manufactures, £27,000,000.

Wilmington (61,431), the chief city of Delaware, has an old Swedish Church that dates from 1698 and marks the first Swedish colony in America, and the first permanent European settlement in the valley. Newark, N.J. (181,820), is interesting because T. A. Edison, the inventor, has his home here, and his workshop—the New Ark of Science. Situated only nine miles from New York, it cannot under its shadow be expected to be celebrated, like the Empire City, for everything under the sun; but from under that shadow Edison's light shines forth a fit compeer in its own sphere, slaying the darkness of night, world, and mind, and creating sights, sounds, and forces.

Our Skycycle having attained the north end of the blue ridge of the Alleghanies, the battle-ground of Gettysburg is near, about 60 miles north from Washington. It has an area of 25 square miles, 400 monuments in bronze, marble, or granite marking the important points. 150,000 men were engaged with 600 cannon (Union and Confederate). The killed were about 5500; wounded, 40,000. Gettysburg (3221) is seven miles north of the former limit line of slavery. Wheeling (35,013), the largest city in West Virginia, turns our eyes west again. Its manufactures are £2,308,000. Next we note Columbus (88,150), in Ohio, which has a State Capitol, in a small park filled with tame grey squirrels. Passing Cincinnati again, and once more over St. Louis, we have described a circle with extended view, fanciful, but descending to facts.

From St. Louis we proceed along the Missouri, 283 miles to Kansas City (132,746), the second of Missouri State, the capital of which is Jefferson City (6742), passed about 125 miles from St. Louis. Three fine bridges cross the river, and on the opposite bank is Kansas City, *Kansas* (38,316), the largest in that State. Omaha (140,452), the "Gate City," 180 or 200 miles to the north, is the largest city in Nebraska, the Antelope State, of which Topeka (31,007) is the capital. From Kansas City to San Francisco is a railway journey of 2094 miles. 135 miles on, the Ogden Monument at Fort Riley marks the geographical centre of THE UNITED STATES (exclusive of Alaska). 42 miles further millions of cattle are grazing, where bunch grass affords food both summer and winter. Fifty miles more bring the Rocky Mountains within sight at Forest View, where they are still 170 miles distant, and, after that has been traversed, we reach Denver, "Queen City of the Plain," 15 miles from the east base of the Rocky Mountains, and capital of the Silver State, Colorado, and its largest city. Only founded in 1858, its inhabitants, 35,630, in 1880 increased to 150,000 (including suburbs). It is in the heart of a rich mining district, and a line of 170 miles of the Rocky Mountains is visible here.

Passing through Utah, round by Salt Lake City (4230 feet), its capital (44,843), and the Zion of the Mormons, encircled by mountains, and Nevada—the "Sage Brush State"—of which Carson (3950), is the capital, California is crossed, and, grandly situated on the shore of a bay and on steep hills rising from it, and extending across a peninsula to the Pacific Ocean, is San Francisco, the inhabitants of which number about 300,000, of whom 25,000 are Chinese. The district where the Chinese reside is divided by narrow alleys swarming with occupants, and the plays in China Town Theatre extend over days and weeks, men only acting. Golden Gate Park is the largest, and has an area of 1013 acres.

BRITISH COLUMBIA.

We have now reached the western terminal point of the flight of our imagination, and from China Town fancy the Chinese Empire visible in the west only as far as we regard the Celestial Empire from Greenwich as towards the east. We therefore leave the western limit of the illuminating range of the Liberty Maiden's torch uplifted by the eastern gate of her Empire State, and turn northwards to Victoria, the capital of British Columbia, where, in the British Empire, we are in the largest territory of our Queen's Canadian Dominion, equalling the combined area of France, Prussia, Belgium, and Bavaria (383,300 square miles). A mountainous district 1250 miles long between the Rocky Mountains and the Pacific and Alaska, with a greatest width of 650 miles, its vast forests contain some of the finest timber in the world. The Douglas fir often attains a height of 200 to 300 feet on the coast. The salmon "pack" in one year was over 20 million 1-lb. tins. It has produced £11,000,000 worth of gold. There are 24,000 Indians, the annual value of whose industries is £140,000.

The city of Victoria is quiet and attractive, and beautifully situated on Vancouver Island, with an old-world air of substantial buildings, well-kept streets, gay gardens, and numerous country houses. The heterogeneous population (about 25,000) includes Canadians, Britons, Americans, Italians, Frenchmen, Germans, Japanese, and Chinese (3000), and there is an Indian reservation near. Vancouver Island is the largest in British Columbia, 290 miles long and 50 to 80 miles wide (area 20,000 square miles). It is mainly mountainous. Victoria Peak is 7485 feet.

On the mainland (of British Columbia), within the Straits of Georgia, is Vancouver, beautifully situated on a peninsula, and surrounded by water on three sides. Made the terminus of the C.P.R. in 1885, it practically dates from that time, last year having a population of 20,000, perhaps 25,000. Stanley Park has an area of 960 acres, and is laid out on a wooded peninsula connected with the city by a long bridge. Across an inlet the white houses of an Indian village are seen, and behind them the snow-capped peaks of the Cascade Mountains. In the environs are forests of noble pines, cedars, and other trees. The Bank of British Columbia, and the Young Men's Christian Association, and various clubs are in the chief thoroughfare, and among public buildings are the Episcopal and Presbyterian churches, the Public School, and the Bank of Montreal.

AMERICAN ALASKA.

From Victoria the distance to Alaska is about 1100 miles. Sitka, the capital, is dotted with green islands in front, and snow mountains behind, and has 1190 inhabitants (244 white, 31 Chinese, 885 natives). It is in the same latitude as Aberdeen, or Riga, and is the official residence of the Governor. Here also is the Russo-Greek Church with green roof and bulbous spires. Visitors are welcomed at the Presbyterian Mission. Notwithstanding the arctic climate there is luxuriant vegetation, fine cedar and other trees. At Pyramid Harbour the latitude is that of Orkney, Christiania, and St. Petersburg.

The territory of Alaska is 580,000 square miles, three times the size of France, and the population is 35,000, one-seventh being civilised. The natives are Eskimo or Innuit, with Aleutians or Haida Indians, the Tlinkets, and the Althabascar Indians, of which there are 20,000 or 30,000. There are 11,000 islands in the chief archipelago, and the chief commercial port is in the latitude of Liverpool, while its southernmost point is that of Brussels. It has the highest mountains, the most superb glaciers and volcanoes north of Mexico, but as yet has only one inhabitant to 17 square miles. In 1867 Russia transferred it to the United States for £1,450,000.

It is divisible into three physically diverse regions, the Sitkan, Aleutian, and Yukon. The first rough and mountainous, with many glaciers, bold coast, numerous fjords and islands, a moist, cool, and equable climate, and dense forests; the second, broad, level areas, with numerous clusters of mountains and volcanic cones, few glaciers, many harbours, luxuriant grass, herbage, and wild flowers; the third has true arctic conditions on the north, a mild summer and arctic winter on its west shores, and a hot short summer and a dry cold winter in the interior, a region of tundra, low undulating grassy mountains, and extensive river valleys, more or less wooded. It was lately said to produce nothing but furs and salmon, with a little placer mining.

KLONDYKE, AND CANADIAN CITIES.

The boundary line of Alaska—between British and American possessions—is at 54° 40′ N. latitude, Mount St. Elias (18,200 ft.), and Portland Inlet, and within this limit Klondyke is in British territory (16 miles).

Mr. Harry De Windt has said, on the authority of Mr. O'Gilvie, the Dominion Surveyor, that there is a marvellous gold zone of 500 miles, and that gold is to be had all over the country, both in American and Canadian territory, and from waters in particular which are in the latter, which produce *some* deposit in every pan when washed. The upper of the three sections of the Yukon River is in the Dominion. In 1897, between 1st January and 1st April £1,000,000 was got by 500 men. The first great gold " strike " in Klondyke was in 1896. Dawson City is 15 miles from the richer creeks. 80° below zero has been experienced, though rare; 70° without the wind (which makes 20° below zero unbearable) is no great discomfort.

Winnipeg is a brisk and prosperous city of 32,000 inhabitants, the capital of Manitoba, and the doorway and commercial focus of the North-West unexplored wealth. In 1870, when it was included in Fort Garry, there were only 240 inhabitants. Before 1881 its name was changed to Winnipeg. Its province, Manitoba, is only a ninth less than Great Britain. The climate is −40° to +95°. The Hudson Bay Company's stores and headquarters are here. They resemble a huge bazaar. For nearly 200 years the Company possessed a monopoly of a tract of country nearly as large as Europe. The Indians with whom they bartered were not allowed to buy spirits.

From Lake Winnipeg, 710 feet above the sea, 260 miles long, and 5 to 60 miles wide, whose waters and those of its companions, Lake Winnipegosis and Lake Manitoba, drain into Hudson Bay, we cross to Lake Superior at Fort-William (3000 feet), the picturesque attractiveness of which brings many summer visitors besides those who here rejoin the Canadian Pacific Railway after crossing Lakes Huron and Superior. Lake Superior is the highest of the Great Lakes, 600 feet above the sea, and is the largest body of fresh water on the globe, being 380 miles long, 160 miles in extreme width, with area 31,500 square miles; 1008 feet is its greatest known depth, and 200 streams run into it. There are numerous islands within it. Isle Royale is a rock-bound one 50 miles long. The steamer takes a course of 200 miles towards Lake Huron, which is 250 miles long and 50 to 200 miles wide, with area 23,800 square miles, and is estimated to contain 36,000 islands within it. The north and east shores alone belong to Canada. From Port-Huron our eastward way leads to London, eighth city of Canada, with 31,977 inhabitants, lying on the pretty river Thames in the county of Middlesex, the street nomenclature of which maintains all the English association with home streets and bridges—Piccadilly, Pall Mall, Regent and Oxford Streets, Blackfriars and Westminster. It is a well-built city with handsome churches, cottages, and public buildings. Windsor, with 10,322 inhabitants, is 100 miles south-east below Lake St. Clair, and is on the bank of the St. Clair river opposite Detroit, (205,876), the U.S. city mentioned at page 40. Lake Erie, 18 miles from Windsor, is the second of the Great Lakes between Canada and the United States, and is 250 miles long and 40 to 65 miles wide (area 9900 square miles). All the waters of the Great Lakes pass Buffalo down the Niagara river between the Canadian and American shores, and over the Falls of Niagara into Lake Ontario, the easternmost and lowest of the Great Lakes, which is 197 miles long and 30 to 70 miles wide, with an area of 7250 square miles. The lake was originally named St. Louis.

Hamilton (48,980), is the fourth city of Canada. It is the Canadian Birmingham and the centre of the fruit district of the western part, while further on is one vast orchard for peaches and other fruits. The seat of the Anglican Bishop, it is here where Dr. Du Moulin, who is always at the front when the St. Andrew Brotherhood is in Convention, has his see residence as Bishop of Niagara. There is also a Roman Catholic Bishop.

OVER NEW YORK STATE.

Places and points on Lake Ontario and the St. Lawrence having been already noted, our thoughts Atlanticwards carry us to New Brunswick, in the direct line to which we pass again over New York State, 412 miles long and 311 broad, having an area of 50,519 square miles. Rochester (133,896), only seven miles from Lake Ontario, has a University (200 students), and the Warner Observatory. The river Erie there forms three falls within the city. Supporters of women's rights and also spiritualists are centred there. Syracuse (88,143), eighty miles on, owes a great part of its wealth to salt springs bordering on Lake Onondaga, which yield three million bushels annually. Its University (800 students) is handsome, and possesses a library of nearly 50,000 volumes. The Erie Canal there lends, by moonlight, a Venetian effect. Utica (44,007), fifty miles further on, is the headquarters of the cheese trade, and twenty miles beyond it Little Falls, with only 8783 inhabitants, is romantically situated on the Mohawk River; through a spur of the Adirondack Mountains, river, rail, and canal pass the gorge side by side, where houses are picturesquely perched on rocky steeps among a series of pretty little falls, the river descending 45 feet within half-a-mile. Fifty miles nearer New York, and about 160 distant therefrom, is the pastoral valley of the Mohawk, the Catskills being visible as well as the Adirondacks. The Mohawks were perhaps the best known of the Indian tribes of the Five Nations Federation in the great lake district of New York.

The other tribes are the Oneidas, Onondagas, Cayugas, and Senecas; and when the Tuscaroras from Carolina were admitted to the league it took the name of the Six Nations. There were 15,000 members, and perhaps 10,000 still exist, the majority in Canada, the others in the Indian Reservation in New York State, where they are peaceable farmers.

Jersey City (163,003) is practically in New York, and would have become part of Greater New York had it not been located on the New Jersey State side of the Hudson River. It contains the stations of half of the railways centering in New York. Adjoining on the same shore is Hoboken (43,648), with Hudson City behind.

NEW ENGLAND.

To reach New Brunswick for Old England we must yet pass over New England, which has an area of 65,000 square miles, and comprises the six eastern States — Maine, Massachusetts, Connecticut, New Hampshire, Vermont, and Rhode Island (the smallest in the Union, 1285 square miles). Excepting Vermont, these were among the thirteen original States of 1776, Maine being then part of Massachusetts, and Vermont joining in 1786. The other nine States were New York, New Jersey, Pennsylvania, Delaware, Virginia, Maryland, North and South Carolina, and Georgia.

Boston (448,477) is regarded as the capital or chief town of New England (see p. 84). It was there where British authority was first openly resisted, Bunker's Hill being the scene of a sanguinary action, and the first engagement taking place at Lexington, about ten miles north, on the 19th of April, 1775. The village of Concord, on the river of that name after the junction of the Sudbury and the Assabit, is of special literary interest as the home of Hawthorn, Emerson, Thoreau, and the Alcotts; and Baedeker describes it as the American Weimar or Stratford-on-Avon, and says it has kept its literary association less tainted by commercialism than either of these places. The free public library contains many interesting autographs. At the bridge over the Concord the British soldiers were encountered on the above date, when the embattled farmers stood and fired the shot heard round the world. (This was ahead of the telephone !) Lowell (77,696), the third city of Massachusetts, is the Manchester of America. Its huge mills and factories are run by water-power from falls on the Merrimac at its confluence with the Concord. The value of cloth carpeting, &c., produced is above eight millions.

New Haven (81,298), in Connecticut, is the City of Elms, and was founded in 1638. Its 5000 inhabitants in 1800 have probably become 100,000. It is the seat of Yale College, founded in 1700 (second in dignity and importance to Harvard only), having 180 instructors and over 1900 students. Whitney, inventor of the cotton-gin, Samuel Morse, Jonathan Edwards, Noah Webster, Fenimore Cooper, and N. P. Willis are among its *alumni*. The library has 200,000 volumes, and there is a fine art school and museum.

Rhode Island State (so called from the insular part

proper, being the Indian Aquidneck, or "Isle of Peace," bought from the Indians in 1639, which connects with the mainland by a road bridge, and a railway one) has for a capital Providence (132,146), the second city in New England, where is located Brown University, and Ladd Observatory on Tip-Top Hill. It has also the Friends' Meeting House (1759), the Tillinghast House (1710), the Whipple House (1660), and other houses of an interesting period.

Worcester (84,434), the second city of Massachusetts and head of the commonwealth, has manufactures of a heterogeneous character to the value of £7,972,000.

Salem (30,800), the quiet and ancient mother city of Massachusetts, is 16 miles from Boston. There the State legislature met the last time under the British Crown in 1774, and there will be found the oldest Protestant church in America (1634). As famous natives, mention may be made of Nathaniel Hawthorn, Prescott the historian, and Maria S. Cummins, author of *The Lamplighter*. Two miles out, Peabody represents the birth-place and burial-place of the philanthropist of that name. At Andover Mrs. Beecher Stowe wrote *Uncle Tom's Cabin*, and Eliza S. Phelps *The Gates Ajar*. In Maine State, Portland (36,451) is the chief city—called, like another, "The Forest City," because of the number of trees in its streets. It has many fine public buildings, and the environs are attractive. Longfellow was born there, and afterwards lived in it. A statue of him is placed in the chief street. N. P. Willis and Fanny Fern were also natives.

As we sight the province of New Brunswick, in

Canada, we part with New England, and finally with the United States; but in recalling the European and British origin of modern America, one is specially reminded that the people of New England are or were mostly descended from a Scottish ancestry as well as an English Puritan, celebrated for industry and enterprise. The region was granted by James I. to the Plymouth Company in 1606, as North Carolina, and the Pilgrim Fathers landed from the *Mayflower* in 1620. In the mysterious unities and continuities, had they and others not landed we would not have known so many scenes of pleasant reminiscences of the United States and of that New Scotland as well as New England.

NEW BRUNSWICK, NOVA SCOTIA, NEWFOUNDLAND.

The capital of New Brunswick is Fredericton, an attractive little city of over 6500 inhabitants. Its five main streets, parallel with the River St. John—there three-quarters of a mile wide—have all royal names. It has other fine elm-shaded streets, the Parliament and many other handsome buildings, and good shops, with the University of New Brunswick on the wooded heights. The New Englanders attacked the town in 1696. The province is 200 miles long and 160 wide, the area being 27,500 square miles, a little less than Scotland. The origin of the population is a third English, a third Irish, a sixth Scottish, a sixth French, and there are 1400 Indians. Christ Church Cathedral is a Decorated Gothic grey stone building, with a spire 1804 feet high. The Episcopalians of the United States donated the east window.

St. John (39,179), the centre of New Brunswick and leading shipowning city in Canada, is picturesquely situated on the great River St. John, and affords the shortest available winter route between Liverpool and Montreal. It has the sixth place among Dominion cities, and is the oldest incorporated. The lumber shipments are immense. One-third of the city was burned in 1877, and nearly six million pounds property destroyed. The landing of the 10,000 United Empire Loyalists, in 1783, is commemorated by a monument in King Square. There is also a Queen Square. Right here, as United States men say, are what are called the "reversible" falls of the St. John's River, which appear to fall with the flow of the river and rise above themselves when the tide rises to fall upon them. We trust the flow of language about this remarkable phenomenon is lucid.

Halifax, the Cronstadt of America and the capital of Nova Scotia, is the naval and military headquarters of British America, with formidable fortifications. The chief winter harbour of Canada, it is the nearest American port to Britain (2170 miles to Cape Clear) and the eastern terminus of the Canadian railway system. It is also, perhaps, the most British city in America. The citadel is conspicuous (255 feet above the sea), and the public gardens are the pride of the city, being about 14 acres in extent, and recalling Boston's beautiful public garden. The climate ranges from $-5°$ to $+90°$. The population (including the imperial troops) is 38,556 (one-fifth Roman Catholic), giving the city the seventh place among Canadian cities.

A seagull fly of 600 miles brings us over St. John, the capital of Newfoundland, which has 29,007 inhabitants, 16,590 being Roman Catholics. It is approached by huge cliffs. The station for signalling vessels as they arrive is on an almost perpendicular precipice on the right 300 feet high, and a hill 400 feet high is on the left. It is 1000 miles nearer Queenstown than New York, and its picturesqueness cannot be surpassed by any city on the American Continent. In 1580 it was a fishing hamlet. It has experienced two terrible conflagrations, the last in 1892. The Roman Catholic Cathedral is the most conspicuous building, and the Church of England Cathedral, designed by Sir Gilbert Scott, is to be one of the finest in British America.

Newfoundland is about a sixth larger than Ireland (42,000 square miles), the population being 202,040 (4000 white in Labrador, and 1400 Eskimo). Although the sentiment of loyalty to Britain is strong, Newfoundland has not yet confederated with the Dominion. Its ramparts of rock, 300 to 400 feet high, are cleft by deep fjords, 30 to 50 miles wide, at the mouths, and running in 50 to 90 miles, with scenery that may some day rival the fjords of Norway. The interior too is diversified by valleys, woods, countless lakes and ponds. Grand Lake is 56 miles long (192 square miles), Red Indian is 37 miles long, and Gander Lake 33 miles, the scenery of both being very fine. Cabot, who discovered it in 1497, five hundred years ago, was really the discoverer of North America. The abundance of fish wealth in its shores, bays, and fjords attracted fishermen of various nationalities.

The cod-fishing is the most extensive in the world —annual value, £1,200,000 dried cod—and seal-fishing comes next. The seals taken vary from 250,000 to 365,000—value £150,000; canned lobsters, £66,000; salmon-fishing, value £20,000; and persons engaged, 55,000. The Great Banks, 600 miles long, are a day's sail, and swarm with fish life; 1100 miles of the Labrador coast is under the jurisdiction of Newfoundland. These fisheries prepared the way and laid the foundations of the empire won by England [Britain] in the New World; the French, however, have privileges still disputed, but the position of the island as the key to the St. Lawrence precludes the idea that it would ever be allowed to pass from the Union Jack— Jack of all treaties for unity and amity.

AWAKE WITH TWAIN IN HAND.

As the Banks of Newfoundland were the first of America seen, or imagined to be seen, so are they the last we saw, or imagined we did, in the transaërial light skiff which we fancy floating now overhead in a starry November night while we wake from our k-night-errant course in the *Lucania* Crescent, where Mark Twain and I were a silent twain, and the reader and I twain too with Cable alongside.

In the cities named and the country gone over there is much of interest which the altitude of our over-States line and the pre-arranged zone of observation prevented us in swift swallow flight descending to deal with in detail, nor were all such so exceptional in such points as were noted as to justify the exclusion of many equally or more important in respect of what has been said, *e.g.*, under shipping, commercial and manufacturing relations, agriculture, education, literary and scientific institutions, political importance, and general amenities. Every place strives to make a name for something for itself which shall be euphonic and stately or elegant. In this transfiguring there is more interest than in the American habit of figuring, although as a tourist I know the value of understanding that 119th Street is a certain number of blocks on from 15th Street, two or three miles distant, over having to waste time and talent discovering Tom, Dick or Harry Street, Royal, Independence or Reform Square, or Paradise Terrace in Slum Road, or the Omaha Post Office at "Dodge Street."

The characteristics of summer and winter and mountain resorts might have been given, and much that is amusing and interesting added, such as 50,000 bathers in one day at Atlantic City, which possesses one of the finest beaches, four miles long. Then there is the National Reservation (the Yellowstone Park), 65 miles long and 55 wide, filled with gigantic natural wonders of every kind, which a detachment of the U.S. cavalry protect during the summer months.

BON VOYAGE.

Nothing transpired to mark or mar the voyage, neither whale nor sail appearing, and on Thursday the notice-board required all telegrams and letters to be posted by 11 p.m. as the mail would be landed at Queenstown about three o'clock on the following morning. As we were approaching Cape Clear we expected to sight the Fastnet light before midnight, but failing to do so, because of the rainy darkness, the ship was slowed and stopped for soundings, the officers being doubly at sea; we then proceeded half speed between frequent stoppages and soundings until two or three in the morning, when most of those who were gazing their eyes out to lend reality to many an imaginary speck went off to bed to sleep themselves to land. I watched the process of casting the lead and reading the soundings with earnest interest, and realised more the hopes and fears and longings of fog-bound vessels out of their reckoning. I succumbed myself to cold and drowsiness, but not until long after many, when I left three in the drizzle and darkness somewhere unknown off the coast of Ireland. I was happier sunk in the sea of oblivion amid other soundings.

On awaking at eight noises on board betokened our arrival at Queenstown. The dawn only had declared the land, and we were five hours later than expected, so that our telegrams and letters were affected by that difference without the chance of rectification. The mails were landed while we were breakfasting. After that the coast line of Ireland, Wales, and England afforded continued interest. Lighthouses and lightships early showed their lights. Of these lights Kipling thus writes:—

" Over sea, and rock, and skerry, over headland, ness, and voe,
The shoreward lights of England watch the ships of England go."

As we neared Liverpool, the bullion-room was opened, and ingots of silver were liberally laid along the open deck, but as a guard was set, and one ingot was sufficient to exhaust a man's strength the shortest distance, all were safe in the little Eldorado.

We cast anchor in the Mersey after sun-set, safe home and well. It was near eleven, however, before we got ashore and clear of the Customs House, and I just caught by a leap, run, and drop, the last ferry across and the last train to Birkenhead Park, where Mr. and Mrs. Clark had all afternoon expected me with a cheery room and kindly fire. Their Brotherhood guest, until Saturday afternoon, I found them only that day receiving my letter from New Orleans, posted two days before my departure. I had outrun, or at least out-sailed, the mail, and by a less direct route.

HOME AGAIN IN ROYAL EDINBURGH.

I reached Edinburgh at 11 p.m., completing a journey of 4500 miles in ten days, a night being spent in New York, and another and a day at Liverpool. A friend was waiting my arrival at the station, with an epitome of news about people and things all being well. He accompanied me to my club in Princes Street, where he left me with a mind at rest, making sure that I had a pillow to lay my bewildered Scoto-American head upon. I beheld again out of the club window after the first long absence of two months for half-a-century the Castle of Edinburgh on its rocky eminence, the sloping steeps and high and massive ridge stretching along the valley. My acquaintance with great Western towns had only enhanced the fair beauty of the city and its romantic site as described by Sir Walter Scott:—

> "Such dusky grandeur clothed the height
> Where the huge castle holds its state,
> And all the steep slope down,
> Whose ridgy back heaves to the sky,
> Piled deep and massy, close and high,
> Mine own romantic town!"

The knowledge of my reception by the American Brotherhood, copied from the *Washington Star*, had preceded me, and at St. Mary's Cathedral on Sunday morning I received the congratulations of my chapter and of its president, the late Dean Montgomery, of Edinburgh, whose sympathies were ever with all Brotherhood efforts. In the same week the Primus and other Bishops and clergy were ready with their appreciation of my delegateship. I had experienced the true regard of the American laity for the Mother Church in Scotland, and the reality of the Brotherhood bond of unity throughout the Communion. *The Daily Picayune*, with an account of All Saints' Day in New Orleans, also arrived with a sample of editorial lionising when the Starry Eagle sights a hair of the British Lion, rampant or passant. Heather from Scotland in St. Louis Cemetery, and the Shadow among the Creoles of a Modern Athenian who had known the City "in old times," was material for a romantic heading. The quaint Crescent City had been to me a magnet, but the editor had Americanised me into a *magnate*. I found myself one of the "eminent men" who had attended the Washington Convention, one who had travelled in all parts of the world, and lastly, but not the least one would best like if true, "a capitalist of Edinburgh"; true enough, however, in the sense of my having been born in the capital of Scotland. We may pardon the proclivity of the eagle to soar rather than sink, to magnify more than lessen, and to regard the mountain not a mole-hill. In a land itself vast, which

Nature made great and wonderful in all its aspects, it is the vocation of man to look for great ideals, to elaborate systems, and to discern forces of nature latent in the land, and proclaim them to the world. True Americanism is the natural succession of our former selves, the flower, the enterprise, the perseverance of our past following the sun shining on a continent kept in store for our racial expansion, when science should bind us all closer in thought and action, in time and space.

Some have suggested that America might have suited my temperament better than Britain, and that energy might have found responsive results. Perhaps. Suppose, instead of being a commander of the Union forces I had lapsed into a raider in the Rockies; instead of being an "eminent" and "travelled" Brotherhood man seeking youth, unity and catholicity, I had been a slave " capitalist," of whom the friends of unbondaged Scotland were ashamed—what then? Where I was born there I hope to be buried; where I have toiled for five decades there I desire to remain. There may be a heroism in remaining at home. Proud of my city, and pleased with my country, although PRESIDENT WASHINGTON is my hero, I was born under a KING. By the glorious reign of a QUEEN, from the sacred resolve of her maidenhood to her magnificent triumphal grace at the zenith of the whole world's applause, I have been benefited. In her Empire "Royal Edinburgh" is one of the fair cities of the world—the fairest on earth if I may believe the veritable magnates of other cities and truly eminent travellers, from all parts of the globe, with whom in my half-a-century reminiscences on Princes Street, I have come into commercial touch. They have been Royal, noble, and landed; English, foreign, and colonial; Cabinet Ministers, Archbishops, and Lords-Justices, Mayors and Provosts; Admirals and Generals; Consuls and Courtiers. Of its men of science, literature, and art—authors, poets, and editors—I have known a few. Some with whom I have conversed are ancient to many too modern to have even seen them. To the time of the city's greatest intellectual orb, but for eighteen months, my tiny existence could touch back, and for half the century I have handled his gems and jewels on the site from which he viewed the battlements, and gazed on the "grandeur" "where the huge castle holds its state" on the rocky throne.

However, when one has once crossed the Western Waves as a traveller, he has a longing desire to see America once more, and more of it. After settling down again at home, he may be more satisfied with his native land and its solid ways and walls, that speak to him as from the past with pleasant memories, and he may then agreeably miss some of the modernisms of the West; but much holds him spellbound to places where he may have met happy and perhaps saintly lives in a sunny though not sinless land, and that brightness may have created within her a lighter world worth living in.

In this new realm I have lived through this Jubilee year, linked, as I have shown it to be, with other sunny memories, when all the world was to me new and bright and beautiful. In a feeble way I have endeavoured to let friends, who could not taste my pleasures, share a knowledge of them in their narration, with the assurance that they too of the "old country" would be received across Western Waves as I was.

VI.

HOME IN A ROYAL CAPITAL.

ROYAL EDINBURGH OR MODERN ATHENS.

EDINBURGH, the Modern Athens, as I remember it, was more on a parallel with my reverie on the tenth day after I had left Louisiana, and found myself repeating history on a re-arrival home, than as I saw it that night from the Scottish Conservative Club. Even the Castle and its rock were changed not by re-volcanic action or glacial flow but by the artifices of man who had taken away the homeness of the hallowed past. It was that of the period of prints before the advent of photographs at the beginning of the Queen's reign in 1837-38, the year when the New Club was opened, before the foundations of the Scott Monument were laid, and seven years before the Queen's statue surmounted the Royal Institution.

Edinburgh's history is that of Scotland, and from points about Princes Street may be recalled the past of the city and its influences in the land. Familiar, however, as I have been with the street from my earlier return home, and hardly a day out of sight of the Castle, my reminiscences here are those of the half-century beginning with a fine May morning in 1848, when I was installed with a pencil into commercial life and entrusted to mark pence on a pile of green pamphlets—"A Word in Season," for Chartists, *et hoc genus omne*, in that year of a French Revolution. The demand for it showed that many were ready to read if not to take a word in season. It was the year of the sudden overthrow of King Louis Philippe and the re-establishment of a French Republic, which excited intense interest in the Scottish metropolis, news coming every few hours by the electric telegraph, then only introduced by a private company, with its office in a flat at 68 Princes Street. The charge then for a message to London was four shillings, and for shorter distances from a shilling, according to place. Then there was the Hungarian Revolution and the insurrection in Vienna, ascribed in great part to Louis Kossuth and his speeches; England, in 1851, after his liberation, receiving him with respect and sympathy, as did also many of the leading citizens in Edinburgh at a hotel in Princes Street, and the United States giving him an enthusiastic reception.

It was a time also of unrest at home, riot and anxiety, many citizens having to be enrolled as special constables to parade the streets and otherwise preserve order, the symbol of their authority and weapon of defence being a white wood baton, which a friend has described as resembling a porridge stick, and which I remember seeing in the hands of a company parading Leith Walk and vicinity.

To quell a mob at the Tron Church the Lord Provost had to call for the military from the Castle and Piershill barracks—infantry and cavalry—and the Sheriff had to read the Riot Act. Military intervention was also necessary for alarming riots at Glasgow. Police and military power were also invoked to poind goods of citizens who refused on conscience to pay the Annuity-tax (the stipends of the city clergy). I remember the cordon of cavalry around the household paraphernalia of an upholsterer, like troops in a drawing-room marshalled for a battle in mahogany. Sword was the defaulter's name, who, for showing his steel, had drawn swords arrayed around his tables as well as chairs with hardly a leg to stand upon, as everything was upside down. This was in Hanover Street, under the eye of the sovereign's statue, and that of King George IV. at the top of the street, both with sceptres. According to statutes, Sword had to surrender for prison or hand over the sovereign s goods on the judgment that determined the penny to be Cæsar's.

In London precautions had to be taken for preserving order as against Chartist demonstrations by enrolling 25,000 special constables, while a special prayer was read in all churches for the preservation of peace. The troubles with Smith O'Brien and others in Ireland were thick, from the "Cabbage Garden Insurrection," backwards, forwards, downwards, and upwards, to trials for high treason, with capital sentences commuted to transportation, the French Provisional Government the while refusing to interfere in Irish grievances, in like manner as England had announced its non-interference with France's internal affairs, the troubles ending, however, with tranquillity in Ireland, although followed by riots in England and the appearance of the little cloud that led to the Crimean War. (Quarrel between Greek and Latin Churches as to Protectorate at Jerusalem.)

The very varied, happier, or marked events of those months included the birth of the Princess Louise (Marchioness of Lorne) on March 18, 1848; the termination of the Kaffir War, Jan. 1; the introduction of chloroform by Professor (Sir James) Simpson, Nov. 12, 1847; public interest in the endeavour to find Sir John Franklin, and the consequent departure of the first of two search expeditions, May 11, 1848;

histrionically, the purchase of Shakespeare's house at Stratford-on-Avon, Sept. 16, 1847 ; and the first appearance of Jenny Lind, the Swedish Nightingale ; ecclesiastically, in England, the consecration of four colonial Bishops in Westminster Abbey, on June 29, 1847, and in Scotland the union of two Presbyterian bodies as the United Presbyterian Church in May, 1847. Within that group of months the death of Dr. Chalmers had suddenly occurred, on Sunday night, May 30th, 1847 ; his funeral, which I remember well, being one of unprecedented public and ecclesiastical solemnity. Four years before I had seen him walking at the head of the Disruption procession ; then I saw him borne at the head of another, around which the thoughts of all thinking Scotland were centred, some represented officially by the whole Assembly of the Free Church, and some unofficially by the Moderator and members of the Established Church Assembly, both being then in session; citizens, by the Magistrates and Town Council and public bodies ; her Majesty's Lord High Commissioner also attending. The rent Church forgot its division to unite, as well by word within the walls, as without by public testimony, to honour the memory of one whom all esteemed. The procession was a mile long.

In the same year and following, the country suffered severely from cholera. In the second a day was observed as a public fast day in "all churches and chapels" on account of its prevalence. Later on the Home Secretary advised the washing of the dirty closes, and since then all courts and closes are annually white-washed, cleanliness having aided godliness. To fresh lime was added fresh air, and after discussion in our Town Council the Meadow parks were opened; then followed houses for artisans, and the re-building of whole areas with widened streets, and a general outcry for play spaces, and green "lungs," the stentorian power of which further threw open to the public the Arboretum, Botanic Gardens, and West Princes Street garden, hills and parks with memorial arches, and kite-runs, golf-courses, cricket grounds, and ponds and burns, *à la* Columbia, only far short of the length the Americans go in providing for what I imagine is included in the inalienable rights which the Declaration of Independence asserts to be those of all men—life, liberty, and the pursuit of happiness. The total area of the twelve open grounds, parks, gardens, meadows, links and hills, is 489 acres, with 37 acres in other twelve squares or small spaces of garden ground. The Queen's Park and Arthur Seat cover about 600 acres.

It was in the year 1848 that the Caledonian Railway to Carlisle was opened with a small station half-way up the Lothian Road (the company this year having duly observed its jubilee), and Trinity College Church (1462) taken down for the North British Railway, that line having only been opened in 1846. The Edinburgh and Glasgow line, with terminus at the Haymarket, was opened in 1842. Upon that important occasion a train of thirty carriages hauled by three engines called Stephenson, Playfair, and Galileo, was hailed by the band of the 53rd Regiment (distinguished in a dozen battles) with "See, the conquering hero comes." The rate at which the hero came was 15 to 25 miles an hour, a reduction in the mail's past from four or five hours to less than two, now accomplished in one. At Cowlairs a thousand gentlemen, including the two Lord Provosts, sat down to a splendid banquet, and rose therefrom feeling that some gigantic power had uprooted the two cities, annihilated their distance and forced them into immediate contact—a natural friendly fancy.

In the same year Queen Street Hall was opened (seating 1000), and the foundation stone of the Corn Market laid. The Music Hall was built in 1843 (seating 1730). These were the past ushers of the future halls, but an "Usher Hall" is now taxing the attention of Council and city, the idea floating at present in the canal basin with a chance of being moored there. It is, however, to some a grave question, whether Port Hopetoun's three-fourths of a century saturated foundations below Downie Place might not carry operations too far down and bring that place down as well, and thus drain the money of the citizens, as the canal did a great deal of that of the shareholders. But according to a meeting of citizens held lately near the site itself, the basin is founded on a rock like the castle. If so, a hall built in the basin would neither sink, rock, nor wreck. The amount donated for the purpose by Mr. Usher was a hundred thousand pounds, and the Town Council have been pounded for doings they ought not to have done and undoings they ought to have done, their wisdom not having as yet ripened sufficiently to *create* a site out of the chaos of opinion.

When I sailed for the Star-land in 1837 I embarked at Port Hopetoun to be fast-towed in the express boat to Port-Glasgow. The steeds were not sea-horses, and Atlantic greyhounds were unheard of. The only other voyage I ever undertook on the metropolitan canal was by the invisible power of electricity to the electrical Exhibition of 1890, which was fast for the short distance and in contrast with the slowness of that for the longest, wherein after ten weeks' sailing on the high seas, Louisiana's Crescent City shore was reached at five o'clock on a Sunday evening the 31st December.

S⁺ Giles.   Bank of Scotland.   Royal Institution.

ORIGIN & GROWTH OF EDINBURGH :—
Probably a Roman Station
under Agricola - - - A.D. 79
Its Province (Newcastle—Sol-
way to Forth—Clyde) called
Valentia · · · · 368
Arthur's Seat called after King
Arthur (p 213) · · circa VIc.
The Station or Hamelit pro-
bably named after Edwin,
first Christian King of Nor-
thumbria (p 371) · · circa 626
Edwin's-burgh or Edwin's Castle
founded by Edwin · circa 626
Made a Royal Burgh by David
I., probably in · · · 1128

Town of Leith bestowed on
Edinburgh by Robert I.
(with Harbour and Mills) - 1329
Cowgate (South Street. Well Gate) 1485
West Port · · · · · 1514
Bristo Port (Gallowgate) · · 1515
Cowgate Port · · · · 1516
City Wall, First 1450, Second, 1513
at Leith Wynd · · · 1520
Great part burnt by the English 1544
Luckenbooths (Krames) · · 1555
Edin. Castle, Palace & Square 1556
Halkerston's Wynd · · · 1560
First Netherbow Port · · 1571
Warriston Close · · · 1583
Port Halkerston's Wynd · · 1680

PRINCES STREET, EDINBURGH. (A)

oners 82 Princes Street

Castle

mes' Court	· · · ·	1727
ortobello (p 218), first house built		1741
:orge Square	- · · ·	1766
. John Street, Canongate	-	1768
thian Road (p 224)	· ·	1784
uth Bridge	- · · ·	1785
ershill Barracks	· ·	1796
ew Barracks, Edinburgh Castle		1796
ink Street, High Street to Mound		1798
ewington begun	· · ·	1806
ankeillor Street 1812, Clerk Street		1818
ontague Street	· · ·	1820
:orge IV. Bridge	· · ·	1827
hnstone and Castle Ter. form.		1825-36
range, 1856 ; Mayfield	· ·	1863
raigmillar	· · · ·	1873

(See view B for New Town Streets.)

Morningside Place	· · ·	1858
Bruntsfield Terrace	· · ·	1858
Greenhill	· · · · ·	1860
Merchiston Park	· · ·	1862
Lonsdale Terrace	· · ·	1868
Glengyle Terrace	· · ·	1868
Tynecastle	· · · ·	1871
Warrender Park	· · ·	1878
So. Morningside	· · ·	1879
North Merchiston	· · ·	1879
Lockharton Gardens, etc.	- ·	1881
S. Bruntsfield Place	· · ·	1883
Gorgie Road	· · · ·	1886
Greenbank	· · · ·	1887
Viewforth, etc.	- · · ·	1890

Related to Queen Street Hall and the Music Hall were the lectures of the Philosophical Institution, founded in the year 1846, the Presidents of which were Lord Macaulay, Lord Brougham, Carlyle, Adam Black, Professor J. Wilson, and W. E. Gladstone, the lecturers being, among many other leading writers, Dickens, Thackeray, Trollope, Ruskin, Kingsley, Stanley, Froude, Freeman, Maurice, Martineau, and Dean Ramsay, all of whom attracted the best society of Edinburgh, as few lived beyond walking distance.

In the '50's and '60's I heard all literary luminaries of the period, thus invited by the philosophers of Modern Athens, as Presidents liked to call us in those days, when, perhaps, wisdom was more fashionable than the latest telegrams, cricket, golf or football matches; cycle or yacht races, which had no records to break; or attendance at smoking concerts, conversaziones, and bazaars. Society was not so fast and sensational, and fiction was not so limp and loose. Subscribers to libraries, perhaps, read deeper, and there was more demand for the solid writers, while all bought as well as read. They could trust the librarian's judgment more in respect of what was worthy a place on his shelves, made no demand for worthless books themselves, and blamed him not for the rubbish he bought and sent them. In book-buying all were guided by the bookseller, who then-a-days everywhere knew much about the inside and cared little about the outside of his volumes, although he knew them upside down and could find some in the dark, for he had a degree of leisure which he cannot well have now, when 6000 books a year are added by England alone to Solomon's estimate of their no-endness.

A PANORAMA OF THE PAST.

It was deeply gratifying to find how attached to Scotland were many of my American brethren, and how gladly they would have had me tell them anything about it. In presenting the views I now do I shall be speaking of Edinburgh in their fathers' and grandfathers' days.

THE VIEW FROM PRINCES STREET (A).

As we look across the Gardens from No. 82 Princes Street, near the New Club, and out of the window where and when I was busy over my green "Words in Season," the Castle of Edinburgh is conspicuous in the morning sun. Nature's green slopes are in shadow and the street is bathed in a flood of summer sunlight. The 1st Royal Scots are on the Esplanade, and perhaps H.R.H. the Duke of Cambridge is inspecting the regiment, as the Royal Standard is hoisted on the Half-Moon Battery, where the flagstaff is no longer, and in its place the one o'clock

time-gun reports the hour to every ship and watch.
The old approach ramparts and Argyll Tower are
improved away, and their peaceful successors adorn
their places. The coach is off to Queensferry, where
the railway has now supplanted it, and at the same
time replaced it on the road with fifty other coach
traps for tourists to see what then it was never
dreamt could exist—a giant bridge over the Forth.
It will cross the Ferry in a boat, and go on to Dunfermline, the occasional residence of the Scottish
kings, 15 miles from Edinburgh, where Malcolm and
his Queen, Margaret, and Robert the Bruce, among
other kings, are buried. The iron horse now accom-
plishes the distance in 36 minutes, while the coach
took three hours and a half.

The street being only macadamised, a cloud of
dust would be raised as the coach hurried on. The
guard's horn has now been silenced by locomotive
science, and in its place have come a thousand car-
drivers' whistles, which in a few months now must
give place in turn to as many or more bells of the
motor men. Dust and noise—clatter and whistles—
silence and bells mark the progress of a revolutionary
era, not to speak of wheels and cycles rubber tyred
out of hearing on wooden ways. When the car bells
awake Auld Reekie I shall hear again the sounds of
Broadway and St. Charles' Avenue.

On a rainy day there would be as many "dubs"
as there are lakes in Minnesota, and the grass in the
channel chinks and round the carriage steps would
gloriously revive. The leisurely habits of the pedestrians and of those in riding habits, as well as the

playful spirit of the two dogs, the racy humour of the one running after the coach, and the dander of the fourth, indicate the summer quietude of the locality and freedom from traffic.

St Giles' Church—" High Kirk " or " Cathedral"— the Bank of Scotland, and the Royal Institution, respectively ancient, antiquated, and modern, are prominent. Round the last, and straight up the earthen mound, was the roadway to the High Street and George IV. Bridge. When in America's Crescent City this view was my idea of home, evolved from a picture painted by my father—doubtless for a St. Andrew's Society man—the Bank of Scotland dome being the dominant peculiarity. Added to this was childhood's recollection of the musical bells in St. Giles' crown steeple and the buttercups and daisies over the stile in the Meadows, where nurse would take us on sunny days—"us"— yes, she whose grave is under the semi-tropical sun made the "us." St. Giles' bells of that decade lately succumbed to general decay. Latterly a monotony in their music was observable, some being more cracked than crack, and therefore with constitutional soundness gone. The long and short about their successors, that now ring the changes, is that they are musical tubes. Within the edifice changes of another sort have been ringing—architectural, æsthetic, liturgical, and pertaining to ritual—such as no one at the time of the view would have believed possible within centuries; the name of "Cathedral" as now used being then an offence against Church and State and the treaty of Union with England.

Like Washington, the city, contrary to all calculations, took a direction diametrically different from the plan of its original self. It consequently could not tolerate the sight of the Bank's back turned to its fair face, and after columns of calumny the directors had to provide it with a new costly and elegant dress of stone with smart trimmings, hood, head-gear and graceful veil to adorn the high and conspicuous place which nature and the ancient royalty had accorded it.

In the Royal Institution are located the Royal Society of Edinburgh, the Board of Manufactures, School of Art, and School of Applied Art, and the Edinburgh Architectural Association. From 1826 to 1856 it had the Royal Scottish Academy of Painting, Sculpture, and Architecture, on the removal of which to the east wing of the National Galleries, the Antiquarian Society and Museum occupied the main portion. The National Portrait Gallery in Queen Street now accommodates the latter on the basement floor and other parts, and also the Royal Scottish Geographical Society. The railings round the Institution are now to be removed to make room for the cable car rails, and so restore the building to its original rank as in the view—railing for railing, present for past.

The fashions of the times are observable. They were less variable, and not so precise as to-day. If the raiment was proof against cold and rain it served its chief end, which was considerably further from the beginning. There was no need in Princes Street establishments for display windows with patent shapes and delicate dyes for summer. Straw bonnets were in vogue, and all were of such magnitude, with lappets to keep the cheeks cosy and set off their roseate hue, that no one could look a lady in the face without first looking into her bonnet—after circumnavigating the bulwarks if one were at sea respecting identity. Ample rear room was left for the hair, not so necessary when ringlets were worn. Ornate Paisley shawls were the right wraps for rich and respectable. Many merchants, as well as professional men, wore dress coats—black, claret, green, &c.—with variegated vests, the seals attached to their watch dangling from a trouser watch pocket ready for sealing letters, gum not being much used. The quill was still the court and noblemen's pen—Hudson's Bays and Swan's, at £2, 2s. a hundred. Umbrellas of gingham and whalebone of liberal amplitude provoked individuality and lent character to the ownership. Young as well as old were only correct when they had tall silk hats : artisans as well as youths respected the Sunday by wearing them. Boots of various kinds prevailed—top-boots and Wellington boots in particular. I forget how I got into the latter, but I remember how difficult it was to get out. Perhaps it was because I had got into the noble Duke's boots that I went to the Horse Guards in 1851 to look at the Waterloo hero. The dress or tail coats of the police were blue and of the postmen scarlet, the former the colour of the impression of the batons carried and sometimes used, the latter of the many impressed seals her Majesty's servants had to deliver. The postmen had cockades on their hats.

Passing up the Mound, a low dyke was on the left, and on the right of the roadway was an open space of considerable width, on the further side of which stood a few workshops, a coachbuilder, carpenter, bookbinder, &c.; a rotunda—the diorama, panorama, cosmorama, and battle of Waterloo, &c.; a theatre for tragedy, comedy, and farce ; Punch and Judy, and an apple and gingerbread stand ; with no end on Saturday nights and popular evenings of showmen, cheap-jacks, itinerant dealers, and caravans.

In high winds the feeble clung to the dyke until some gallant arm piloted or towed them through the ill wind that sometimes did the rescuer good.

The tall tenements of nine storeys high at the top have been conspicuously palatial in the illuminations of the past, to which spectacles no city in the world could better lend itself. The westmost half was rebuilt, after one of Edinburgh's conspicuous fires, in 1858. The fires best remembered during the century have been those in the High Street, in June and November 1824, which splendidly illuminated the tall ridges and spires as seen from Princes Street, the spire of Christ Church (the Tron Church) being itself on fire on one of these dates. Old Greyfriars' Church in 1845 was also a great conflagration, as were too the great establishments of Nelson & Sons, publishers, in 1878, and Jenner & Co. in 1892, both of which firms immediately rose, Phœnix-like, from their ashes to a life commercial, lofty, extending, and more perennial and perpetuating.

Behind, in the Lawnmarket—the High Street as continued to the Castle—was finished in 1844 the Victoria or Assembly Hall of the Established Church of Scotland (Presbyterian), having the most graceful spire to be found in Scotland, and to which that of

Christ Church (Morningside), one of the Edinburgh Episcopal churches, built in 1876, has been compared.

At the top of the Mound the College and Assembly Hall of the Free Church of Scotland were also erected 1846-50. The latter was opened for the Assembly of the year 1859, up to which time Tanfield Hall was annually occupied. From these heights, upon which Allan Ramsay's house stands, is obtained

A VIEW OF THE NEW TOWN OF EDINBURGH (B).

The spire is that of St. Andrew's Church, and the column (the Melville monument), rising from St. Andrew Square, is similar to Trajan's column at Rome. Usher Hall eyes are on every leading and misleading site, and have coveted these also—twins in affliction. The American ideal would be the square, but the square would become too loftily American for Scottish Athenian taste. The alternative would displace the parish church, historically linked with an event common to both the Established and the Free Church of Scotland—the creation of the latter and revival of the former.

From that edifice the Disruption of the State Church took place on May 18, 1843. On that date, after the whole of the General Assembly and the Queen's Lord High Commissioner had arrived in military procession from St. Giles' Church, the Moderator, before the usual procedure of making up the roll, rose and read a document giving reasons for protesting against the House proceeding further, and for the step which he and those of like mind were to take. He then left

St. Andrew's Church, accompanied by Dr. Chalmers, and a numerous band of protesting members (clerical and lay). Surrounded by a great crowd of citizens they walked in procession to Tanfield Hall, where three thousand people awaited their advent. Dr. Chalmers was then chosen the first Moderator.

As this now historical ecclesiastical procession passed down Dundas Street, I was standing near in charge of a maid, and was fortunate in thus seeing something to remember. The Established Church Assembly continued its proceedings in the even tenor of its way. It had naturally, however, lost its young and ardent spirits both among the clergy and adherents, though now it can number as many within as there are without.

Upon the open ground on the Mound the twin buildings of the National Gallery and Royal Scottish Academy now stand, the foundation-stone of which was laid by Prince Albert in 1850. It is difficult to imagine the view without the exquisitely beautiful Scott Monument that has adorned Princes Street for over half-a-century, and to think of the East Gardens as a somewhat waste valley—a toom for excavations from Princes Street, and partly at one time let as a nursery—but the monument was only proposed on 5th October, 1832, and was not begun till 15th August, 1840. It was inaugurated on Scott's natal day, August 15, 1846, with Masonic honours. My perch on my father's shoulders, right in front, enabled me to observe the whole proceedings of unveiling the marble statue. Adam Black, the Lord Provost (afterwards M.P. for Edinburgh, and whose statue is only sixty yards from the monument), in his speech on behalf of the city, to which the monument was that fine day formally handed over, said :—

"I congratulate you and the countrymen of Sir Walter Scott, on now seeing placed on its pedestal, in this magnificent monument, a statue worthy of its shrine. This tribute of a nation's gratitude to one of the most honoured of her sons, adds a new feature of beauty and of grace to his native city, but the halo of his genius sheds a far greater lustre over the name of Edinburgh and of Scotland. As one burning torch not only illuminates the sphere of its own brightness, but kindles the latent fire in others, so who can tell how many dormant spirits have been roused to arduous and successful exertion by the honourable example of Scott? Even here, we see how the glowing genius of the poet has stirred the soul of the architect, and awakened the talents of the sculptor, whose skilful chisel has moulded the rude block into the all but breathing form and features of Scotland's darling son. The sister-arts of architecture and sculpture here vie with each other in presenting the richest offerings to the genius of poetry, history, and romance, and they are themselves singularly honoured in combining to honour him who has contributed so largely to the instruction and enjoyment of the human race. This Monument and Statue, admirable for beauty and durability, I trust will long adorn our city; but though they crumble into dust, the author of *Waverley* has reared for himself monuments of more surpassing beauty, and more lasting endurance and more excellent celebrity. The forked-lightning may dash these turrets to the ground, the tooth of time will corrode these marble features, but over the monuments of his mental creation the elements have no power—

THE WAVERLEY NOVELS	STATUETTES IN THE SCOTT MONUMENT	MINSTRELSY OF THE SCO. BORDER
The Abbess Amy Robsart Lucy Ashton Lady of Avenel Balfour of Burleigh Baron Bradwardine Rose Bradwardine Geo. Buchanan Caleb Balderston Charles I. Prince Charles Stuart, Claverhouse Constance Oliver Cromwell Dougald Dalgety David Deans Effie Deans Jeannie Deans Dandy Dinmont Meg Dodds Dougald Cratur Laird of Dumbiedykes Edith of Lorne Q. Elizabeth. Ellen Douglas, Lady of the Lake Fair Maid of Perth Glee Maiden Halbert Glendinning Gurth Hall o' the Wynd Dick Hatterick		Mause Headrigg Geo. Heriot Ivanhoe James VI. Baillie Nicol Jarvie John Knox Last Minstrel Earl of Leicester Queen Mary Flora M'Ivor Helen M'Gregor Julia Mannering Meg Merrilees Richie Monoplies Montrose Edie Ochiltree Old Mortality Peter Peebles Ravenswood Rebecca Richard Coeur de Lion Robert the Bruce Rob Roy Saladin Dominie Sampson Sir Percie Sha'ton Wayland Smith Knight Templar Magnus Troil Minnie Troil Friar Tuck Dianna Vernon Madge Wildfire
TALES OF A GRANDFATHER	Poetical Works: LADY OF THE LAKE LORD OF THE ISLES LAY OF THE LAST MINSTREL MARMION. ROKEBY BRIDAL OF TRIERMAN	MISCELLANEOUS PROSE WORKS

these will continue to be honoured at home and under distant and more genial skies. Continents as yet unexplored will be taught by the wisdom of Scott, and enlivened by his wit, and rivers unknown to song will resound with the lays of his minstrelsy, but nowhere will his memory be cherished with fonder attachment and more enduring delight than in the cities and in the hamlets of his own beloved Scotland."

Beyond the Rotunda already mentioned, now seen in this view, was the little mound, since improved and become the Waverley Bridge. On its further side, amid thistles and dandelions, was the station of the Edinburgh and Northern Railway, *alias* Edinburgh, Perth, and Dundee line, *via* Granton Ferry. It occupied the hollow, and was chiefly an engine-house with cable to haul trains up the tunnel from Scotland Street; those descending being entrusted to brake-wagons in front to regulate the momentum. An upholsterer's wareroom occupied the space further east, its roof being level with Princes Street, as is now the roof-garden above the Waverley Market area. After the line to Granton and Leith was diverted round the Calton Hill, mushrooms were cultivated in the tunnel. The entrance to the station was at the top of Canal Street, until a wooden stair down from Princes Street was added; the goods offices were further down, with some other unimportant buildings and tenements that carried the foundations up to the North Bridge level, where the New Buildings, seen to the right, then stood. On the right were the slaughter-houses and markets until the North British Railway acquired the north portion, when the slaughter-houses being removed the markets continued, with entrance from Market Street. Railway progress and station requirements have absorbed the whole old area of the market, which is now held under cover where the Northern Railway terminus and the above upholstery shop were. The Waverley Market, as it is now named, has become an institution for public banquets and gatherings, national, political, floral, musical, cyclical, and recreational, accommodating thousands, and as many as 10,000 seated. Where the entrance to the Market now is, Campbell, the old piper, had his little box, in which he skirled the bagpipes to the English tourist's delight at seeing a real Highlander, and one who could intelligently interest them.

Canal Street received its name in view of the Union Canal being brought, as projected in 1776, along the Princes Street valley, thence to Greenside, at the head of Leith Walk, where an immense harbour would have converted the New Town into a sea-port by the further extension of the canal by locks to the sea. It was supposed the Leith traders would abandon their sea traffic, and that the chief ports of Europe would send shipping into the heart of Edinburgh! The public were to be gratified with a pleasure ground made out of the valley nurseries and waste ground, and the transformation of the Nor' Loch into a canal was to be not only ornamental but of great benefit to the citizens—perhaps for curling, skating, and boating, and as coaling depots, as well as mud and manure loading banks, all which the city finds it hard now to tolerate, at

Port Hopetoun, once a delightful suburb at Fountain-bridge in the midst of groves of pretty trees now hopelessly lost to the town. On the 25th March of that year twenty labourers scored historical mention by beginning work at the banks. It is well the contractor did not go over the score; the Scotsman, however, who is to find the North Pole might have disembarked by the Castle rock under a scientific salute of the great guns of the capital, as was lately accorded by the Royal Scottish Geographical Society *inter muros* near that rock to Nansen and Peary the Norwegian and American Arctic explorers.

The splendid and picturesque view of the Forth, with the Fife hills and sunny shores opposite, Inchkeith, and North Berwick Law, reminds one of the regular route to London up to 1846, which was by sea even for long after the railway was opened, until the aversion to the tedious train journey was overcome, and its advantage over time and weather realised. The first royal visit of Queen Victoria in 1842 was made by sea, and so uncertain was her hour of arrival, owing to weather, that her Majesty's unexpected appearance threw the magistracy and the whole city into consternation on the morning of the first of September, which happened to be St. Giles' Day, and the ter-centenary of Queen Mary's arrival from France. The royal cortege passed on to Dalkeith for want of the city keys, which were formally handed to the Queen during her deferred public royal progress through the city on the 3rd.

The approach of a London steamer (paddle-boat) was known by the smoke on the horizon. The first man who ran to Edinburgh with the intelligence of it received a gratuity, and something extra to tell the man at Nelson's Monument to hoist the flag. This was the signal for cabs to go to Granton, and indicated to merchants the early delivery of their weekly bales and boxes, tidings so important that a former assistant of Renton & Co. remembers three ladies waiting in the shop at one time for the arrival of silk goods which the flag had foretold the advent of. After dark, and on Sundays, a gun was the signal.

Besides the Nelson Monument, erected to incite Scotchmen to die for their country and, telescope like, that they might see their distant duty, there is on the same hill the National Monument, designed to be a tribute to the gallant and illustrious past, and an incentive to the future heroism of the men of Scotland. It was to have given the new Athens the Parthenon of the past one, in glorious remembrance of soldiers and sailors who fell in the French War, and in particular at Waterloo. It cost £1000 per pillar, base and frieze, and was honoured with the King's personal patronage, a grand procession, royal salutes from Castle, Crags, and Fort, and from the Royal Squadron in "Leith Roads." (Leith Walk is a road, but Leith Roads is the near waterway in the Firth of Forth.) Built in 1822, it had not come of age when the view was taken, but the greater age that has come upon it since has done more for the realisation of the city's ideal through its pillared pose than could have been done had the nation added to its number of pillars, and made that which was not as if it were. To perfect would have been ruin. The Royal Observatory, as seen on the Calton Hill, was then under Professor Piazzi Smyth, of Pyramid fame. The building still remains as the City Observatory, while the Royal Observatory is now an imposing erection on the Blackford Hill, its equipment being second only to Greenwich in Great Britain.

The North Bridge New Buildings on the right are now being replaced by the North British Railway Station Hotel. The bridge itself has already been re-erected in steel, with stone piers, not a piece of the past being left to tell its story unless the coming New Zealander finds the foundation stone the nineteenth century failed to discover. (There is perhaps a base still hidden beneath Mr. Hyde's room, G.P.O.)

The trees in the view conceal its site; perhaps some have survived its demolition. It lived a century and a quarter. It may not have latterly thought itself worthy of the high level which nature and the city had placed it at, nor have looked or felt very graceful after the iron epaulets its sturdy old-fashioned frame had to don; but it had weathered storms, borne royalty and loyalty along it, and carried the traditions of Auld Reekie as heirlooms to a new Victorian city it made a Queen. It leased to that Queen for ever, unmolested with winding closes and hovels, a valley of picturesque beauty which she should herself grace with a fair face as became a terrace city jewelled with the fortunes of the past.

Behind the bridge (north end), on the east side, was Shakespeare Square, with stairs to Canal Street; and the Duty House; and near it Sarah Sibbald's fruit and speldrin stand, herself and her stand with considerable latitude, natural and allowed, until she and barrow had to give place in the stream of humanity that has since swept the old bridge away, the new one being erected on a level with the time and its ways, with double cable car lines characteristic of the world's iron progress at the century's close.

In the square stood the Theatre Royal, occupying its whole central space. With this Sir Walter Scott and other distinguished men of the time were associated. At the period of half-a-century ago W. H. Murray was the lessee. He was the brother of Mrs. Siddons, the former lessee (with whom he was associated in the management), the refined lady and the irreproachable member of society whose financial anxieties were allayed by the timely help of Sir Walter Scott, ever the player's friend, and others. The production of the Waverley dramas, inaugurated with Rob Roy, and honoured with the presence, on the first night, of the Great Unknown himself, was the beginning of a new career for her. I have lately received an account of this first production of Rob Roy from a relative, whose box was next to Sir Walter's. She says it was evident, the moment he entered, that all knew the writer; the ovation was one to be ever remembered. The same relative was a great favourite of Hogg the Ettrick Shepherd, and to her father's suggestion of Hogg to Sir Walter Scott and his own help (acknowledged in the preface) is due Hogg's Jacobite Ballads, which collection Sir Walter Scott was then the originator of.

The whole property around was bought by the Government for a new General Post Office, £5000

New Club   R G & Son   St Andrew's Ch.   Royal Institution   Melville's Mon^t

PROGRESS OF NEW TOWN :—
North Bridge founded (p 207)   (1763)-66
Rose Court, Thistle Street   ·   1766
Princes Street commenced (p 273)   1767
Leith Walk formed (p 221)   ·   1774
St. James' Square   · · ·   1775
Earthen Mound begun (p 274) ·   1783
Princes Street built to Mound ·   1784
George Street, East Div. (p 245)   1784
Frederick Street (p 264) ·   ·   1790
Castle Street (p 261) ·   ·   ·   1792
York Place   · · ·   1794
Charlotte Square   · · ·   1800
London Street   · · ·   1803-1818
Heriot Row   · · ·   1803-1818
Howe Street   · · ·   1807-1819

Picardy Place (p 222)   · ·   18
Albany Street   · · · ·   1800
Regent Bridge   · · · ·   18
Waterloo Place planning ·   ·   18
North Bridge, New Buildings ·   18
Great King Street, Fettes Row   18
Royal Terrace   · · · ·   18
India Street, Gloucester Place, etc. 18
Moray Place Coates Csescent, etc. 18
Scotland St., Mansfield Place, etc. 18
376 private buildings erected   - 1822-
Howard Place   · · ·   18
Henderson Row   · · ·   18
St. Bernard's Crescent   · ·   18
Annandale Street   · · ·   18
Haddington Place   · · ·   18

T GARDENS EDINBURGH (B)

s & Stationers 82 Princes Street

Register House   Dug^d Stewart's Mon^t Playfair's Nelson's
                       Observatory.   Mon^t   Mon^t

Regent Terrace 1825, Hope Cresc.	1826	ROOMS, HALLS, THEATRES :—
Dean Bridge - - - -	1833	Assembly Rooms, (1) 1720 ; (2) '56 ; (3) '87
Clarendon Crescent - - -	1850	St. Cecilia's Hall (1) 1728 ; (2) 1762
Oxford Terrace - - -	1854	Music Hall 1843, Queen Street Hall 1849
Chester Street - - - -	1862	Free Assembly Hall (p. 272) - 1858
Osborne Terrace, etc. - -	1863	Oddfellows' Hall - - - 1873
Grosvenor Street 1865, Crescent	1869	U.P. Hall, Castle Terrace - 1880
Manor Place, West Side - -	1866	Albert Hall - - - - 1886
Abbeyhill - - - - -	1868	M'Ewan Hall - - - - 1897
Coltbridge Terrace, - - -	1872	Usher Hall don. 1896 ; site (p 335) 1898
Dalry - - - - -	1872	Theatre, Carr. Cl. 1735, Canongate 1746
Albert Street - - - -	1872	Theatre Royal, Shakespeare Sq. 1769
Drumsheugh Gardens - -	1875	Amphitheatre, Head of Leith
Glencairn Crescent, etc. - -	1876	Walk, (Corrie's Rooms—
Parson's Green - - - -	1880	Pantheon—Adelphi Theatre) 1790
Inverleith Gardens, etc. - -	1882	Lyceum Theatre 1884, Empire - 1892

being paid for the theatre, which ceased after ninety years of a chequered course. It was closed the day after the Queen's Birthday, with a farewell address, written by Lord Neaves, one of the Scottish Judges, the entire assemblage joining in with the celebrated actors in singing the National Anthem.

As the National Anthem ended the curtain fell, and the theatre passed from sight, and the site into her Majesty's service. But ere the stage vanished in its final transformation scene, the religious mission of that year alighted on its boards. Then as secretary of the Y.M.C.A., and associated through it with the forward religious social movements of the day, I appeared one night, and "for that night only," among the company behind the scenes, and before an audience come not to plots and players with their cues, but to other p's and q's—Preaching, Prayer, and Psalms, with questionings and qualms of conscience. The chief actors on this stage, which had the world as its scene, may have been from Chicago, at that time not a supposed Nazareth out of which no good could come. This was my first and only appearance before the foot-lights, if such lights were required when American luminaries came. I was curious about the caverns and the wooden clouds with painted skies, but the side winds and cold currents from below with the traps and pitfalls made the region very aerie.

The new General Post Office for Scotland was opened in 1866. The laying of its foundation stone and that of the Museum of Science and Art in Chambers Street, on 23rd October, 1861, were the last public acts of the lamented Prince Consort, ALBERT THE GOOD. It was built on a site appropriate to its purpose, being the most centrally situated and conveniently placed of any public building. The association of the site with men of letters and *belles-lettres* of former times is of a piece with its purpose. With the occasion the letter-carrier's scarlet coats and tall hats with cockades disappeared.

Opposite the theatre was the Register House—now the old one in contradistinction to the New Register House, since built behind in 1860, and about to have another building added to its service. There all ancient and modern records are arch-hived or pigeon-holed. Deeds of all kinds are kept, and events of births, marriages, and deaths recorded with great exactitude and fidelity to fact; the Great Seal and Privy Seal are there, and the armorial bearings of all entitled to such in Scotland. There are to be found the Lord Lyon, and the Unicorn may be heard of. The first is the head, and the other is one of several assistants or heralds, &c. They are not the crowned lion and crowned unicorn in the arms of Scotland, although the first has his name from the emblem. But when the kingdom is in arms against any power, or the Crown decrees a holiday or a new coin, they and their *confrères* make proclamation of such at the Cross in great pomp in silk picturesque costumes, with military guard, band, and trumpeters, who flourish forth her Majesty's will. For a fair fee the Lyon will provide arms with a differentiation for a member of any family having arms, or for about £50 or less he will create arms for any one whose family never had any: of course they are paper or parchment ones. In H. M. General Register House are kept the Barons' letter to the Pope in 1320, declaring that "so long as one hundred Scotsmen remained alive they would never submit to the dominion of England," and the Act of Settlement of the Scottish Crown upon the House of Stuart. In 1869 there were in 21 chambers, 42,835 folio record volumes.

As we continue towards the Calton Hill, the former Post Office building is passed. It was opened for business in 1821, and some months before its occupation, by order of the Depute Lyon King of Arms and the Usher of the White Rod,* the new coat of the royal arms of Britain put thereon was torn down and removed as derogatory to the independence of Scotland—*i.e.*, giving England precedence. A correct coat of arms was substituted. In Scotland the lion rampant occupies the first and fourth quarters, the English lions the second, and Ireland's harp is in the third quarter.

At Waterloo Place is the entrance to the Calton Burying Ground, where was lately erected a red granite monument to the Scottish-American soldiers who fell in the Civil War, 1860-65. It is 15 ft. high, surmounted by a statue of Lincoln 9 ft. in height.

The view from the Calton Hill has ever been *par excellence* the grandest that any eye, without or with telescope or any scope at all for observation or imagination, can conceive. City, sea, and landscape are all there, by day; and when the moon sheds her silvery lustre o'er the valley a fairy scene supervenes; but

* The Walker Trustees (St. Mary's Cathedral) are hereditary owners.

when there is superadded a royal illumination of the banks, ramparts, buildings and edifices, with dome or spire or crown, then fairy land itself is not equal to it, at least by night.

VIEW OF ARTHUR'S SEAT AND HOLYROOD (C).

After treading ground associated with Scott and Shakespeare, a trio is completed when we reach Burns' Monument, now also a museum of Burns relics. The monument was erected in 1830. But about the half-century ago, I am inclined to think, either because the illustrious Scott was in the zenith of Scottish poetry or owing to the thought-currents of the time, when Church questions and religious feelings were dominant, and prejudices against light literature were strong, Burns was not in Edinburgh more than a minor poet. In some Princes Street shops his works were relegated to a high place in the shelves, for which steps had to be taken to reach them. Still though the stream was low, it trickled o'er the bonnie braes of Scotland, percolated the valleys, and flowed quietly through the villages until nature—human nature—gladly drank in showers that fell and flowed in fullest sympathy with the land, and made Robert Burns rise again in power to refresh humanity and nourish the national bond with which St. Andrew had girdled the world of Scotland.

Arthur's Seat and Salisbury Crags rise on the farther side of the valley, the highest point being 822 feet, "to which the ascent is easy and from which the prospect is unrivalled." The way to the top from Burns' Monument has always been by Jacob's Ladder down, past Holyrood, up by St. Anthony's Chapel on the knoll and Salisbury Crags, and on and up with "a stout heart tae a stey brae" until the crown of Arthur's Seat is gained, and the city, a thousand years old, curtained in smoke, lies below—"Auld Reekie." It occupies the spot where, half a thousand years before its existence, King Arthur, of Tennysonian and legendary fame, fought, as is said, one of his battles in defence of the liberty and faith of his people; but be that as it may, Arthur was a king of the ancient Britons, and may have made victorious expeditions to Scotland, Ireland, Denmark, Norway, and France, and have defeated a great Roman army, all as is assigned to his arms. Whatever, however, his valour and conquests as a king, or his legendary power among the Knights of the Round Table, the symbol of his name, and allied fancy that he still lives, the soul and conscience of an ideal, surrounded by knights and ladies, patterns of valour, breeding, and grace to all the world, may well suggest a hill worth climbing in life, for "the prospect from the top is unrivalled." So far the externals of these virtues are sought in Arthur's Seat on May Day morning, when young men and maidens—some not altogether young—ascend the hill at sun-rise in gay groups to perambulate its sides searching for the dew by which grace and beauty are promised them. In the past octogenarians even have deigned to have an early wash with the rising sun and air of heaven at this altitude, among them being the founder of the *Morning*side Asylum in 1826, at the age of 81, and J. Burnet, 19 stone, who ascended in 15 minutes "on a hot summer day."

On the unique imperial night of the Victorian Diamond Jubilee, June 22, 1897, both on Arthur Seat and Salisbury Crags, huge bon-fires blazed in the galaxy of the terrestrial stars that were visible from Edinburgh to the number of fully fifty, representing a radius of 20 miles, burning in concert with all other hills throughout the United Kingdom, the total being 2500, to the wonderment of the planetary namesakes of gods and goddess: Mars bewildered, knowing only Scotland's fiery cross of war; Mercury astonished at the blazing eloquence of the land over commercial progress and prosperity; and Venus in her silvery robe surprised and confused, for she had known no empress so honoured in the history of the world or since the creation of the universe.

The level ground upon the north and west, called the Queen's Park (which, with the hill, has an area of 600 acres) has gradually assumed during the half-century a royal air, the houses at the base and those adjoining the Palace, as well as a number opposite, being long ago cleared away, and a morass at St. Margaret's Well made a loch.

Two grand National Volunteer Reviews have taken place in the presence of the Queen, on the ground beyond the Palace, the first in August, 1860, and the second in August, 1881—the first as fortunate in regard to weather as the other was unfortunate. The numbers reviewed were 22,000 and 30,000 respectively, while the spectators on the hill-sides and prominences, computed at 600,000, presented a sight as wonderful, and to an extent as interesting, as the uniformed mass below in review order. At that of 1881, in response to the royal salutes fired as the Queen and cortege reached the saluting ground, the pluvial descent that pattered Her Majesty's and people's umbrellas and parasols and battered the uncovered battalions was such as Scotland had never experienced in the Queen's reign; for, until then, it had enjoyed unbroken sunshine wherever and whenever her sovereign appeared, such as the whole of the United Kingdom rejoiced in on the Diamond Day when the British Empire was in the meridian. Still the untruly yclept fire-side soldiers stood water as they proved they were prepared to do fire, while the spectators turned back under cover and fled, the whole hill appearing a moving mass of mushrooms, more of a lively than of a deadly nature, especially in the Hunter's Bog. The Queen kept her post by the colours till the last, and sat out the march past in an open carriage long after the mushrooms had scrambled, marched, or run away, after the rain of terror had done its worst.

There was no Queen's Drive at the time of the view, that being only formed in 1846, to give employment to many idle hands at a time of much distress. It makes the circuit of the hill, gradually ascending as it winds round the east by the place where the smoke is seen, and descends again at the west side. The view from it is said to be second to none in Europe. When I made the drive in 1895 it was most happily associated with the present Bishop of Niagara, his wife and son, and their enjoyment of the scenery, as well as my own delight, was a ratification of its deservedness of a reputation.

To attempt any professed reference to Holyrood Palace and Abbey, so prominent in the view, in a few lightning lines would be a transgression, for their history and associations and the events of Edinburgh Castle, royally linked as that is with Holyrood, are such as to warn wayfarers off unless they are prepared to deal with matters of the deepest and far-reaching interest. The characters and events that cluster about their walls belong to sterner times of Scottish interest more or less related to and even affecting the welfare of the whole kingdom; while the elaborately carved fountain so beautifully reproduced from that within Linlithgow Palace, under the directions of the late Prince Consort, and placed in front of Holyrood in 1858, carries one further afield to the room in which Queen Mary was born on 7th December, 1542, in the palace, with the Parliament Hall, which was the favourite residence of the Stuart kings. Of that palace, burnt in 1746 and in ruin, although not uncared for by the Government, Sir Walter Scott writes:—

> "Of all the palaces so fair
> Built for the royal dwelling
> In Scotland, far beyond compare
> Linlithgow is excelling."
>
> *Marmion.*

The Abbey of Holyrood owes its origin, according to the legend, to David I. being saved from an angry stag in the hunting forest of Drumsheugh by the sudden interposition of a cross, St. Andrew appearing after in a dream instructing him to found

Published by R. Grant & Son B.

Drawn by W Banks.

N. Berwick Law & Aberlady Bay.   Piershill Barracks.   Portobello.   Palace of Holyrood

ROYAL, POLITICAL AND MUNICIPAL EVENTS:—		
Edinburgh in hands of Picts		653
Conquered by Northumbrians		IXc.
Given up to Indulphus King of Scotland		956
Queen Margaret widow of Malcom Canmore died in the Castle, 10th June		1093
First Parliament held in Edinburgh		1215
Alexander II. died		1249
Alexander III. married to the daughter of Henry III.		1251
Alexander III. Killed by a fall from his Horse		1285
Margaret the Maiden of Norway, d.		1285
Castle besieged by Edward I.		1296
Re-taken by Earl of Moray		1313
David II. died in Castle		1371
James II. buried in Holyrood		1460
Mary of Gueldres, Q. of Ja. II., buried in,Tri. Coll. Ch. (p217)		1463
Jas. IV. m. to d. of Henry VII.		1503
James IV. buried at Holyrood		1513
Holyrood Palace erected by Jas. V.		1528
James V. buried at Holyrood		1542
Queen Mary leaves for France		1548
Mary of Gulse died at Castle		1560
Qu. Mary returns from France married to Darnley at Holyrood		1561 1565
James VI. born in Edin. Castle		1566
James VI. enters by West Port		1579

St Anthony's Chapel.   Arthur Seat.   Burns' Monument.   Salisbury Crags

arl of Morton, Regent, beheaded	1581
ımes VI. and his Queen Anne of Denmark land at Leith (p 2)	1590
:. Elizabeth Bapt. at Holyrood	1596
liver Cromwell arrived in Edin.	1650
arquis of Montrose executed	1651
arquis of Argyle executed	1661
ımes II. proclaimed King	1685
'illiam and Mary proclaimed	1689
James VIII." proclaimed King	1745
ɛith created a Barony	1555
ıperiorities—Newhaven 1511; Leith 1565; North Leith, Broughton, Canongate, and Pleasance 1636: Portsburgh	1648
xtension, including Portobello	1896

RELIGIOUS FOUNDATIONS:—

Holyrood Abbey f. by David I.	1128
Blackfriars Monastery f. by Alex. II	1230
Hospital of Our Lady, Leith Wynd	1479
Convent and Hospital of the Virgin Mary, St Mary's Wynd	1499
Convent of St. Catherine of Sienna	1517
Church and Monastery of Carmelite Friars, and Hospital of Greenside	1520
St. Mary's Chapel, Niddry's Wynd	1504
St. John's Baptist Chapel	1517
St. Roque's Chapel, Canaan	1530
Magdalene Chapel, Cowgate	1547
Archbishop Beaton's House	1619
Edinburgh made an Episcopal See	1633

a monastery on the spot. The monarch's grateful endowment included the canons' privilege of erecting the Burgh of Canongate, partly seen in the view, St. Cuthbert's, and other churches, and Canon Mills, as well as a tithe of whales and sea-monsters that visit twenty or thirty miles of the coast, very few of which have made themselves known in that part this century. The bell of the Chapel Royal is now in St. Paul's, York Place, on loan from the old Barons of Holyrood, and is, I believe, the only church bell beside the parish ones allowed by law in Scotland. It was originally in the Cowgate Episcopal Chapel.

There is not, perhaps, any kind of royal important event which Holyrood has not been the scene of, alone or in connection with the Castle. There was baptized on the 1st December, 1596, Princess Elizabeth, daughter of James VI., Queen of Bohemia, from whom Queen Victoria is lineally descended, James VI., in whom were united the crowns of England and Scotland, being born in the Castle. The marriage of Queen Mary with Darnley was celebrated within its walls, and, as every visitor is told and made visibly to understand, therein Rizzio met his tragic fate. Thereat resided or have been buried many kings and queens, the last burial being the re-interment from Trinity College Church, on the 15th July, 1848, of Mary of Guildres, Queen of James II., who died in 1463. This burial reminds me of the funeral of Lieutenant John Irving, R.N., of the Franklin Polar Expedition, who died in 1848 or 1849, and was buried in the Dean Cemetery, Edinburgh, in January, 1881, with naval and military funeral honours. Dying at the age of 33, his fellow-officers and companions, who bore him to the grave, were men of about 70. His remains, found in the Arctic regions, were sent home by Lieutenant Schwatka, of the United States Navy, and the America Searching Expedition.

The Palace and Abbey were at various times attacked, surprised, laid waste, and burnt, the Abbey being destroyed, and finally ruined in varying tumults. The chapel was twice restored for service, the last time with "abominations of surplices and chanting choristers," which offended the people. The Palace was the scene of important public transactions during the reigns of Queen Mary and James VI., and was the residence of Charles Edward Stuart before and after the battle of Prestonpans, 1745. To the French exile, Charles X., in 1799, it opened its walls, and again in 1830-32. Founded, erected, and restored by royal favour, it is the residence of Queen Victoria when her Majesty visits her royal Scottish capital, and is annually occupied in semi-royal state by her Majesty's Lord High Commissioner to the General Assembly of the Established Church of Scotland.

Portobello, where the sea laps the land, is two miles beyond Holyrood, and those two miles of road and the sea suburb are now within the Greater Municipality by which this Edinburgh-by-the-Sea has made the capital at last a kind of seaport, although, as yet, it can only boast of a pier and sea craft of the build of pleasure boats and bathing coaches. The latter, however, have a gloriously wide sandy beach with which to adorn and enliven the scene with their sea-cabins. Besides trains every few minutes, the narrow isthmus or neck of road between the county fields, thus connecting the city and its postscript, gives a constant service of cars, which is a complete contrast to the single 'bus that, fifty years ago, plied once an hour to primitive and polite Portobello, which one may hope will retain its amenity, though cast into a city not without a rough element alongside of its culture and refinement.

BATTLE OF PRESTONPANS.

Prestonpans is six miles beyond Portobello—*i.e.*, that distance from sea-side Edinburgh, or ten miles from Edinburgh Castle. The battle of Prestonpans was fought on the 21st September, 1745. Charles Edward Stuart (son of James Francis Edward, the son of James II. of England and VII. of Scotland, better known as "The Chevalier de St. George") had a few days before had his father proclaimed at the Market Cross "James VIII. of Scotland, England, France, and Ireland," with the support of the Cameron clansmen, the heralds and magistrates (some perhaps unwillingly), a number of ladies on horseback, with swords drawn, acting as a guard of honour, and afterwards, with other Jacobite ladies, enlivening the Holyrood apartments at a ball. On the night before the battle Charles slept in a little house at Duddingston, a village on the east of Arthur Seat. The battle was of short duration, the Highlanders—suffering under great disadvantage—gaining a signal victory over a well disciplined and veteran army, and sweeping it from the field. By the speed of their horses the cavalry escaped, but the infantry were killed or taken, with their colours, baggage, and £6000 in the military chest. Sir John Cope's cannon were captured on a wooden tramway, the first known in Europe. This victory annihilated the only regular army in the kingdom, excepting that in Edinburgh Castle, Stirling Castle, and some petty forts. It caused a panic in London, and a run upon the Bank of England. 105 fugitives reached the Castle, but 1500 prisoners, of whom 80 were officers, were marched through Edinburgh on the following day, preceded by a hundred pipers, playing "The King shall enjoy his own again." In the triumphal procession, which the Prince did not accompany, were the captured colours of the 13th and 14th Light Dragoons, the 6th, 44th, 46th, 47th, and London Corps. The Old Chevalier was proclaimed James VIII. in all large towns, and his concealed friends avowed their sentiments, the ladies especially, while even doubtful people became Jacobites.

The year 1745 is vividly impressed on the Scottish mind. Down to the days of Burns and Scott the whole land was filled with melodies for the lost cause and fallen race, while not one song is known in favour of the victors, and now, wherever Scottish song is known—and that is everywhere in the kingdom and in America, as well as in the distant colonies—Jacobite songs mingle with those of Burns in praise of Scotland, its past and its people.

The illustration of the battle of Prestonpans is from a mezzotint drawing by my father, done about the centenary of the event. The central figure, falling

Highlanders   BATTLE OF PRESTONPANS, SEPTEMBER 21, 1745   *Army under General Cope*

from his horse, is Colonel James Gardiner, a Scotsman who passed into the English army in 1702, was severely wounded in 1706, and fought with distinction in all Marlborough's battles. In 1715 he gave proof of daring courage. In the picture his dragoons will be seen to have deserted him, upon which he placed himself at the head of a handful of infantry, and fought till cut down with a Lochaber axe, when he was borne to the manse in the village of Tranent, in the background, where he died in a few hours not far from his own house, near which the battle was fought.

VIEW OF EDINBURGH FROM THE NORTH (D).

From the Queen's Park we thread our thoughts through fields, now thickly set with tenements, and these teeming with tenants. The whole of Leith Walk, which we cross, we now see as an avenue of stores and storeys, while the nurseries known in our childhood are known no more, for they are rooted out, and the zone which divided port from city and lent bracing air or cooling breeze to refresh the up-coming pedestrian, is no longer. In a few months the interregnum of horse tram cars will end, and a thousand cable horseless ones will dominate, from every direction, the great artery between city and port, where almost alone, and at no hurried intervals, an omnibus long held a leisurely course to the Tron Church, and round it; then an improved service to Punch and Judy at the foot of the Mound; and then, somewhat accelerated, to the Four Lamps at the west-end, now an illuminated clock surmounted with the city arms; after that to Haymarket, the Ultima Thule of the town, so termed then, when no one thought of its importance as a city.

We have come round the Calton Hill from the Canongate by Greenside, where the port was projected; touched the site of the past village of Picardie, through the barony of Broughton and Canonmills village to Inverleith, in order to introduce the view of the city from the Botanic Gardens. The peacock and the lady painter in the picture indicate the taste and culture that, half a century ago or a little earlier, pervaded general society as generally and relatively the same spirit and restful study of the beautiful in art and manners does not do in these hurrying, competitive, whirling cycle days.

Tanfield Hall at Canonmills is among the trees in the middle of the view. It was originally erected in 1824 for the Oil Gas Co., of which Sir Walter Scott was the chairman, and who suggested its design —that of a Moorish fort. There the Free Church of Scotland was organised or constituted in May, 1843, on its renouncing State bonds; and there till May, 1856, its General Assembly annually met for eleven days, as the Established likewise annually does in its Assembly Hall for ten days. The building has been variously occupied since. For long a wool-store after the faithful flock had left it, it is now a bonded warehouse for spirits of other sorts before being taken out of their State bonds. By it now runs a rectified and purified Water of Leith—an *eau-de-vie* for the fish now freed from a fifty years ago filthiness. Once more the river, teeming with piscatorial life, is the scene of fishing rods that

are not spared, in lashing the stream, by the too
ardent juvenile offenders against the decree of the
Magistrates to keep the water again a river resort of
the true angler.

By the cable car line, the first introduced into the
city in 1887, amid much popular prejudice, we pass up
Brandon Street, the point where, on the morning of
September 1, 1842, the Queen entered the city, the
Royal Archers, her Majesty's Body Guard, narrowly
escaping being too late to make their loyal bow and
present their silver arrow, while the Magistrates insuffi-
ciently on the *qui vive*, waiting with the keys at the
Council Chambers, missed their presentation that day.

Continuing up to Princes Street, we are again at the
Royal Institution, with the statue of the Queen in
State as there erected in 1844, and the starting point
of our panoramic views at the foot of the Mound,
where culture and commerce met and law and leisure
intersected each other.

VIEW WEST END PRINCES STREET—ST. JOHN'S (E).

By turning to the right, and passing along three
blocks or divisions, St. John's Church is reached, at
the junction of the street with the Lothian Road, and
the general aspect of that part of Princes Street in
the time of the View E understood.

Of services in St. John's and other Episcopal
churches I shall speak further on. Here I only note
that the church was erected in 1818, at the same
time as St. Paul's, York Place—the proposal that
the two congregations should build one large central
edifice giving place to the opinion that it would be

better to have one at the west end and one at the east, and a subsequent arrangement to have a common fund for their erection being also abandoned. The tower originally terminated in an open lantern, which fell during a tempest in January 1818, doing great damage to the interior. Of this Sir Walter Scott wrote to a friend that "the Devil never so well deserved the title of the Prince of the power of the air, sincè he had blown down this handsome church and left the ugly mass of New Buildings on the North Bridge." Sir Walter's graceless mass, after eighty years' grace, is now scattered to the winds by the peaceful progress of the Victorian era, which has also, in the eyes of the railway shareholders, crushed the debris into golden dust. To St. Paul's building fund Scott subscribed £50. Lothian Road, " nearly a mile long by 20 paces," was made in a day, in the winter of 1784, between sunrise and sunset. The scheme was executed with consummate ability with the aid of several hundred workmen, who had also to fill up a great hollow. The inhabitants knew nothing about the plan, and had to succumb to the invaders, who swept dykes and cottages before them. Neither house, nor byre, nor cows, nor pipe, nor pot was left to the old woman, who had gone to the market but a few hours before. The road was raised again at its lower end in 1869, and various important buildings razed away to give place to the wooden Caledonian Station of that year. Thus disappeared Braehead House, Croall's Bazaar, St. Cuthbert's Poor's-House, The Riding School, Royal Military Academy, and Dr. Candlish's Church, rebuilt at Stockbridge.

Princes Street

GARDENS, &c.
Walk round Salisbury Crags - 1815
Calton Hill Walks - - - 1816
West Princes Street Gardens 1818 1876
Queen Street Gardens - - 1822
Royal Botanic Gardens (p 222) 1824
New Leith Pier commenced - 1826
Royal Terrace Gardens - - 1831
Queen's Drive (p 215) - - 1846
East Gardens, Princes Street 1850-54
Waverley Market - - - 1877
Arboretum - - - - 1881
Blackford Hill 1884 ; Braid Hills 1889
Harrison Park - - - - 1887
Water of Leith purified (p 222) - 1889-94
Inverleith Park - - - - 1891

MONUMENTS AND STATUES:—
Charles II., Parliament Square 1685
Nelson's Monument (p 206) 1807-1815
Melville Monument - - - 1821
National Monument f. (p 206) 1822
Professor John Playfair - *circa* 1825
Dugald Stewart (p 316) - - 1830
George IV. (p 206) - - - 1831
William Pitt - - - - 1833
Robert Burns (p 112) - - 1833
Fourth Earl of Hopetoun - - 1834
Frederick Duke of York - - 1836
Queen Victoria (Royal Inst.) - 1844
Sir Walter Scott 1840-44, Statue 1846
Duke of Wellington - - - 1852
Prof. Wilson (Christopher North) 1854

JRGH FROM THE LOTHIAN ROAD.
Ilers & Stationers, 82 Princes Street. (E)

Princes Street

Allan Ramsay (p 291)	- -	1865
Catherine Sinclair	- - -	1867
. Watt (p 316) 1854, tr. H. W. Coll.		1873
'rince Consort Memorial (p 210)		1876
Dr. Livingstone (p 316)	- -	1876
Adam Black, M.P., etc. (p 316)		1877
ir James Y. Simpson (p 316)		1877
Dr. Chalmers (p 200)	- -	1878
Dean Ramsay (p 345)	- -	1879
Duke of Buccleuch -	- -	1887
Vm. Chambers, LL.D.	- -	1891
Scottish American Soldiers	-	1893
8th Highlanders Ind. Mutuny of 1857-58		
2nd High. Afghan Campaign of 1878-80		
Col. Kenney 92nd Highlanders		1873
John Knox in Free Church Coll.		1896

SOCIETIES, ETC. :—
Merchant Company Inst. -	-	1681
Board of Trustees for Manuf.	-	1727
Speculative Society -	- -	1764
Society of Antiquaries	- -	1780
Royal Society of Scotland	-	1783
Royal Company of Archers' Hall		1776
Highland Society	- -	1784
Chamber of Commerce	- -	1786
Royal Caled. Horticultural Soc.		1809
Roy. Sco. Society of Arts	-	1821
Royal Scottish Academy -	-	1826
Royal Sco. Geographical Soc. -		1884
Misc.: Geol. Arbor. 1834; Botanical 1836; Meteorological 1855; Horticultural 1877; Sco. History 1886		

PRINCES STREET, PAST AND PRESENT.

Of the shops or stores on Princes Street flourishing, as their continued longevity till to-day would suggest, when my pencil was busy with the verdant "Word in Season," ten still continue as then designated, with other three as then known and recognised by sexagenarians. These are given below in the order of their establishment, with the respective years of their appearance in Princes Street, and other data. Their assessed rental in the year of 1847-48 was £1485, which would be equivalent to a real rental of £1856, and that of the same firms in other or enlarged premises, including Jenner and Co.'s entire building stretching up St. David Street, was this year (1897-98) £13,617, the full rental. In 1847-48 the assessed rental of Princes Street was £16,493, the full rental being say £20,616. It is now £95,919, nearly five times what it was half-a-century ago. The difference in the figures for 1847-48 arises from only four-fifths of the rental being rateable fifty years ago, and I think that was in relation to some limit which an Act prescribed. The only practical difference must have been in the City Chamberlain's Office, where simpler figures were at hand in dealing with the real rental. To the citizens it would be six under the one system, and half-a-dozen under the other, or rather *vice versa*.

1848—1898.

PRINCES STREET FIRMS 50 YEARS AGO,

still continued under same (or similar) designation, with names of present proprietors.

GEORGE COTTON & SON (Estab. 1775), No. 100. In 1825 at No. 16; 1833 at No. 23; 1870 at No. 100; formerly in 1775 (*George Cotton* till 1842), at Crosscauseway; 1816 at 12 North Bridge. In 1834, tobacconist to the King; 1838, to the late King; 1840 to Her Majesty; 1841, purveyor of cigars and snuff to Her Majesty; 1842, tobacconist to the royal household. GEORGE COTTON (great-grandson of the founder).

THOMAS DUNCAN & CO. (Estab. 1797), No. 55). In 1806, at No. 18; 1808, at 24; 1811, at 55; 1816, at 58; 1828, at 59; and in 1877-98, at 54; formerly about Lothian Street (*Aird & Duncan* till about 1808); in 1816, bootmaker to the Prince Regent; 1822, to His Majesty; 1835, to the King; 1838, to the Queen; 1844, to the Queen and Prince Albert; 1862, to the Queen, the Prince of Wales, and the Royal Family. THE EDINBURGH ROYAL

Hotel Company, Limited (purchased in 1897 from *Thomas Duncan*, grandson of the founder).

ROBERT GRANT & SON (Estab. 1804), No. 107. In 1834, at No. 82; 1854, at No. 54; 1871, at No. 107; formerly in 1804 (*R. Grant* till 1830), at No. 12, in 1811, at No. 23, and in 1822, at 36 Lothian Street; 1830 (*R. Grant & Sons*—1830-34), at 8 Nicolson Street, booksellers, stationers, circulating library, publishers, binders (from 1804 till about 1840, quill manufacturers). Arthur Giles (partner from 1861, survivor in 1887).

JOHN SMITH & SONS (Estab. 1815), No. 79. In 1847, at No. 54, and also then in High Street (see below) (*John Smith* till 1876); in 1852, at No. 78, and in 1878, at No. 79. In High Street from 1815, at 37 Netherbow; in 1823 to 1860, at 227 High Street, and from 1860, at 38 North Bridge, umbrella and parasol makers. John Smith and A. C. Smith (sons of founder).

DUNCAN, FLOCKHART & CO. (Estab. 1820), No. 139. In 1846, at 139, and also then, as still, at 52 North Bridge from 1820; (*Duncan & Ogilvie* till 1832, then *Duncan & Anderson*, and in 1838, present designation); now also, since 1890, at 104 and 106 S. B. Canongate, chemists to the Queen. JAS. BUCHANAN, JAS. HERON, ROBERT DICK, ALEX. NOBLE, JAS. EWING, WM. INGLIS CLARK, D.Sc. (partners in continuity of firm).

H. C. BAILDON (Estab. 1821), No. 73, and also in 1881 at 148, and since 1893, at 144*a*. In 1828, at No. 73; formerly in 1821 at 20 Waterloo Place as *T. Butler & Co.*; 1826, *Butler & Stone*; 1828-1832, *Butler & Co.*; 1833, present designation, chemist and druggist; 1826-31, chemist to His Majesty. ROBERT AITKEN (sole manager of the firm for ten years, 1877-87).

COWAN & STRACHAN (Estab. 1825), No. 15, silk mercers, &c. WILLIAM RUSSELL (surviving partner) AND WILLIAM RUSSELL, JUNR. (son of same).

J. W. MACKIE & SONS (Estab. 1825), No. 108 from 1840 (*John W. Mackie* till 1865). Formerly in 1825, at 18 Greenside Street; in 1829, at 9 Scotland Street; from 1835-1840, at 8 S. Hanover Street, baker and confectioner; 1840, purveyor of rusks and biscuits to the Queen; also in 1863, to H.R.H. the Prince of Wales. J. W. MACKIE AND GEORGE MACKIE (sons of founder).

STURROCK & SONS (Estab. 1826), No. 97. In 1842, at No. 33, and in 1895 at No. 97; also since 1872 in London; and since 1847 in Glasgow; formerly in 1826, at 27 Duke Street; (*Sturrock* till 1838); in 1838, at 25 and 27 Duke Street; 1842, 27 Duke Street, and at 33 Princes Street; 1842, perfumers and hairdressers to the Queen; in 1856, to the Duchess of Kent; 1863, to the Prince of Wales; 1886, to the Duke of Edinburgh. JAMES STURROCK (son of the founder).

JENNER & CO. (Estab. 1838), No. 47 in 1838 (*Kennington & Jenner* till 1861); in 1847, extended to No. 2 and 6 S. St. David Street; in 1848, added No. 48, also 8 and 10 St. David Street; in 1880, No. 47 to 49 Princes Street and Nos. 2, 4, 6, 8, 10, 12, 14, 16 St. David Street. Silk mercers and drapers. JAMES KENNEDY AND DONALD KENNEDY (surviving partners).

M'LAREN & RENTON (Estab. 1839), No. 12 and 14 (*W. Renton & Co.* till 1895), mercers and general drapers. DUNCAN M'LAREN (nephew of founder).

DICKSON & SON (Estab. 1840), No. 63; in 1840 at No. 60; 1849, at No. 63. Gunmakers. JOHN DICKSON (grandson of the founder).

IRVING BROTHERS (Estab. 1827), No. 99. In 1847, at No. 97 (*Walker & Irving* till 1849); in 1849, at No. 80; 1867, at No. 78; and in 1892, at No. 99. Portmanteau, trunk, and brush manufacturers to Her Majesty. PETER IRVING (brother of founder), and JOHN IRVING (nephew of James Irving, founder).

The order in which the above firms appeared in Princes Street is T. Duncan & Co. (1808), George Cotton (1825), Cowan & Strachan (1825), H. C. Baildon (1833), R. Grant & Son (1834), Kennington & Jenner (1838), W. Renton & Co. (1839), Dickson & Son (1840), John W. Mackie (1840), Sturrock & Sons (1842), Duncan, Flockhart & Co. (1846), John Smith (1847), Walker & Irving (1847).

Cowan & Strachan is the only firm continuously in the same number in Princes Street (upstairs at the first), where it commenced business under the same designation, continued now for 73 years. Other firms that have continued in the same shop under one name are H. C. Baildon (65 years, estab. 77 years), and Duncan, Flockhart & Co. (52 years, estab. 78 years). The firm which is still in the same shop and family (58 years, estab. 73 years) is J. W. Mackie & Sons. The firms that have changed their designation, but which occupy the same sites, are Kennington & Jenner (now Jenner & Co.), rebuilt on site of 60 years ago, and sites adjoining westward and northward; Renton & Co. (now M'Laren & Renton) in same premises of 59 years ago, with enlargement and extension eastward. Those that continue under the same name, but have occupied two shops, are Dickson & Son, No. 60 (9 years), No. 63, since 1849, estab. 58 years; John Smith, No. 54 (5 years), No. 78 (26 years), and in No. 79 (since 1878), estab. 83 years. Three shops —George Cotton, No. 16 (8 years), No. 23 (37 years), and 100 (since 1870), estab. 123 years; R. Grant & Son, No. 82 (20 years), 54 (17 years), 107 (since 1871), estab. 96 years. Six shops—T. Duncan & Co., No. 18 (2 years), No. 24 (3), No. 55 (5 years), No. 58 (12 years), No. 59 (49 years), No. 54 (21 years), estab. 101 years. One firm for two years differently designated, Walker & Irving (now Irving Brothers), has occupied three shops, No. 97 (2 years), No. 80 (18 years), No. 78 (25 years), estab. 51 years. The one firm in the same hands continuously since its occupancy of Princes Street (56 years) is Sturrock & Sons, estab. 72 years. All the original founders are dead, and there is only one alive of the proprietors of fifty years ago (Mr. Sturrock). The only member of a firm that has been personally acting continuously in the same business, including apprenticeship, &c., for the past half-century is the proprietor of R. Grant & Son. At May 13, all the firms are continuations of partnerships, family or other relation, excepting that of Duncan & Co. The Royal Hotel Company's absolute purchase of that firm, being the only break in such continuity, and that only since the previous May 13.

To literary firms I shall refer further on, but of others, John Purdie, established in 1804, and in Princes Street in 1809, will be recognised in Methven, Simpson & Co., and William Roughead, hosier, No. 69, who came to Princes Street in 1824, by the new designation of Laurie & Mackenzie; Mr. Laurie, the sole partner of the present firm, having entered as an assistant of the late William Roughead in 1867. The old business of Robert Bryson & Sons, established over a century ago in the Old Town, and which occupied No. 66 Princes Street from the year 1841 until 1894, is now merged in that of Hamilton & Inches, goldsmiths, who thus four years ago became the clock and watchmakers to the Queen for Scotland, they themselves having been established at No. 90 Princes Street in 1866, from which they removed to their own property at No. 87 in 1888. Of this firm Mr. Robert Kirk Inches is the sole partner. He was elected in 1896 a "Livery" of the Clockmakers' Company, and is a freeman of the city of London, of which company, I believe, the first Master was "a Scottish man," David Ramsay, 1632. Mr. Inches is the only royal tradesman in Scotland holding that honour. The business of James Bryson, optician, first in 1850 at No. 65, and from 1855 at No. 60, has been continued, by the founder's own arrangement, by Turnbull & Co., established at 60A in 1880, who in 1894 incorporated their own business with it. The latter thus now trade as opticians and fishing-tackle makers, with a reputation in American angling circles. They were awarded the highest possible medal and diploma of honour at the Chicago Exhibition, 1893.

In the autumn of 1848, Thomas Thomson, draper, removed from No. 2 Shandwick Place, where he founded the business in 1845, to No. 135 Princes Street, and in 1890 the style of the firm became Thomson & Allison.

About the same time, half-a-century ago, R. & T. Gibson, grocers to the Queen, opened at 98 Princes Street, and in 1859 moved to No. 93, an extension being made in 1889 to 5 Frederick Street, which has continuous connection with the Princes Street premises. The latter are now further enlarged with double frontage.

Some long-established firms, that were in Princes Street in 1848, have left it during the half-century for other chief streets.

Boog & Rogers, established at 20 North Bridge prior to 1797, as Maxton, afterwards Maxton, Boog & Co., removed in 1876 from 80 Princes Street, first to 132 and in 1890 to 117 George Street. The firm is now John H. Rogers & Co., saddlers, &c.

There readers of *The Heart of Midlothian* will find the veritable "Sign of the Golden Nag" which indicated Saddletree's shop, of whom Maxton was the prototype. It adorned Princes Street above the door of No. 80, at the foot of the Mound, for forty years as a curio to the young and a familiar landmark or street mark to those who had been born in the city. I had naturally thus a knowledge of the Nag before I went to rub shoulders with it two doors off, and to the circulation of the *Heart* that told its pedigree. We were somewhat on a level, up the same number of steps. Our ground was so at least, as he was more of a wingless Pegasus above, golden and glittering, surveying the Athenians below as they passed or congregated or parted up the Mound.

Boyd, Bayne & Co., fruiterers, were established at No. 41 in 1810, and in 1891 went to No. 16 Shandwick Place, a number which will be altered next year when the Magistrates change the name of Maitland Street on the south side and number it in with its sister on the north side. The firm is not to be confounded with its original shop, which structurally remains unaltered from its origin.

John Cotton, who occupied No. 35 Princes Street in 1848, and No. 122 from 1858 to 1884, is now at 7 Frederick Street. The present proprietor is in the direct line from the original tobacconist business established at 231 High Street, in the shop occupied by James Gillespie (*circa* 1807), the founder of Gillespie's Hospital, now James Gillespie Schools.

A. Young, Queen's cutler, No. 79, moved in 1861 to 58 North Bridge, and in 1880 to 57 and 61 Forrest Road. The firm is now Archibald Young & Son, with a branch at 7 Hope Street, and was established in 1805.

Edwin Millidge, established in 1820 by Jonathan Millidge at 82 South Bridge, came from 13 North Bridge, in 1834, to 28 Princes Street. His was the first shop of the kind to continue in the street, as it was only in 1854 that the traditional relationship of jewellers to the Bridges in succession to their High Street Krames or Luckenbooths reputation as bankers, in knee breeches and buckles, began to give way in favour of Princes Street by the coming of Mackay & Cunningham from the New Buildings in 1854, followed at intervals by others from the North Bridge—George Street, and even Leith Street, having been early privileged to possess those gold and silver stores. Crouch

& Son were the last jewellers, as also about the last firm, to leave the now doomed upper division of the Bridge, and I believe theirs was the first shop opened there.

Millidge's business was acquired in 1891 by Thos. Smith & Sons, who buying that of G. & M. Crichton (estab. at 63 North Bridge in 1839), removed in 1895 to their premises in No. 18. In 1896 they also bought the business of Jas. Crichton & Co., George Street, late Hamilton & Crichton, whose premises were formerly those of James and Walter Marshall (estab. early last century). *See* Smith & Sons, page 251.

Cowan & Co., besides occupying No. 17 Princes Street (1831 to 1864), had for a long time large paper warehouses opposite. When they retired from their Princes Street shop in 1864, they built their extensive wholesale premises in West Register Street, their mills (established in 1771) being at Penicuik, and their envelope works at Craigside. Their original warehouse was in the Canongate (1793).

W. B. Mackenzie, the Shetland warehouse, established in 1830 at 121 Princes Street, was transfered by the founder in 1860 to John White (now White & Co.), 10 Frederick Street.

Adie & Son, opticians, established last century, now Adie & Wedderburn, were in 58 Princes Street from 1830 to 1842; No. 50, 1842-77; 37 Hanover Street in 1877, and No. 17 in 1882.

Alexander Bell, ironmonger, who commenced at No. 98 in 1845, went to 7 Frederick Street in 1860, and in 1880 to 81 George Street; now Bell, Donaldson & Co. Mr. Bell practically continued Bancks & Co. (1794).

Sanderson & Laurie, grocers, established at No. 78 in 1817, who went to No. 101 in 1849, removed from thence to 20 Hanover Street in 1866.

Scott & Orr, chemists, established at 100 South Bridge in 1819, moved to 67 Princes Street in 1822, to 78 in 1844, and to Dundas Street in 1853, when they amalgamated with Pugh & Plews (established in 1825, at 33 Princes Street). The business is now J. Innes Fraser, 9 Dundas Street, formerly Symington & Fraser.

In 1855 Andrew Barrie & Son, watchmakers and jewellers (now 4 George Street), occupied No. 24, from which they removed in 1859 to No. 43, where they remained till 1885. The business was established by David Whitelaw in No. 16 Princes Street in 1816. It was styled D. Whitelaw & Barrie in 1845, at which time it was in St. Andrew Street (1844 to 1855).

Considerably more firms of corresponding longevity have come to Princes Street, and continued to the present time. These are given below according to their present designation and the date they appeared, with that of their establishment :—

1850.—No. 133, John Summers & Sons, bakers (1844); also at 24 Maitland Street.
1852.—No. 110, John Taylor & Son, Ltd., upholsterers, &c. (1840), from 51 and 54 George Street (Assembly Rooms).
1854.—No. 74, late Mackay, Cunningham & Co. (No. 54, 1854-71 ; No. 62, 1871-80), from 47 North Bridge (prior to 1793), now Jas. Hardy & Co., jewellers (est. Aberdeen *circa* 1850).
1854.—No. 78, Thornton & Co., Ltd., India-rubber manufacturers, from 48 Nicolson Street (1853); also at London, Leeds, Belfast, &c.
1857.—No. 30, Mossman & Sons, jewellers (1813), from 32 North Bridge (re-est. 1813 by a descendant of Jas. Mossman, goldsmith burgess, 1576).
1857.—No. 46, E. Lennie, optician, &c. (1834), from 14 Leith Street.
1859.—No. 126 and No. 45, W. & J. Milne (1844), heraldic stationers, &c., from 33 Hanover St.
1860.—No. 24 and 25 (1870-80), now at 134, Wm. Marshall & Co. (1804), goldsmiths to George IV. (1820), William IV. (1830), and the Queen (1890), from 62 North Bridge.
1862.—No. 59, 60, W. R. Clapperton & Co., of Clapperton & Co., High Street (1798), in continuation of A. Lauder (13 Hanover Street, 1848), (*or* C., Oliver & Co., 1865-72).
1867.—No. 103 (No. 89 in 1867-77), Edwin Pass & Son, hairdressers and perfumers, from 47 Frederick Street, originally Gianette & Pass (hairdressers to the Queen in 1839), established 1839.

1871.—No. 102 (No. 111, 1872-81), James Robertson & Son, goldsmiths, silversmiths, jewellers (1801).

1872.—No. 123, J. Allan & Son, with which is now combined Bell & Son (1834), bootmakers, established in Leith Street, 1783.

This business was originated by Forest Alexander, whose successors in 42 and 44 Leith Street were David Green & Co., Green & Blyth, and Greenoak, whom Allan & Son succeeded. An account of Mr. Alexander is given in *Some Edinburgh Shops* (Thin, 1894), wherein it is shown that he was one of Edinburgh's extraordinary men. He was famed for his manufactures, including the Hessian boot with silk tassel at the knee, which some remember Sir James Gibson-Craig wearing. He opened a tannery in the Pleasance, purchased all the building area of Arthur Street, &c., and introduced "a new order of things in the system of banking in Edinburgh." With his friend Robert Cox of Gorgie, he founded at Picardy Place the Commercial Bank of Scotland, and afterwards the Caledonian Insurance Company.

1878.—No. 57, Mackay & Chisholm, jewellers (1826), from 49 North Bridge.

1880.—No. 62, Romanes & Paterson, tartan manufacturers to the Queen, &c., from 59 North Bridge (1805).

1880.—No. 67, R. Anderson & Son, fishing tackle makers to the Queen (estab. Dunkeld 1840).

1885.—No. 131B, James Ritchie & Son, watch and turret clock makers, as a branch of 25 Leith Street (established 1809). *See* page 259.

1890.—136A, John Ramage & Son, bakers and confectioners; also at 4 Albert Place, originally John Thomson (Potterrow, then College Street), afterwards Albert Thomson, College Street, who was the grandfather of the present head of the firm.

This firm claims to be the oldest firm of bakers in the British Isles (established 1804).

1898.—No. 32, Crouch & Son, jewellers (1821), from 40 North Bridge.

The later established firms that have come to or commenced in the street, and are now prominent in respect of their extensiveness, attractiveness, or position, are the following, given in similar order to the preceding :—

1852.—No. 76, 77, Thos. Stevenson & Son, hosiers, haberdashers, &c. (1852).

1860.—No. 15, Thomas Methven & Sons, seedsmen, nurseries (1850)—Leith Walk, Warriston, Inverleith.

1860.—No. 117 (No. 99, 1860-68), John C. Pottage, homœopathic chemist (1860). Patronised by the Homœopathic Medical Faculty.

In 1890, kola, the valuable article of diet, was introduced to Europe and America by Mr. Pottage, and has now become one of the favourite dietetic beverages.

1860.—No. 124, Henry, Darling & Co., silk mercers, late Donald Reid & Co. (1860-93), (1860).

When No. 124 was the dwelling-house of John Donaldson, W.S., the late Principal Cairns was the family tutor there.

1860.—No. 122 (No. 107 till 1870, afterwards in No. 108 and 74), Singer Manufacturing Co., sewing machine manufacturers (New York, 1856).

Tom Hood, who died in 1845, whose comedies are forgotten, and whose fun and fancies are floating into forgotten land, wrote three poems destined to linger long. One, "The Song of the Shirt," sung into ears and sown into hearts, stimulated if it did not lead to the invention of the sewing machine as now perfected, for the notes of the song, vibrating through Britain, are said to have struck the heart of one seated penniless on a pile of boards near Boston, U.S.A., one sultry August midnight fifty years ago, when he formed in his brain the missing link that should transform the attic needle into the treadle of happy homes over the whole civilised world and even to some uncivilised lands. From this penniless singer, meritorious in action, and Isaac Merritt by name, has grown the Singer Manufacturing Company, with 4500 agencies, one-third of which are in the United States.

1861.—No. 50, Colin Sinclair, fancy stationer (1849).
1863.—No. 29, James Dow & Sons, hosiers (1863).
1864.—No. 130A, W. Jamieson, fruiterer and Italian warehouseman (1860).
1870.—No. 80 (No. 23, 1870-80), James Aitchison, goldsmith to the Queen, Prince and Princess of Wales, and Duke of Edinburgh (1859).
1870.—No. 95, Thomas Lugton, bootmaker, succeeded to the business of R. Macleod (1840), and later on to that of R. Rutherford & Co., George Street (1823). *See* Henry, page 263.

1872.—No. 10, A. Jenkinson, china merchant (1872).
1872.—No. 125, Scott Brothers, linen drapers (1872).
1880.—No. 101, A. Sprengel (Arcade, 1880-98), acquiring in 1884 Soutter, Son & Co.'s Bazaar, Nos. 98 and 102 (1856).
1880.—No. 24, A. Ritchie & Son, confectioners (1861).
1881.—No. 70, Edinburgh Café Company (1881).
1881.—No. 111, M'Nab & Shepherd, drapers, silk mercers, &c., to the Queen (1857).
1884.—No. 144, John Downie, seedsman, &c. (1848).
1886.—No. 106, North British Rubber Company, Limited (1856). Works at Castle Mills, Edinburgh. Branches in London, Liverpool, Manchester, Leeds, Newcastle-on-Tyne, and Glasgow.

This business was founded by an American. Goodyear (America), Hancock (England), and Mackintosh (Scotland), are specially identified with the India-rubber development. The last mentioned was the originator of "the Mackintosh," celebrated for wet weather comfort, along with Prof. Syme, Edinburgh.

1886.—Nos. 31, 32, Redfern, Limited, ladies' tailors (Nos. 51, 52, 1886-90); Cowes (1872), London (1874), Manchester (1891); also New York, Washington, Saratoga, Newport, R.I., Paris, Nice, &c.
1888.—No. 99, M'Kechnie & Co., dressmakers, &c. (1882).
1889.—No. 129, West End Café (1889), now a branch of Aitchison & Sons, Limited. *See* page 254.
1890.—No. 139, Wilson & Sharp, jewellers, are successors of several firms in the same shop.

1890.—No. 39, John Ford & Co., glass and china merchants (estab. S.B. Canongate, 1815).
1892.—No. 105, Wight & Co., mantle warehousemen, &c. (1882).
1895.—Nos. 146-149, &c., Robert Maule & Son, furnishing drapers, &c. (estab. Leith, 1872).
1895.—Nos. 33, 38, Cranston & Elliot, silk mercers, house furnishers, upholsterers, &c. (1866).
1895.—No. 81, G. Ballantine & Son, tea dealers and wine merchants (1827), from North Bridge.
1897.—No. 115, George M'Crae, hatter and hosier (1879); also 37-39 Cockburn Street.

Many well-known names long in the street have disappeared in the retirement or death of their principals, whose businesses have been absorbed by other or later developed firms. Among these are :—

Clark & Beatson, ironmongers, 1859-89, George Street, 1889-90; Doull's Restaurant, &c., 1819-64; Gray & Macfarlane, silk mercers, 1862-98; Grieve & Oliver, hatters, 1810-85; Harvey's Bazaar, 1825-60; Hay, jeweller, 1832-87; Howden & Son, jewellers, 1807-64; Levy, furrier, 1816-56; M'Lean & Son, fruit merchants to the Queen, 1818-89; Graham More, hairdresser, 1828-72; Philip, watchmaker, 1814-53; William Pike, silk mercer, 1838-60; Purves & Co., tailors and clothiers to the Queen, 1805-67 (this firm was not Purves & Son); J. & J. Ritchie, clothiers (Ritchie & Craies, 4 George Street, 1862-71), 1829-71; Russell, M'Nee & Co., coachmakers, 1807-86; Rutherfurd, fishing-tackle maker and auctioneer,

1839-68; Sanderson & Son, lapidaries, 1800-86; Francis R. Sim, cut-glass manufacturer, 1853-96; R. Stephenson, comb manufacturer to the Queen, 1827-65; Summers, shawl manufacturers, 1829-79; Tait & Craven, lacemen, 1846-86; Charles Trotter, upholsterer to the Queen (*or* Young & Trotter, 1804; 1853-60, Potts, Cairnie & Rae); Truefitt, hairdresser, 1827-79; Andrew Wemys & Co., portmanteau and trunk makers, 1836-60.

During the half-century a few other firms located themselves in Princes Street, and left again for other chief streets :—

Bowie & Thomson, ladies' outfitting, &c., No. 123, were established in Leith Street in 1839. The Princes Street shop was opened in 1861, and after being 18 years there the firm removed to George Street, and in six years returned to Princes Street for other 14 years. It has again removed this year to 69 George Street.

J. & G. Cockburn, wine merchants, established 1853, occupied No. 135, 1862-68, and are now at 2 S. Charlotte Street.

Macgill, artist's colourman (1841), at No. 103, from Hanover Street in 1860, was succeeded in 1867 by Westren, jeweller (1849), who removed to 70 George Street in 1886.

Hugh Paton & Sons, of Adam Square (1827), printers and printsellers, were in No. 10, 1854-62; No. 9, 1862-68; No. 115, 1868; and No. 122, 1884-93, when they left for their St. James' Square premises.

G. & H. Potts, painters and mosaic tile agents (1851), were in No. 92 from 1854 to 1884, when they removed to 5 Frederick Street, now in No. 23.

H. Salomon & Co., bootmakers, and Madame Salomon, corsetier, &c., in Princes Street from 1849-90, afterwards in George Street till 1895, are now at 8 Castle Terrace (estab. 1845).

Somerville & Craig, hosiers, &c. (1855), were in No. 35, 1858-82; G. D. Craig, who occupied No. 145 (1882-90), being now at 109 George Street.

Simpson & Co., trunkmakers (1870), who succeeded former firms (estab. 1851) in No. 97, are now in 15 Frederick Street and 13 Maitland Street.

GEORGE STREET, PAST AND PRESENT.

There are so many important and long-established firms in George Street that a certain reference to them, and also to others around, is a natural sequence to those in Princes Street.

The princely airiness of the one that has as its portion the summer slopes of a royal region will not prevent our admiration of the kingliness of George Street, chaplained at its head in queenly Charlotte Square by St. George's stately church, and by the Church of St. Andrew near its feet, tending it as it were on one side, while the Physicians' Hall (at one time opposite) cared for it on the other, the Royal Bank supplying a restful base, and St. Andrew's bells, not jangling as they may have done on Disruption Day and distressing the whole body, but chiming to its soul, as they were directed to do in 1789, or "rung in the English manner." It would seem to have had an earlier and a later character—that of a shabby royalty before the erection of its statues, and a very different kind after. According to the early writer of *Provincial Antiquities of Scotland*, "although otherwise handsome," "its extreme breadth" rendered it "comparatively mean," and the author of *Modern Athens*, published prior to 1829, characterised it as "the most gloomy and melancholy street that can well be imagined." But James Grant, in his *Old and New Edinburgh*, records that previous to other brilliant streets and squares of the New Edinburgh, it "was said to have no rival in the world," and that now, "whether viewed from the east or west, it may well be pronounced unparalleled," so that its fossilness has been rooted out with the finding of the great fossil tree in it in 1852. It has been compared with Sackville Street, Dublin, from which, so far as my observation goes, it differs on a Sunday. My home for seven years was in the Assembly Rooms division, and from its duplex semi-cul-de-sacness it may on an east-windy cold winter Sunday rather deserve its austere name, while meriting most its complimentary one when business lends external briskness and variety of life, more so now than when the grass always grew in the sedate sideways.

The businesses in this royal George Street that have continued there through the half-century are :—

40, James Ballantine & Son, painters (1834).
42, Ballantine & Gardiner, glass stainers (1834).

The founder of these businesses was James Ballantine, author of the *Gaberlunzie's Wallet*, and a popular volume of songs with music. He was selected by the Royal Commissioners to execute the stained-glass windows of the House of Lords at Westminster.

87, Brook & Son, goldsmiths to the Queen, the Princess Louise, and the Company of Royal Archers.

This business was conducted in No. 87 from 1835 to 1887 under the name of Marshall & Sons. The original firm was established in the Lawnmarket early last century.' It removed first to the Luckenbooths, then to a shop lower down the High Street, and in 1806 to the old North Bridge, then to the New Buildings (No. 62), which premises were burned in 1832. The firm occupied 54 Princes Street during alterations on 87 George Street.

55, W. Bryden & Son, bellhangers and electricians (1809).
57, A. Cruickshank & Sons, hosiers, &c. (1790).
61, D. Foulis, late W. P. Steele, ironmonger (1745).
28, A. Gibb & Son, umbrella warehouse, &c. (1805).
85, J. Gray & Son, ironmongers to the Queen (1818).
102, H. Healy, bootmaker (1800), with the business of J. James & Son (prior to 1800).
6, Holtum & Welsh, clothiers, &c. (1852).

118, Christian Jockel & Co., Berlin warehousemen, &c., established at 43 Princes Street, 1839. This was the town house of the Earl of Caithness.

60, R. M'Dowell & Sons, bakers and confectioners (estab. at 57 in 1848; *or*, Porteous 1827, Tait 1840); and at 15 Frederick Street, 1 Wemyss Place, 26 Torphichen Street.

39, A. Matheson & Co., black silk and crape merchants to the Queen (1838).

93, Andrew Melrose & Co., tea merchants to the Queen and the Prince of Wales (est. 1812).

Some Edinburgh Shops begins with Shepherd, the arch-grocer of his time, with spacious premises in South Bridge, next or near the arch, and choice assistants. The heads of the four departments given in the order of their precedence, tea, sugar, butter, and coffee, commenced business on Shepherd's retirement. The whole flock, Melrose, Richardson, Christie, and Law, eventually found pasture and pence in the promising, and in course realised, fields of the New Town. The first and fourth are famed to this day; Christie is transformed into Wood, Hanover Street; Richardson left his pasture in Greenside for the Waterloo Arch, and then pushed on to Glasgow and Greenock as the first in the trade with branches in the East and West Indies, sugar having been his first care. One cannot say whether tea, sugar, butter, or coffee rose highest or became more celebrated. The articles were of a homely nature, and, like them, the four friends were social and harmonious. As the senior of the quartette, Andrew Melrose, continued at the Arch, opened two shops in the High

Street and Canongate, then in 1834 crossed the valley to 39 George Street. Tea being his speciality, he so developed his relations with China as to make his cargo arrivals eventful even in Liverpool and Hull, and he warmly espoused the cause of China Missions. The duty on tea up to 1834 was 3s. 1½d. per pound, its price per pound early in the century being 12s. to 15s. for good qualities. It was reduced that year to 2s. 2¼d. per pound, and now stands at 4d., the home consumpt being 230 millions of pounds. Melrose's teas to-day make the school board boy trip in his geography; he answers that Melrose is celebrated for tea, and he is quite right socially.

78, Morison & Co., upholsterers, billiard table makers, &c. (1822).

The original close relation of this firm with Glasgow, Ayr, and Mauchline circles, accentuated by the head of the firm, in 1845, being made a burgess of Glasgow, is continued by *clièntele* there.

85, Mortimer & Son, gunmakers (say 1698).

This firm is descended from a witness mentioned in the State trials (London), two hundred years ago. It was established in Edinburgh 1835. In 1801 it received a £10,000 order for a present to the Bey of Tunis from the American Government.

27, Paterson & Sons, musicsellers to the Queen, &c. (Paterson, Mortimer & Co., North Bridge, 1819.)

35, James Robertson & Co., chemists and druggists (1830).

10, J. & T. Scott, upholsterers, billiard table manufacturers, warehousemen, &c. (1833).

16, P. & R. Wright, linen manufacturers, &c. (J. & P. Wright, 1822).
9, R. Whytock, Reid & Co., cabinetmakers, warehousemen, &c., formerly Richard Whytock & Co. (1806).
This firm came to 7 George Street in 1826. It is said to have been the first shop in the street.

After these may be given others of equal or similar duration, some from the Old Town and some from other streets in the New :—

12, Banks & Co., lithographers, engravers, &c., also Grange Printing Works; formerly Lizars, St. James' Sq. (1817); Back of the Guard (1780).
65, Bell, Rannie & Co., wine merchants (Leith 1715).
37, Robert Blair & Son, restaurateurs, &c. (1793).
58, Thomas Bonnar, painter and decorator (1708?).
A representative of a family and firm of painters since his great-great-grandfather.
17, Brown Brothers, clothiers (1855).
82, Croall & Croall, coach-makers to the Queen (1845).
126, Croall & Son, coach-makers (1845).
132, W. Dall & Co., glass and china merchants. Succeeded Jas. Brown, 4 Hanover St. (1834).
23, G. Dobie & Son, painters and decorators (1850).
90, Doig, Wilson & Wheatley, fine art dealers to the Queen (1851).
135, Dymock, Howden & Co., Italian warehousemen (1830).
120, Field & Allan, marble and slate merchants, &c. (1793).
83, R. Grieve & Co., carpet warehouse, &c. (1810).
8, Thomas Hall, painter and decorator (1830).

94, W. & A. Hogg, clothiers; originally G. Murray, 4 St. Andrew Street (1820).

105, W. M'Kimmie, tailor and clothier, successor to Rausch & Co. (1826).

77, Moxon & Carfrae, painters (early last century).

63, C. Muirhead, late Carter, Hanover Street (1829), wine merchant.

52, R. S. Richardson & Co., cutlers (1828). Mr. Richardson is the father of our cycle trade.

47, Thomas Smith & Son, goldsmiths to the Queen, and silversmiths to the Highland Society. *See* Princes Street, page 236, Millidge.

89, Smiths & Co., Ltd., purveyors of oils and lamps to the Queen, electricians, &c. (1770).

This firm for many years held the contract for lighting the city, which at first was with oil lamps, the men parading daily to receive wick and oil for the cruses and flambeaux. Leith Walk and a part of Leith was one night in total darkness through sailors of a Russian squadron climbing the lamp-posts and drinking all the train-oil. Gas was first used for streets in March 1820, its introduction into the High Street being as important an event as the electric lighting of Princes Street on 11th April, 1895, when Princes Street was crowded with citizens of all ages. The table in the Rutland Hotel, from which the light was turned on by the wife of the Lord Provost, has a brass plate with inscription of the event. Lamps and candles continued in shops and houses for a while as gas does now, which, in shops at least, will ere long give place to the newer illuminant, created out of nothing, although generated by the fire of pent-up sunshine and by water. The founder of the business was the inventor, along with Stevenson, of the system of reflectors for the May Island light adopted by the Board of Northern Lights. Mr. Stevenson and his sons, according to the above book, "have made the Scottish light system famous over the world." The improved and Government lighting of "May," once private property and still belonging to no parish, originated with the Edinburgh Chamber of Commerce in 1786, the Government lending a cruiser, the *Royal George*, for the committee's two days' "voyage" to the island and its "safe return" in one. (It is 25 miles from Leith.) The Chamber has a minute of gratitude for the committee's return, with "families and friends," who thus went forth a-May-ing on the water.

13, Stewart & Rae (Hume & Melville, 1817).
88, J. Stewart & Son, clothiers to the Duke of Edinburgh and to the Royal Archers, late Purves & Son, formerly Fraser & Anderson (1802).
107, Taylor & Turnbull, clothiers, hosiers, &c. (1638). The firm claim to be successors to a series of firms of celebrated citizens, and possess the golden anchor that hung above the earlier shops when signs were a necessity.
79, Townsend & Thomson, music-sellers (1825).
7, Tullis & Co., wholesale stationers (1827), succeeded Durham & Co. (1804).
41, James Walker & Son (1853), linen-drapers, successors to H. Ferrel (1483).

W. Wilson, in No. 55 Frederick Street, painter, is the successor of James Sheppard & Co. of 107 George Street (1835 to 1897).

The names of firms long continued in George Street, and long established, that have disappeared through deaths, &c., are Allardice & Sclanders, 1807-65; Blanc et Fils, 1841-91; T. & J. Blackwood (founded two centuries ago), J. J. Gaugain, 1822-53; Graham & Gowans, 1848-85; Haldane & Rae, 1833-58; D. R. Hay, decorator and painter to the Queen, 1833-66; Hay & Addis, 1825-58; Peter M'Gregor, 1805-84; R. Waterston & Co., 1813-69; Willis & Williams, clothiers to the Queen, 1818-50; Wilson & Co., 1813-69. The wine branch of Menelaws, established in 1822, is continued by Bryce & Son, Hanover Street.

Gardner & Ainslie, formerly James Gardner (1786), apothecary, at No. 58 (1804-96), are now dispensing chemists at North Berwick (1896).

Hamilton & Müller, No. 116, the organ builders to the Queen, &c. (established 1823), are now at 4 Hope Street Lane as C. & F. Hamilton, organ builders. This firm built the first organ among the Presbyterians of Scotland in that of Old Greyfriars' Parish Church (1865), and another in the following year at Park Church, Glasgow. Mr. Hamilton opened the one in the presence, unofficially, of the Lord Provost and Magistrates, and many clergymen of different communions ; the other was opened by Mr. M'Farlane and Mr. Peace, one of the most accomplished city organists, at a crowded service of sacred song. The first mentioned had 20 stops with 1205 pipes, the last 36 stops with 2236 pipes. Scotland's, thirty-three years ago, prejudice to the "kist o' whistles," which up till then was confined to the Roman Catholic, Methodist, and Episcopal or "Whistle Kirk," were then blasted by those 3441 pioneer pipes, sounding in the ears of the people of the capital and of the western commercial metropolis. General Assembly and Kirk Session fulminations against mechanical praise services have died down, and the smoke has cleared away before these pipes of peace, while instead rises the incense of song in the cathedrals of those great cities and elsewhere throughout the three dominant bodies. Hamilton & Müller were the first to convert a whole residential house in George Street into business premises, and were grealy laughed at for their supposed folly. The firm was there 1838-95.

Queen Street, the other parallel chief street, which will always remain a street of offices, has long had at its west end a few select shops. Of these continue Muirhead (1822), poulterers to the Queen ; Aitchison & Sons (Ltd.), confectioners, with a branch at 129 Princes Street, West End Café, 1790 ; Carmichael, now Johnston & Co., poulterers and game-dealers (1780) ; J. Jameson & Son, fishmonger, &c. (1834), have gone round the corner to 58 North Castle Street. Sydney Smith lived in No. 79 in 1800. The stationer's shop opened at No. 78 by Tully in 1853 has been successively John Murray's and John Reid's, the present proprietor. The confectioner's at No. 63, now Jameson & Co., was formerly Mackenzie & Middlemass (1851), and afterwards Forrester.

At the east end, Smart & Sons, bootmakers, No. 1, have been established for 70 years.

Thistle Street has no traditional stores, lawyers' and printing offices dominating it. Hill Street is entirely lawyers, doubtless with traditional stories ; and Young Street, once a quiet residential quarter, follows the legal character of its neighbour. In 33 Rose Street there is the bakery established in 1812 by Tait, now A. Wright ; and in No. 113 J. Kelly & Son, smiths and lockmakers, dating from 1840.

Leith Street and Hanover Street, as continuation streets north respectively from the North Bridge and the western Mound, in the one case to Leith and, the east part of the New Town, and in the other across the middle of the New Town, down towards Newhaven, Trinity, and Granton, ranked as business streets next in importance to the Bridges and east Princes Street. There, therefore, were located well-grounded businesses, several of which are found among the longest established in the New Town. Those that have continued in these streets during the past half-century, and link one's thoughts to the time when their street names were among the dignified, and their pavements were frequented by the George Street and Queen Street nobility and Royal Terrace magnates, are, in Hanover Street, A. Boswell, trunk and brush manufacturer, No. 8 (1790); James Dickson & Sons, seedsmen, No. 32 (1801); Gulland & Kennedy, clothiers, No. 55 (1844); John Small, basket maker, No. 33 (1847); William Vallance, confectioner, No. 13 (1849); G. Waterston & Sons, wholesale stationers, &c., No. 56, and at 12 St. John's Hill (1752).

No. 53, Robert Christie's, long known as a tea shop (established at No. 48 in 1826), is now William T. Wood & Co., who have modernised, extended, and enlarged the premises—the original corner shop down three steps, in antique and dusty keeping with the industrious past, indifferent to reputation other than that of honest and plodding Scottish worth, being clean swept away save in the garnered memories to which even cobwebs are dear, and their mysterious net-work the meshes of many thoughts. Next to it is a down-steps shop of lengthy and honourable reputation, No. 51, established opposite in 1839 by A. Johnston, victual dealer, now John Jack. Knox, Samuel & Dickson, hosiers, &c., No. 15, of happy Father Christmas memories, established in 1843, is now a memory only; the name, however, remains allied with Henderson, Adam & Co., No. 33, upholstery warehousemen and trimming manufacturers.

Bryce & Sons, No. 44 (1824), have succeeded Menelaws (1822), wine merchants, and Carter (1824). To No. 7 have come, from 17 North Bridge, J. F. Macfarlan & Co., manufacturing chemists (1780); and No. 4 is Jas. Goldie's hat shop, late J. & T. Mackay of 64 North Bridge, established at No. 3 by P. Mackay in the reign of George III.

In Leith Street the city-famed Littlejohn, the confectioner, &c., established in 1811, is now occupying No. 31, 33, and 35; and James Ritchie & Son, the patentees of electro-sympathetic clocks, No. 25, established 1819 (whose branch in Princes Street is already noted), have an electrical reputation far beyond Leith Street, as they have an electrical relation by land from Edinburgh, and by sea from Leith. It is from their office that the firing of the Edinburgh time-gun and the dropping of the time-ball for the shipping in the Forth are regulated. To them the Royal Observatory communicates the true time, and upon them devolves the daily arrangements for the time signals transmitted to various parts of the country. For that purpose their wires connect with the time-gun clocks at the Edinburgh General Post Office and Glasgow Post Office; also with the west end city clock, as well as with numerous other public and private ones, so that no one need be second in minute attention to engagements and slow in business if punctuality is its soul within and the timely exercise of the soles without makes it go like clock-work.

William Brown, hosier, &c., No. 43, has been established since 1803. A. Cunningham & Co., glass merchants, No. 18, succeeded J. Russel, formerly

John Baxter (1817); and J. Robertson & Son, umbrella makers, No. 32, opened in 1850.

The half-century firms that remain in east cross streets are James Dickson & Co., stationers, established 1807 (see below), 10 South St. Andrew Street; J. Miller, baker and confectioner, 1 North St. Andrew Street (1843); A. Watt & Sons, saddlers, No. 1 South St. David Street (1843). In Frederick Street the long past is represented at No. 16 by J. Bryden & Sons, bell-hangers, &c. (1809); at No. 45 by Hill, Thomson & Co., (1793), wine merchants to the Queen; Laird & Sons, nurserymen, No. 17 (1848); Robb & Sons, grocers, No. 9-11 (1849); with later come, though long established, firms, No. 6, Young & Sons, clothiers, &c. (1834); No. 59, Ciceri & Co., mirror manufacturers, &c. (1841); No. 39, S. Duncan, representing the long ago Buckmaster of 35 George Street, Edinburgh (1810), celebrated here, and more so in London and Dublin, as the Army clothiers, and as such figuring in fiction (see Professor Aytoun's, *How I became a Yeoman*, &c.); also Millan & Mann (1838). To those prominent, though later, firms may be added, Dickson & Walker, plate-glass merchants, No. 31 (1858); R. Cockburn & Co., grocers, No. 51 (1860), and Alexander Henry (Limited), gunmakers, No. 18 (1850).

St. Andrew Square claims W. & G. Law, tea and coffee merchants, No. 31, as its commercial fathers, established in Hanover Street 1825, and in the Square since 1830; A. Black & Co., brushmakers, No. 30 (1841). W. & A. K. Johnston, Geographers to the Queen, established in the

High Street in 1825, occupied 4 St. Andrew Square 1838 to 1879, when they removed to 16 South St. Andrew Street, and are now located at No. 20, their extensive printing works being at Easter Road. The head of the firm in 1848-51 was Lord Provost of Edinburgh at that period.

In St. Andrew Square are now settled several very old firms. J. Christie & Son, clothiers, &c., dating from 1792, occupied No. 11 in 1875, after being sixty years in 16 George Street. Harrison & Son, clothiers, another long-established firm, of date 1838, came in 1896 from the North Bridge, in advance of the demolition which has now widely separated neighbours long located there together. The late Sir George Harrison, the head of the house, was Lord Provost of the city in 1882-85. The business is the successor of many firms, the earliest dating from about the middle of the last century. A. & D. Padon was founded by A. Padon, bookseller and stationer, in Dundas Street (1834), who, along with his brother, opened No. 13 in 1852, now entirely a stationery business, bookselling being dropped in 1867. The large building of Alexander Cowan & Sons, Ltd., papermakers (1775), is at 38 West Register Street.

St. Andrew Street has attracted Marshall & Aitken, clothiers, established in 1816, North Bridge neighbours of a firm just mentioned, who came to No. 12 in 1895, when that tenement was the earliest taken down to give place to the southmost pier of the new North Bridge, the site being historical as that of the General Post Office to 1821 ; also John F. B. Donaldson, goldsmith, &c., No. 19, from the same quarter (established 1818). The trunkmaker's shop in No. 6, now Cleghorn, was Raeburn's in 1844.

Waterloo Place, notwithstanding its now out-of-the-wayness since the General Post Office, successor to the above, left it for the Bridge north-east corner, and the removal to George Street of Wood & Co., the great music centre of the time, retains at No. 1 Dickson & Sons, seedsmen, founded prior to 1770, and Caldwell Brothers, stationers, at Nos. 11, 13, and 15, established in 1840.

To say that Duncan & Flockhart, established in 52 North Bridge since 1820, are still there would be assigning the Queen's chemists at this moment a place in thin air—a chimerical position which would make them spirits of the past hovering over the sites of the newer New Buildings. Walls around their renascent store there they claim, but there will not be a roof above them for some months. When, however, the firm occupies No. 5, they will be "fathers of the Buildings," new and older. There will return with them from the present emergency buildings—to No. 4, D. M. Dunlop, hatter, who in 1861 occupied No. 3, and then No. 64, in succession to another hatter, which in 1848 was William Wright's; Lipton (Glasgow, 1873), Limited, tea merchants to the Queen, of unlimited area of operation (London 1888, Edinburgh 1889, and 360 U.K. branches)—his name lately on everybody's lips, from royalty downwards, and many lips in his teas from the cheapest upwards, will also be there. The rebuilding and levelling up of the North Bridge, and the levelling to the

ground of the old buildings that flanked its original
sides, and the substitution of Victorian Age street
architecture will run a New Town tongue into Auld
Reekie's historical "lands," but into that past these
pages do not profess to enter, excepting in references
to where ancient firms in modern avenues sprung
from, and to the half hundred North Bridge exiles,
some of whom have perhaps preferred death to exile
or an inglorious existence apart. The visitation of
progress presents to us at this moment a plague-stricken
street where leisurely pace is not required to read the
commercial epitaphs of some gone here and others
gone there and a' airts. My friend who sings the
"Auld Hoose" may now add the Auld Brig.

After 1860, when the population began rapidly to
increase, the New Town to extend, and unfeued sites
in the best residential streets were built up, family
businesses came from the Old Town, and all tended
westward, while the suburban building at Morningside, Merchiston, Murrayfield, and across the Dean
Bridge gave an impetus to the extension and improvement of the central shopping area, and with it the
enlargement of the commercial district, and by the
time the tramway system was introduced Princes
Street was transformed from a pleasant and quiet
promenade—such as it was fifty years ago—to a city
and county centre of activity in winter, and a garden
street in summer, to which the world's tourists wend.
In this way the shorter west streets that lead into
Princes Street have come to share its advantages,
and there have appeared in Castle Street, Maitland
Street, Shandwick Place, and Queensferry Street

handsome shops equal to many in the primary street, some firms of which are also among the oldest in the New Town, while the eastern transverse ones, as well as Charlotte Street and Hope Street, have thus also had added others of traditional reputation.

At No. 9 Castle Street, Douglas & Foulis, booksellers, &c., of and from Edmonston & Douglas, opened in 1877, and Mr. Douglas of the same firm has for a considerable time had his publishing office at No. 10. (Further reference will be made to the firm after.) Wightman & Son, musicsellers, established in St. James' Square in 1840, have been in No. 13 since 1885; Aitken Dott & Son, carvers and gilders, established in 1842 at No. 26 since 1874; and A. Muirhead & Son, painters, established in 1820, at No. 14 since 1890; John H. Bell, No. 13, is successor to John Taylor, bookseller (1848); G. Cockburn, No. 21, wine importer, &c., was established 1853; William M'Gregor, No. 7, watchmakers, &c., in 1862; Alex. Reid, optician, &c., No. 31A, in 1866; and No. 45, R. Graham, glazier, in 1845.

The new shops of Charles Wilson & Sons, butchers, at No. 19 (and 298 Lawnmarket 1854); and Hector Laing, fishmonger (established 1819), at No. 15, have been finely fitted up in the most attractive manner with complete sweetness of arrangement, similar to which is J. Anderson & Son, fishmongers, &c., to the Queen (1830), in No. 29.

No. 39 Castle Street is the house where Sir Walter Scott lived from 1800 to 1826. In 1797 he was in 108 George Street, and in 1798-9 in 19 South Castle Street.

Charlotte Street, Hope Street, Shandwick Place, and Maitland Street were residential streets a quarter of a century ago. Shops already run the full length of the two last, and have gained a footing in the other two, while Queensferry Street has been able to hold and extend its old businesses, and thus several half-century firms and their successors are found there. In No. 2, George Brown, baker (1808); No. 3, Johnston & Waters, butchers (1825); Nos. 5 and 6, Young & Saunders, grocers (1822); No. 10, William Patterson & Co., upholsterers, &c. (1837); No. 19A, Andrew Aikman, corn dealer (1848); No. 22, J. Kirkhope & Sons, wine merchants (1835); Nos. 23-25 and 4 Charlotte Place, R. M'Vitie, baker (1839); No. 35, Miss Rogers, bookseller, &c. (1838).

Shandwick Place and Maitland Street may now be called one street, as the latter, which is on the southern side, is in a few months also to be called Shandwick Place. There will be found Adams & Son, ironmongers, established in 1823 by Robert Adams, Hardwell Close; Henry, the bootmaker, the shop at the corner, established in 1833, which is now a branch of Lugton's, Princes Street; D. & G. Glen, house furnishers (1854); D. Fender, hosier, &c. (1863); Simpson's portmanteau shop, already noted under Princes Street; and Sibbald & Sons, ironmongers to the Queen, for 40 years in George Street (1790); G. Watson & Co., artistic furniture manufacturers (1857); and Boyd & Bayne, of Princes Street celebrity, already noted.

TERRACE AND VALLEY AND BANK.

About half a century ago Princes Street shops only extended to Frederick Street, beyond which there were only one or two in the next division and about half-a-dozen in the furthest west. Houses were at first turned into shops without altering the flooring of the basement or area, and thus many were either up or down steps, some five or six one way or the other, a main door making one up steps and either one or two in the area, according as the upper shop door was put in the middle or retained at the side as originally placed. Shop window panes were all small, some as dirty as cellar ones until cleaning day came, and desks and fittings were removed and deceased bluebottles and spiders respectfully transferred to the dust bin. A narrow iron gallery gave access to the windows for putting on the shutters or for outsiders to inspect any article or advertisement, but few showed any wares because of the sun, there being no sun-blinds, as wire gauze frames with name, number, and business were only necessary. Sometimes dummies were resorted to. The bookseller and stationer would have a row or two of imitation backs of books with standard titles, Shakespeare, Bacon, Milton and Josephus, &c., or boards of works padded to thickness with some inflated packets. A baker found it of advantage to have wooden ginger-bread packed for window service, but once one of the wooden cakes was sold to a gallant who desired something sweet for lady friends. When he next visited the fair recipients they ventured to suggest the toughness of his attentions; eventually, however, they obtained a real cake, the donor's intention being set right in such well bred and flavoury language that it made amends for all their pining. Renton & Co. were the first to have plate-glass windows down near to the ground.

One private house was in the New Club division betwixt Hanover Street and Frederick Street, that being No. 81, occupied by Mr. Tyndall Bruce of Falkland, the Queen's Printer for Scotland, while only one or two shops were in the next, Mr. Mackie's being the most conspicuous, with an oriel shop frontage. Others might only have porches, with the areas open and their windows flush with the original wall. At the extreme west there were about half-a-dozen shops, where a dozen tenements still indicate by their unaltered upper flats the elevations and style of houses as originally built. A scattered few in other parts convey the same idea, which will be better understood by examining views B and E. No. 119 is the only whole tenement of pristine Princes Street now left. As far down as 1851 there were 79 private dwelling-houses with main doors, 22 of which were whole tenements, all perhaps in the western half (opposite the West Gardens), which up till then maintained its residential character—109 was occupied by Professor Munro, 110 by Mr. H. Home-Drummond, of Blair Drummond, 114 by Professor Gregory, 123 by Sir Henry Jardine, 124 by Lady Foulis, and 144 by Dr. Sibbald.

No street has undergone so much change, excepting the present wholesale sale and flight of the North Bridge and all its roundabout belongings, its street and new buildings, now levelled to the dust, and taking with it the south side of Princes Street. The greatest changes were contemporaneous with my firm's removal in 1854 to No. 54, one of the Princes Street shops with saloons, *i.e.*, with large show stores behind. This removal meant a doubled rental, and ten years later the same shop and saloon all but doubled again, until the proprietor, requiring it, my partner and I in due course returned westward to a more commodious shop and premises at No. 107, to which, with separate entrance from the street behind, we were able at the time to remove our binding workshop, then in Hanover Street, and greatly increase its plant. The removal of whole tenements for first-class shops, hotels, and clubs began in the Sixties, when street architecture became a feature of the day. From 1854 to 1871 my daily vocation was under the early morning shadow of the Scott Monument, exactly opposite where the Adam Black statue has since been erected. With that living personage I had had converse in No. 54 and elsewhere. Prior to that my daily duties at No. 82 were exactly opposite where the monument and statue of Allan Ramsay is erected. My converse with that bookseller could only have been among the leaves of *The Gentle Shepherd*, pastoral and past.

Edinburgh, a semi-courtly legal and cultured centre, and also a political and ecclesiastical if not a cathedral city, having had within or about it the great Scottish lights, was even in May, 1848, a conspicuous summit in the world of departed *literati*, as when in the western horizon the after-glow lends transcendence to the scene. Burns was but half a century away—for immortal poets cannot die—and his friend, Professor Dugald Stewart, twenty years. Scott had only departed sixteen years, Ballantine fourteen, Blackwood thirteen, Alison nine, Campbell four, Sydney Smith three, Dr. Chalmers but a year. James Thomson was a century in the grave, but Allan Ramsay, Bruce, Falconer, and Fergusson had lived within that period. Hugh Miller was alive editing *The Witness*, as well as writing books, and Russel, who had before been given the direction of *The Scotsman*, had begun to edit it; while Wordsworth, of the

English "Lake School"—an appellation of *The Edinburgh Review*—was the Poet Laureate, and Tennyson rising as a brilliant star, who, in a couple of years, was to succeed Wordsworth in the poetical firmament. Ten years, however, were still to intervene before the *Idylls of the King*, one of the noblest poems in our language, were to be heard of and received everywhere with enthusiasm.

Sir William Allan was President of the Royal Scottish Academy; Macaulay had already been and was destined again to be M.P. for the city; Black was Lord Provost; Jeffrey, editor, and one of the projectors, along with Sydney Smith, . of *The Edinburgh Review*, as well as a contributor of two hundred articles, and Cockburn had been fourteen years on the bench; while on Princes Street were seen Christopher North, Sir Thomas Dick Lauder, Aytoun, both William and Robert Chambers, Sir James Gibson-Craig, George Thomson (the composer of the music to Burns' songs), Charles Kirkpatrick Sharpe, Lord Moncreiff, Thomas Maitland Murray of the Theatre Royal, Hamilton (architect of High School, &c.), Archdeacon Williams (first Rector of the Edinburgh Academy), Principal Lee, Bishop Terrot, Dr. Candlish, Dr. Guthrie, and other celebrities of the times to be found among the 96 Modern Athenians of Crombie's portraits of memorable citizens of Edinburgh, the last survivor of whom died in 1883. Of those therein mentioned who passed along the Avenue of Edinburgh in my verdant apprenticeship days there are 73, whose characteristic green or brown umbrellas and canes, hats of varied contour, coloured coats, &c., as shown in Crombie or in Kay's Portraits, are more or less within my memory. To these I may add the remembrance of Sir William Hamilton, while Sir James Simpson, only then approaching his prime, now of world-wide celebrity, besides many others, who are still within the recollection of some, were going out and in among the citizens. Miss Ferrier, who enjoyed Scott's friendship, was living in the New Town, De Quincey was at Lasswade, and Louis Stevenson was not yet born.

Mrs. Oliphant in her *Royal Edinburgh* (a city royal in event, prospect, name and letters), has called the "grey metropolis of the North" the city of a thousand various associations. She has indicated the necessitous disparity of the new Edinburgh with the old, and nature's solution of the problem how to make a happy partnership betwixt the unlike, so that the incongruous may be harmonised and the light and fancy of fashion and taste of the present be relieved by the darker and ponderous past with its comfortable indifference to inconvenience and undesirable surroundings.

It is where the ancient and the modern join hands between the massive and the buoyant that our ideas blend to make a great picturesque landscape, city and garden. But not less orderly arranged are edifices that speak of stirring times of warfare by word or weapon, or of the progress of commerce, science, art, and literature, everyone of which has a story of its origin, purpose, and period.

That which could tell the oldest story, and story upon story, from Edwin to Albert Edward Prince of Wales, whose birth it heralded on November 9, 1841—of war in the land, tumult in the city, of attack and defence, successful and unsuccessful siege, of royal imprisonment and escape, of royal birth, tutelage, and residence—is the citadel on the great hill opposite; while the monuments on the eastern hill stand ready to narrate decisive battles and great naval engagements in times that have passed away; for tower and castle have now scientists with leisure to loiter in the sun and tell forth to the city and the sea by descending ball and resounding fire in simultaneous signal the passing hour of peace and luncheon.

The time-ball dropped from Nelson's monument, and the time-gun fired by electricity from the Royal Observatory were installed, the one in 1854, and the other in 1861. The inauguration of the latter ended, or rather didn't end, in smoke, owing to the defective trial-days' cartridges, supplied by the Government. One of the company who were present at the Observatory on the occasion, duly provided with cake and wine, said that the professor's thunder-struck and dumbfoundered expression, in an unhappy moment, was a sight superior to the surprise of expected sound. Next morning's papers' description were those of a "signal failure."

From war by weapon our thoughts pass to the arena of warring words, more deadly in their effect than those of bloody feud, because embosomed within them lie causes of battles with their accompaniments of hate and wrong, injury to lives and souls, proceeding from excited lips or bitter tongue, and which now an electric spark from hemisphere to hemisphere may fuse into world-wide bloodshed. No hasty words or angry tongues beneath St. Giles' tower in 1637 set the celebrated stool of Jenny Geddes whirling in the kirk at the dignitary who dared, according to her understanding of matters, to read prayers from an *English* book. But from the bristling of her missile an ecclesiastical storm spread over Scotland, and eventually helped to rend the then National Church and to transfer the State's care from an Episcopal to a Presbyterian form of government; while the disestablished, disendowed, and disabled former Church of Scotland became by law only a body claiming to be the Church in Scotland, but obliged to call itself the Scottish *Episcopal* Church.

An epoch of various Church discipleship and discipline obtained until the "Ten Years' Conflict" (1833-43), of rival parties within the Presbyterian Establishment ended in the two dividing all their Churchmen into those professing State dictation of their ministers and those demanding the right of congregations to determine their own pastors, the latter being termed Non-intrusionists, and forming in 1843 the Free Church (*vide* p. 200). Then arose the towers of the Free Church College, with the Assembly Hall on the height above the Mound to contain the elements of mingled rivalry of good works and bad feeling between brethren to be shot across the Castle warpath to the Victoria Hall of the State General Assembly.

The end of these estrangements would seem to be a vision of the State Establishment in conflict with Jenny Geddes' ghost and a magic-lantern view projected on the screen of Time of the earlier dissentients from the Established Presbyterian Church, themselves united half-a-century ago (*v.* p. 189), again in union with those who uphold the principle of State relations, but with a latitude to both within the united principles. In a lesser way this is the method proposed in the Lambeth quadrilateral for the greater union of Christian Churches, and it

St. Giles' Cathedral, Edinburgh, and the Restored City Cross.
As in "Scotland, Picturesque and Traditional." (Cassell & Co.)
From a Photograph by A. A. Inglis. Block kindly lent by Messrs Cassell & Co.

would point to hard-headed laymen feeling the irksomeness of disunion in theological science when practical religious science, common philanthropy, and social duties are throwing them so much together in their common interests and opportunities for the amelioration of life. From the west end of Princes Street, the headquarters of the United Presbyterian Church are visible across the gardens in Castle Terrace.

Princes Street as planned was to have been called St. Giles Street, but George III. disapproved of it, because of associations of the name in London, and thus the ancient Athenian lost the titulage of the magnificent terrace of the capital, which was then named after the two Princes, the future George IV. and the Duke of York. It is worthy of any Princess, but after none such has it been registered. Its name is Princes, and the patron saint of the city is satisfied with his ecclesiastical crown and the little crook beside it yclept St. Giles' Street. The roadway was greatly improved in 1877, when the foot pavement was widened from 6 to 10 feet and made 18 feet wide throughout, that on the garden side from 7 or 9 to 12 feet, and the carriage-way made 68 feet wide instead of 57. To do this 10 feet were taken from the West Gardens, which had a new walk made within it, from end to end, half way down the bank, an ornamental railing being erected along both gardens. This improvement cost the city £33,244, the Tramway Company expending £5000 additional. The electric lighting of the street and other main thoroughfares three years ago has perfected the street by night and enabled many shops to dispense with the inconvenience of window shutters, always so dreary on a Sunday and holiday.

The West Gardens were set out in 1820, when the Nor' Loch was drained. 77,000 trees and shrubs were planted under the superintendence of Dr. Neill, the printer, secretary of the Horticultural Society from first to last, and of the Wernerian Natural History Society, the former having the Experimental Gardens (dating from 1809), now amalgamated under Government with the Botanic Gardens (dating from 1823). Dr. Neill was also an archæologist and a defender of architectural relics, and was the means of intercepting the demolition of the Flodden Wall amid "city improvements." He was one of those who wore knee breeches and buckles.

In 1830, after fifty years' tipping, the earthen mound had received two million and a half cartloads of New Town excavations, which might be valued at £50,000, two thousand piles being driven for the founding of the Royal Institution in 1823, completed in 1834. The three varied ways of communication between the hill and valley towns by great bridge, lesser bridge or mound, and greater mound, while respectively serving a purpose, have contributed not a little to enhance the *tout ensemble*. It is to be regretted that the treatment of Princes Street re-erections and altered fronts has been a departure from the classical order to a commercial order embracing the Pyramidal to the Jenneresque or modern attic, now overtopped by castle later or higher attic. The Royal Institution, however, with the National Gallery and Scott Monument, serve to divide the attention, and prevent the tourist's being too much directed to the idiosyncrasies of individual designs or advertising signs of the times, which relegate taste to the attractiveness of windows for raising the wind, and to the streamers, national and native, that flutter above on four and twenty flagstaffs.

As we take our summer evening stroll on the higher walks of the East and West Gardens, by the statues of Livingstone, Scott (canopied in the monument to his genius), Adam Black, John Wilson ("Christopher North"), Allan Ramsay, and Sir James Simpson, and see the iron horse with its weighty freights or living multitudes careering along the valley, our reflections lead to the conclusion that no other city could present a hollow where a railway station could so naturally and so unobtrusively find a lodgment as the North British system has done within that beautiful and withal unspoilt valley.

It would seem as if Nature had designed it as a smiling welcome to people from all lands who visit the shrines and haunts of Scott and Burns, while the Caledonian is not less fortunate in the possession of a path into the most fashionable city centre at its western end. How different the mode of departure and arrival little more than half a century ago. In the Directories of the period, there are the hours of the stage coaches to Aberdeen, Carlisle, Newcastle, and Dumfries—not to accentuate those for Perth, Melrose, Jedburgh, and Innerleithen, the former runs occupying respectively 11, 15½, 10, and 9 hours, the others 6½, 4, 5, and 4 hours, nor to particularise the steam and packet vessels from Granton, Leith, and Glasgow to the principal ports of Scotland, Newcastle, London, Liverpool, and Irish ports, some for Dundee, Stirling, and Alloa leaving Granton Pier, and some for Dysart and Largo the Chain Pier at Trinity. With some the mails would go in 1848, but to London and other distant places the railway was partly open, a letter reaching London in 15 hours. Trains were first denominated Express, Mail, and Parliamentary, the fares varying, and the parliamentary taking 11 hours to reach Aberdeen, and 20 for London. Canal boats left Port Hopetoun for Glasgow twice a day—1st cabin, 2s. ; 2nd cabin, 1s. 4d. To Linlithgow the fares were 10d. and 8d., with different hours of despatch, for they could neither steam nor sail; the hours also varying for Falkirk, Winchburgh, and Ratho. The fly-boats were, I believe, towed by two horses and postilion. The coach to Glasgow, which took 4 or 5 hours, would be discontinued on the opening of the railway in 1842, but in 1848 one still ran to Lanark, and, besides those above named, to Dumfries, Dundee, Galashiels, Hawick, Inverness, Kelso, Linton, Moffat, Peebles, and other less distant places. I am informed that the last stage coach that was run in Scotland may be found at the base of the Bass Rock, on board a vessel wrecked there, before it could get a stage further on its way to London for exhibition as an old stager of Scotland. The coaches, with one or two exceptions, started from Croall's Office, Nos. 2 and 10 Princes Street.

America would call Princes Street the Monument Avenue, but George Street, wide and noble, immediately north of it on the New Town ridge, has, like its sunny sister, also become a Monumental Street. It has also undergone as well a vast change from a residential to a commercial character during the last half century. Although the grass had liberty at one time to grow in the western half beyond Frederick Street, the commercial importance of its eastern half was perhaps equal to Princes Street, the

North and South Bridges being also dominant. Lothian Road was a nondescript semi-rural road to the links, which were visited chiefly by red-coated golfers, red-coats from the Castle being also drilled there. At some of the George Street crossings badged porters, strung round with an ample quantity of rope for heavy emergencies, were always to be found upon their forms, and near by might be a sedan chair to serve either lady invalid or aged lady, or the damsel ready for the evening party. There is a story of the bottom of one having come out, and the occupant continuing inside walking, for "the fashion of the thing." Some families possessed chairs of their own, and it was a common enough practice for infirm people to be taken in them to church.

Charlotte Square, at the west end of George Street, one of Adam's grand architectural compositions, is the finest in the city, and is still of an entirely residential character, but St. Andrew Square at the east end has now been entirely transformed into a commercial region, with imposing insurance offices recently added to the banking houses. It is indeed, with the eastern end of George Street and the Stock Exchange adjoining it, the banking and insurance centre of the city. The monuments in George Street and the squares are those of Prince Albert, George the IV., William Pitt,

Lord Melville, Earl of Hopetoun, and Dr. Chalmers; St. George's Church—resembling St. Paul's, London—on the further side of Charlotte Square, with St. Andrew's Church in the east division, and other public buildings, enhance the monumental completeness and dignity of the street as viewed from either end.

My home, soon after my translation from an American to an English boy, before I had again become an acclimatised Scotch one, was next the Music Hall (which, along with the north side of Charlotte Square, is also chalked for the Usher short leet), and from the back windows I used to peep over the shoulder and chimney-pots of Princes Street, straight across to the Castle, and round to the heights of Arthur's Seat. No. 82, grown so tall now, intercepts the view, as the rising generation of Princes Street houses has also that of the two squares.

The suite of tall tenements, now in sweeter High Street surroundings than in 1848, with the windows of the Municipal Chambers overlooking the valley, recalls the progressive painstaking devotion of the magistrates and town councillors to the city's interest, as well as many acts by which it has been made what it is, and preserved from disfigurement. When Councillor Grant, the founder of my firm, was one of their number, I saw how closely they had to attend to civic duties. Since then these duties have multiplied, and later acquaintance with many of the present councillors convinces me that the citizens have no conception of the toil with which they have to overtake their task. Their observant powers are but typified in the altitude from which their windows, like their eyes, overlook the greater part of the city, as well as the Forth, of which their chief is the Admiral, although, notwithstanding, never at sea—at least as a magistrate. Their civic predecessors grievously erred, however, when they sanctioned the proposal of some one to erect houses on the south side of Princes Street, and defended the feuars in the Court of Session. What Lord Provost Drummond and his Council had done in founding, in 1772, the historical North Bridge — now oratorical from its dust—was on the verge of ruin by land in 1774 when that proposal was made, and again in 1776 by water, when the canal scheme was begun. Within those half dozen years verdict was given for a queen city, and her fortune secured to her fair face. These land and water escapes, however, did not exempt it from another danger in our own scientific utilitarian day, that of the inroad of electricity on our ways after the transatlantic fashion, which, however adapted either to United States or Canadian cities, where utility thrusts out amenities, does not kindly lend itself to historical, quaint, or show cities. In return for the withdrawal of a thousand horses from the streets, the system would have had to plant hundreds of high poles along our finest avenues to carry the overhead wire work, which only a snowfall could wrap into picturesqueness. It is to be hoped that electric advertisements about beef and mustard, and soaps, salts, or pills, or of starch and blues, are not to disturb our after-dinner contemplation of Edinal palatial lights and fairy scene, especially after we have had enough of them all by day, whether we read, ride, or ramble.

The Bank of Scotland conspicuously represents the banking business. It is curious to note that although the Bank of England was founded by a Scotsman (William Paterson, a native of Dumfries), the Bank of Scotland was projected by a retired London merchant, John Holland, in 1695, according to Paterson's scheme. The other banks are the Royal Bank of Scotland (1727), the British Linen (1746), Commercial (1820), and National (1825), with chief branches of the Union and Clydesdale, whose head offices are in Glasgow. The total authorised bank-note circulation of the ten Scottish banks is £2,676,350, but the average circulation last year was £7,293,283, coin being held against the difference. About 1848, the authorised notes represented £3,087,209, and the average circulation was £3,571,636.

Insurance companies are prominent in Princes Street, although equally large offices are located in St. Andrew Square and George Street. The largest are perhaps the Scottish Widows', North British, Standard, Scottish Provident, Caledonian, Scottish Union, Life Association. There are nearly 300 agencies.

"THE SCOTSMAN."

In the domain of literature and journalism, the high blocks of warehouses and offices near the municipal buildings signify the press with its talismanic power, as represented in Cockburn Street by *The Scotsman*, the leading journal in Scotland, possessing an influence as wide as any in London; and in the High Street by Messrs. Chambers, the precursors of cheap literature.

The Scotsman newspaper was established in 1817. At first, a weekly paper of insignificant size, giving only a tenth of its present news for ten times its present cost, it was issued at the price of 10d. (6d., plus 4d. duty stamp), and contained all the latest news from London, that three days back, from Paris ten days, and from New York forty days, the last about Monroe (of "Monroe Doctrine") being elected President, the fashionable intelligence including reference to quadrilles becoming favourites. In 1823 it was issued twice a week at 7d., the duty being still 4d. On the reduction of the duty to 1d. in 1836, the price was made 4d., and in 1840, 4½d. In 1855, when the stamp duty was abolished altogether, it appeared daily and weekly, as well as, for a short time, bi-weekly, some still preferring semi-weekly news budgets; in 1886 *The Evening Dispatch* (½d.) was added. The total weekly circulation is now 700,000, the daily impression being 100,000, printed on web paper in rolls five miles long, at nearly 60,000 per hour, weekly 70,000, with *The Evening Dispatch* 40,000 daily. For one ton of paper in 1817, and twenty in 1835, it now consumes 1800 tons per annum. Advertisements numbered about six daily the first year, chiefly about books, the Government duty being 3s. 6d. In 1820 there was an average of 16, in 1830 44. In 1833 the duty was reduced to 2s. 6d., but the number of advertisements was only 50. In 1848 they would be about 60, but on the repeal of the advertisement duty in 1854 the daily number averaged 150, of the annual value of £3000. In 1884 the total for the year was 434,800, when one day's issue contained 3913, probably more than in any paper in the world. On May 5, 1883, they filled 77 columns out of 112, a seventh larger than that of *The Times*. There were 34,000 lines, or 300,000 words, in such an issue, or two millions of distinct types.

The proprietors of *The Scotsman* have now bought for £120,000 the site of the whole of the west side of the new North Bridge Street. It is their intention to occupy the north portion—one of the most commanding positions in the city—which will give the paper a position unequalled in the kingdom. Being the end facing Princes Street, it is practically the site of the General Post Office previous to 1821, after it was removed from the Parliament Close, and before it was transferred to Waterloo Place. From 1823 to 1851 the same relative site was occupied by Adam and Charles Black, the eminent publishers and proprietors of all Sir Walter Scott's works, after Cadell, and of the *Encyclopædia Britannica*, as also, after Constable, of *The Edinburgh Review*, to both of which publications, as also to the *Quarterly* and *Blackwood*, Russel, the brilliant editor of *The Scotsman*, for some years contributed.

The offices of Messrs. Chambers enter from the High Street. Their *Journal* and works about Edinburgh and Scotland are well known, but their crowning enterprise was their *Encyclopædia*, begun forty years ago, and unrivalled by any in Europe or America as a handy yet comprehensive book of reference.

In the same street *The Scotsman* had its

offices from 1817 to 1868. There chiefly, in
1848, were several newspapers issued at 4½d.,
these being published some twice and some
thrice a week, representing one or other political or ecclesiastical party. *The Scotsman* has
survived them all.

In the High Street were situated the howffs
of the *literati* of the periods of Burns and
Scott. It was there Constable began business
just about a century ago, and where Creech
followed those who, in 1752, succeeded Allan
Ramsay, who opened the shop, in 1718, which
became the rendezvous of all the wits of the
day. There in 1725 Allan Ramsay established
the first circulating library ever known in Scotland, that from which, when it was in later
hands, Sir Walter Scott, according to his own
statement, read with avidity in his earlier years.
According to Kay's "Portraits," the library latterly contained 30,000 volumes.

Coming fifty years nearer to modern times,
when the Mound, although formed, was as yet
incomplete, and down or over to Princes Street,
we find the first house of William Tait, the
bookseller, which was at the corner of Hanover
Street, as seen in view *B*, facing up the sunny
side of the Royal Institution, that building
being only finally completed however in 1836.
Of the Royal Society, which afterwards occupied
that part, Sir Walter Scott was President from

1820, the same year when he received the baronetcy, until 1832, the year he died. In Tait's shop about that time might be seen the boy who read with avidity from the Allan Ramsay library become the author of *Waverley*. We are told that although Carlyle never met him, he saw him once sitting in Tait's.

From that point a fine view is obtained of Ramsay Lodge, the residence of Allan Ramsay, built by himself in 1743, but Professor Geddes's somewhat pious residential scheme has externally divested it of its "goose-pie"-ness by its incorporation with other elevations, whereby its prominent distinctiveness is lost along with the past of Allan's first house and shop in the High Street, this year taken down.

William Tait occupied that conspicuous corner from 1818 to 1840, when he removed to No. 107, a division and a half west, on the site of which I now write, my late partner having bought the tenement built upon it. Tait's occupancy of No. 107 continued to 1846, when he retired; but the premises were un-altered until 25 years later, when in 1871 my firm rented the new block, with a sub-let to the Edinburgh Street Tramways Co. for head offices, on the introduction of that system, and next to the Mid-Lothian Conservative Association.

There is not at the present day any occupant of a Princes Street shop who lives on the premises, the upper floors, where separate, being let for other business purposes. Fifty years ago, however, there were several, and William Tait's house, 1840 to 1846, would be in the same block, which although also a bookseller's shop, would appear to have remained as originally built, Tait's immediate predecessor, Mr. Vans Hathorn, W.S., having resided in it for thirty years before that. The son of Tait's successor remembers it was his father's residence down to 1861, and it would probably be that of the following tenant down to 1870. There was a fine stone portico and balcony at the entrance, which was also the passage to the dwelling-house, and an exquisite balustrade ran along the front of the house, the windows being some feet back, with an area between them and the balustrade.

LITERARY SOCIETIES.

In Oliver & Boyd's Almanac for 1848, the Scientific and Literary Institutions therein mentioned that continue to the present day well established are The Royal Society of Edinburgh (1783), The Society of Antiquaries of Scotland (1780), Royal Scottish Society of Arts (1821), and The Royal Scottish Academy (1826), and to these may be added as like them having a place of abode and library, &c., The Royal Scottish Geographical Society, founded in 1884 for the purpose of popularising and diffusing geographical knowledge in Scotland. Diplomas are granted by all these respectively, represented by the initials F.R.S.E., F.S.A., F.R.S.S.A., R.S.A. and A.R.S.A., and F.R.S.G.S. In addition to these there are the leading scientific and professional colleges and institutes, the more important of which also issue diplomas.

Of Literary Societies for the issue of a certain series of publications there were five, all of which long ago completed their course in fulfilment of their intention : The Bannatyne Club (1822), for "Works illustrative of the History and Antiquities of Scotland"; The Maitland Club (1828), for "Works relating to Historical Families and remarkable Historical Books"; The Calvin Translation Society (1843), for "Original Translations of John Calvin's Writings"; The Wodrow Society, for "Works of the Fathers and Early Writers of the Reformed Church of Scotland"; and The Spottiswoode Society, "for the Revival and Publication of Works of the Bishops, Clergy, and Laity of the Episcopal Church of Scotland." Of the three ecclesiastical, the office-bearers in the first consisted of six noblemen as patrons, a lay editorial secretary, and London and Edinburgh bankers; the second, a noble president and vice-president, a banker as treasurer and secretary, and

LINLITHGOW PALACE (*Page 216.*)

MARY, QUEEN OF S(

EDINBURGH CASTLE AND NATIONAL GAL
Blocks kindly lent

SIR WALTER SCOTT BART.

39 CASTLE STREET. (*Page* 262.)

LLAN RAMSAY'S HOUSE, 1860. (*Page* 286.)
ng Co., Edinburgh.

a council of one Scottish judge, six ministers (clergy), and four elders (laymen); the third having Dean Ramsay as its president, a clergyman as its vice-president, an advocate for secretary, an accountant for treasurer, together with a council of other three deans, five clergy, eighteen advocates, six writers to the signet, three landed proprietors, one major, two medical practitioners, and one architect. It is almost needless to say that none of these survive.

Looking up the North Bridge to the further end of the South Bridge, where eminent booksellers in the past were located, the dome of the University (gifted this generation by Mr. Cox, W.S.) is seen. It is surmounted with a gilt bronze figure of "Youth," holding aloft the torch of knowledge, the complement of the American Liberty maiden, enlightener of the world; for without knowledge in the land liberty would be as in a tempestuous sea, while without flame in the heart even electric light would penetrate but a cold soul. The educational system of Edinburgh, everywhere celebrated, has the University as its head, attracting 3000 to 4000 students from all parts of the world, its medical school being renowned among the nations. There are 42 professors, and about 200 fellowships, bursaries, and scholarships, value £8000. The library has 150,000 volumes and 1000 manuscripts.

EDINBURGH BOOK STORES,
STATIONERS, PRINTERS, ETC.

Celebrated as "Modern Athens" has been for its men of literary genius, by whom in 1790-1820 it deservedly acquired its cultured name, and at a later period became beautified by memorials of their living presence—reputed too at home and abroad for its printers—its book stores (an American term very appropriate in its application to shops of intellectual treasures) may justify particular mention, as also print and music stores in Princes Street fifty and more years ago, within a century's touch of the time when it was a straight country road, the "Lang Dykes," beside farm and thatched cottages, and the plough in the furrow, growing corn, browsing cattle, grunting pigs, and doubtless whistles, laying fowls, with ducks in the Nor' Loch, water rats, and eels.

The King's High Street had had its Bassandyne, who, along with Thomas Arbuthnot, printed a folio Bible in 1574. At Bishop's Land had resided Archbishop Spottiswoode, the Primate of Scotland in 1615, who took fifty journeys to London long before the "Flying Scotsman" was heard of, to promote Episcopacy as James VI. designed. At the Netherbow John Knox—according to someone—perhaps composed the Confession of Faith, and there Archbishop Sharpe resided, and before him George Durie, Abbot of Dunfermline and Archdean of St. Andrews (1539). In Byer's Close, Adam, Bishop of Orkney, lived, and elsewhere in the street were the birthplaces of Falconer and Fergusson, the poets; the abodes of David Allan, the historical painter and Scottish Hogarth; Chepman of Ewirland, who introduced the printing press into Scotland; and of Lekprevik, an early Scottish printer, Andro Hart, and others. Then there were the bibliopoles that assembled at Allan Ramsay's and Provost Creech's shops, whose publishing and bookselling successors there—Constable, Cadell, and Manners & Miller, with Blackwood and Tait—sustained and led the *literati* of the times across to sunny Princes Street to found, as Blackwood conceived, an Albemarle Street related to the City's Paternoster Row.

Allan Ramsay's first shop and home (1686-1758) was near the Netherbow, a bow from which have been projected arrows of literature and commercial lines that reach to our own day. In 1725 he removed to the Luckenbooths, a name next or equal in ancient esteem, although the buildings are now no more. From each date some of our leading goldsmiths, and have come some of our library treasures —jewels intellectual and ornamental.

Allan Ramsay was hairdresser, wigmaker, poet, and bookseller. His vocation thus embraced the outs and ins of a man's intellectual parts, as he himself was supposed to consider it did. Adam Black remarked that according to Williamson's *Edinburgh Directory* there was a disparity in 1777 between the number of hairdressers and barbers, and that of booksellers, respectively representing the withouts and the withins of the head, the former numbering 98 to cut and curl and score the hair, and the latter only a score to adorn the mind; but that by 1867 the scales were turned, and for 128 booksellers there were only 43 whose daily toil was the toilets of others.

William Creech's shop occupied a commanding position at the east end of the Luckenbooths, and so situated, in the centre of the Old Town beside the Parliament House, it was a natural centre of literary intercourse as well as a convenient market for the book world. His literary breakfast levees at his house in 5 George Street, though crowded, were select. He continued 44 years in business (1771-1815), having been at first designed for a medical practitioner. His apprenticeship was served with Kincaid, whom he joined in 1771 and eventually succeeded. Creech was Lord Provost in 1811-13.

Constable, who began business in 1795, published in 1802 the first number of the *Edinburgh Review*, edited by Sydney Smith at the beginning, but after a year or two by Jeffrey—they, with Brougham, being the promoters. In 1805 he started the *Edinburgh Medical and Surgical Journal*, and in the same year he published, in conjunction with Longman & Co., the first of Scott's works, *The Lay of the Last Minstrel*, of which 44,000 sold before 1830, as well as, in conjunction with Miller of Albemarle Street, and Murray then in Fleet Street, the first of the Waverley Novels. In 1814, when, after several changes, Cadell was his sole partner, the *Encyclopædia Britannica*, the largest publication in the kingdom, was being issued. Chalmers' *Caledonia* and Wood's edition of *Douglas' Scottish Peerage* were also successful publications.

Beginning with Constable's shop in the High

BOOK STORES, STATIONERS AND PRINTERS.

Street, Lockhart, in *Peter's Letters to His Kinsfolk*, says of it :—

"On entering one sees a place by no means answering, either in point of dimensions or in point of ornament, to the notion one might have been apt to form of the shop from which so many mighty works are every day issuing—a low dusky chamber, inhabited by a few clerks, and lined with an assortment of unbound books and stationery—entirely devoid of all those luxurious attractions of sofas and sofa tables, and books of prints, &c., &c. . . . The bookseller himself is seldom to be seen in this part of his premises; he prefers to sit in a chamber immediately above, where he can proceed in his own work without being disturbed by the incessant cackle of the young Whigs who lounge below. . . . The bookseller is himself a good-looking man apparently about forty. . . . He is one of the most jolly looking members of the trade I ever saw, and, moreover, one of the most pleasing and courtly in his address. . . ."

Going on to the next, he says :—

"If one be inclined, however, for an elegant shop, and abundance of gossip, it is only necessary to cross the street, and enter the shop of Messrs. Manners & Miller—the true lounging place of the blue-stockings and literary *beau-monde* of the northern metropolis. Nothing, indeed, can be more inviting than the external appearance of this shop, and more amusing, if one is in the proper lounging humour, than the scene of elegant trifling which is exhibited within. At the door you are received by one or other of the partners, probably the second mentioned, who has perhaps been handing some fine lady to her carriage, or is engaged in conversation with some fine gentleman. You are then conducted through a light and spacious ante-room, full of clerks and apprentices, and adorned with a few busts and prints, into the back shop, which is a perfect bijou. . . . Upon the leaves of these books, or such as these, a group of the most elegant young ladies and gentlemen of the place may probably be seen feasting, or seeming to feast, their eyes; while encomiums due to their beauties are mingled up in the same whisper with compliments still more interesting to beauties, no doubt, still more divine. . . .

In the midst of all this the bookseller himself moves about doing the honours of the place, with the same unwearied gallantry and politeness, now mingling his smiles with those of the triflers, and now listening with earnest civility to the dissertation, complimentary or reprobatory, of the more philosophic fair. One sees, in a moment, that this is not a great publishing shop; such weighty laborious business would put to flight all the loves and graces that hover in the perfumed atmosphere of the place. A novel, or a volume of pathetic sermons, or pretty poems, might be tolerated, but that is the utmost. . . . This shop seems to have a prodigious flow of retail business, and is, no doubt, not less lucrative to the bookseller than delightful to his guests. Mr. Miller is the successor of Provost Creech, in something of his wit and many of his stories, and in all his love of good cheer and good humour, and may certainly be looked upon as the favourite bibliopole of almost all but the writers of books."

In Nicholson's Memoir of Adam Black, among the youthful "collecting" reminiscences of booksellers' shops at the end of the last and beginning of the present century as given by Mr. Black at the booksellers' annual dinner, he says, speaking of the booksellers in Parliament Square:—"On the south side was Manners & Miller's shop, the most fashionable in town. Robert Miller was generally cicerone to any distinguished ladies or gentlemen who visited Edinburgh. He was himself an amiable man, with an aldermanic presence, witty, sang a good song, and whistled like a laverock."

Of another Peter writes:—

"The daily visitors of Mr. Laing (for that is the name of its proprietor) seem rather to be a few scattered individuals of various classes and professions, among whom, in spite of the prevailing spirit and customs of the place, some love of classical learning is still found to linger—retired clergymen and the like, who make no great noise in the world, and, indeed, are scarcely known to exist by the most part even of the literary people of Edinburgh. The shop, notwithstanding, is a remarkably neat and comfortable one, and even a lady might lounge in it without having her eye offended or her gown soiled. . . . Mr. Laing himself is a quiet, sedate-looking, old gentleman. . . . But his son is the chief enthusiast—indeed he is by far the most genuine specimen of the true old-fashioned bibliopole that I ever saw exhibited in the person of a young man. David Laing is still a very young man, but W—— tells me, 'that he possesses a truly wonderful degree of skill and knowledge in almost all departments of bibliography.'" [This is the late Dr. David Laing, for 41 years Librarian, Signet Library, 1837-78.]

In the ebbing year of the last century there were only two booksellers in the New Town, William Whyte in St. Andrew Street, whose trade was chiefly music and musical instruments, and Kinnear in S. Frederick Street, who, along with Mackay in the High Street, had the only circulating libraries. The last mentioned, Alexander Mackay of Blackcastle, bought in 1803 the library founded by Allan Ramsay in 1725. It had been purchased by Sibbald in Parliament Square in 1780, at whose death in 1803 it was acquired by Mackay, who greatly enlarged it. It was called the "Edinburgh Circulating Library." Not finding a purchaser for the whole, Mackay, when he retired in 1832, disposed of it by public auction, and in that way a large portion of it eventually formed a part of Wm. Wilson's, 44 George Street (1812-51; W. Moffat, 1851-57), the morning dusting of the books of which, at the back windows, I used to hear in early days from No. 50—a sentimental recollection of sight and sound. A co-assistant in Grant's Library would be one of the 1848 in-dust-rious youths.

Between 1800 and 1834, New Town booksellers increased from two to fifty-four out of a total hundred in the city, though, as Mr. Black said when he thought of the 128 in 1867, and might have said with emphasis in the present days of book*selling* in the land in sight of the 144 booksellers in modern Athenian ways, "those only who dealt in folios, quartos, octavos, and duodecimos were dignified with the name," their stationery beginnings being left behind. Then, indeed, some only of the hundred, as of the gross, would have been acknowledged when but quartos at two guineas were of any pretensions, the first edition of *The Lady of the Lake* being greedily bought up at £2, 2s. 6d., and a 6$^{dy.}$ edition "in Lilliputian times" not being conceivable. *A propos* of this, thousands immediately rushed off to Loch Katrine to view the scenery it describes, and the post-horse duty in Scotland rose to a degree.

William Blackwood, who had served his apprenticeship with Bell & Bradfute, commenced business in 1804, at No. 65 South Bridge, and soon became the agent for John Murray and several other London publishing houses. It was in 1817 when he issued the first number of *Blackwood's Magazine* (in point of fact, however, No. 7, when the six numbers of its predecessor, the *Edinburgh Monthly Magazine*, are reckoned in). The first contained the famous Chaldee Manuscript by Professor Wilson. The magazine was the monthly model upon which so many of the high-class magazines have been started in England.

Blackwood's shop, which was the one presently occupied by Mr. Elliot, Peter-the-above describes as "the only great lounging book shop in the New Town":—

"The prejudice in favour of sticking by the Old Town was so strong among gentlemen of the trade, that when this bookseller intimated a few years ago his purpose of removing to the New, his ruin was immediately prophesied by not a few of his sagacious brethren. He persisted, however, in his intentions, and speedily took possession of a large and airy suite of rooms in Princes Street. The length of vista presented to one on entering the shop has a very imposing effect; for it is carried back, room after room, through various gradations of light and shadow, till the eye cannot trace distinctly the outline of any object in the furthest distance. First, there is as usual a spacious place set apart for retail business. . . . Then you have an elegant oval saloon, lighted from the roof, where various groups of loungers and literary dilettanti are engaged in looking at, or criticising among themselves, the publications just arrived by that day's coach. In such critical colloquies, the voice of the bookseller himself may ever and anon be heard mingling the broad and unadulterated notes of its Auld Reekie music. He is a nimble, active-looking man of middle age, and moves about from one corner to another with great alacrity, and apparently under the influence of high animal spirits. . . In the present day, I look upon periodical writing as by far the most agreeable species of authorship. . . . . The happy man who is permitted to fill a sheet, or a half-sheet, of a monthly or quarterly journal with his lucubrations, is sure of coming into the hands of a vast number of persons more than he has any strict or even feasible claim upon, either from the subject matter or execution of his work. The sharp and comical criticisms of one man are purchased by people who abhor the very name of wit, because they are stitched under the same cover with ponderous masses of political economy, or foggy divinity, or statistics, or laws, or algebra, more fitted for their plain, or would be plain understandings; while, on the other hand, young ladies and gentlemen, who conceive the whole sum and substance of human accomplishment to consist in being able to gabble a little about new novels and poems, are compelled to become the proprietors of so many quires of lumber, *per quarter*, in order that they may not be left in ignorance of the last merry things uttered."

Blackwood removed in 1816 to 17 Princes Street; William Tait in 1818 occupied a large house at No. 78; and Constable came to an elegant mansion, No. 10, in 1822. Manners & Miller were at No. 92 by 1825, and John Stevenson, who is reputed as being in a special manner a correspondent of Sir Walter Scott, and his adviser and agent in buying books, began at No. 87 (down steps) in 1826. In 1831 Thomas G. Stevenson succeeded his father at No. 87, and Laing & Forbes succeeded Manners & Miller at No. 92 (up a few steps).

Constable's shop in 10 Princes Street was at the east corner, next the Register House. It was at a point visible from the lower end of the North Bridge to anyone strolling down from the High Street and Old Town, as the *literati* of the day would likely do. It had been built by his father-in-law about fifty years before—that is to say, in 1769—and was the first house erected in the street.

William Tait's was similarly situated relative to the Mound, by which people would come over to Princes Street from the upper part of the High Street, and from George Square after George IV. Bridge was built (founded 1827, completed 1836). *Tait's Edinburgh Magazine* was started in 1833.

To 19 Waterloo Place (opposite the late G.P.O.) came in 1833—apparently after Constable had been there and ceased publishing—the eminent publishing house of William and Robert Chambers, by which time *Chambers's Journal* had been established a year

(4th February, 1832). This was the turning point of the two brothers, for the journal, then a folio, immediately obtained a circulation of 50,000, which rose in 1845 to 90,000 in 8vo form. This precursor of cheap literature was soon known throughout Scotland, England, and America, and early imitated.

WHITSUNDAY MDCCCXXXIV.

In the year 1834 John Menzies commenced business at the shop No. 61 Princes Street (up steps), to which he added in 1851 a suite of warerooms entering from No. 63. In both of these numbers he continued until 1859 (see below).

In the same year (1834) R. Grant & Son removed from Nicolson Street to No. 82 Princes Street, where they occupied a shop with perhaps the most steps up of any, rented, down to 1854, at £100, with the westmost half area down steps at £25, Tait, a hairdresser, having the other half area—a renewal of the *tête-à-tête* relation which Allan Ramsay had begun, the interiors being treated above, and the exteriors trimmed below.

Of the seven earliest bookselling occupants of Princes Street shops, there were thus in 1824—Constable (10), Blackwood (17), Tait (78), of whom only Blackwood remains; in 1827 the same, with John Stevenson (87), Miller (92), late Manners & Miller, added; in 1834 Tait (78), T. G. Stevenson (87), and Laing & Forbes (92), late Manners & Miller; with the additions of John Menzies (61), and Grant & Son (82), Blackwood having gone to George Street, and Constable & Co. become printers (from

1842 printers to the Queen). Of the number the two last firms and Blackwood still exist—Blackwood and Grant & Son being the oldest and of equal longevity (1804), exceeded only by Bell & Bradfute in the Old Town, the oldest booksellers in Scotland.

W. & R. Chambers continued in Waterloo Place until 1841, when they removed to the High Street, with which for many reasons they will ever be linked. William Chambers was Lord Provost of Edinburgh from 1865 to 1869.

In 1834 James Stillie, who was established in 1826, was in 140 High Street, and came from 6 North Bank Street in 1843 to 78 Princes Street, the second shop from the corner (in the same tenement as the corner one, which still belonged to Tait, and was sold by his trustees in 1879, along with No. 107). Stillie's name is associated with the passing of the proof sheets of the Waverley Novels betwixt Sir Walter Scott and Constable, and with visits made to him by Mr. Gladstone on that account, and for other antiquarian information.

The leading publishers and booksellers left in the Old Town were A. & C. Black (Adam Black, 1807 to 1834), in 27 North Bridge, the G.P.O. of 1821; Oliver & Boyd, Tweeddale Court, originally in John Knox's House, Netherbow (1806); William Oliphant & Sons (William Oliphant, 1818 to 1833), 7 South Bridge; Waugh & Innes, 2 Hunter Square; Nelson & Sons, 2 West Bow; and Bell & Bradfute (established in 1734), for about 70 years in 12 Bank Street, the corner of which is now to be affected by the cable tramways companies alterations thereon.

The last mentioned firm was even earlier originated by Alexander Kincaid, who became Lord Provost of the city in 1776. It was at first styled Kincaid & Bell. In the *Courant* and *Scotsman* of June 25, 1824, is an advertisement to the effect that Bell & Bradfute's stock of books having been laid in the Old Church (one of the four churches in St. Giles' at the time) during the calamitous fire in the Parliament Close on the 24th, and it being found impossible to remove them for some days, "the magistrates, ministers, and session have agreed that DIVINE SERVICE SHALL NOT TAKE PLACE IN THIS CHURCH NEXT LORD'S DAY"! The books were largely or entirely law books, and the booksellers and magistrates had the law therefore in their own hands, their actions securing the law in the church opposite to its "lug."

In 1834 Princes Street had six booksellers, besides Alexander Hill the printseller, then in No. 50, and two musicsellers, J. Robertson in No. 39, and John Purdie in No. 83. In the same year George Street had eight booksellers, including Blackwood in No. 45, Thomas Clark (established as a law bookseller in 1822 at 8 Parliament Square) having occupied No. 32 in 1825, and No. 38 in 1829; Whyte & Co., from 12 St. Andrew Street, going into No. 13 in 1825; William Wilson, in No. 44 in 1812, with the remnant of what was Allan Ramsay's circulating library, forming a part of his own (*v. supra*), being still there, and others started. Paterson, Roy & Co. had occupied No. 27 as musicsellers since 1827. In Hanover Street there were six booksellers, in St. Andrew

Street five, St. Andrew Square three, Waterloo Place two, and Leith Street three, while other nine smaller streets near had a total of nine. These last twelve would not be of *Encyclopædia Britannica* calibre, but some were progressive, and would have a fair share of school books, now supplied by School Boards without money and without merit, besides post paper, ink, wax, wafers, quills, pencils, chalk, paints, brushes, &c., down to pictures, 1d. plain, 2d. coloured. The important establishments not here indicated were Charles Smith & Co. (1823) (Charles Smith, 1828-47, founder of Edmonston & Douglas), No. 25, and Waugh & Innes, No. 41 Hanover Street, also 1811 to 1837 in 2 Hunter Square (*vide* p. 317); Elder & Ogilvy in 1 Hope Street, the founders of John Maclaren, now Macniven & Wallace (*vide* p. 317); William Elgin & Son, in N. St. Andrew Street (1829, Davidson & Elgin, now G. Elgin, Elder Street); Robert Cadell, 31 St. Andrew Square, the publisher of Sir Walter Scott's works; and in No. 12 Waterloo Place (1822 to 1860), Wood & Co., musicsellers (established in 1797), formerly Wood, Small & Co., musical instrument makers to the King, 1819-1831. Wood & Co. removed to George Street in 1860.

MAY MDCCCXLVIII.

Fourteen years brings us to 1848, when I was myself within a field of view the most favourably situated in respect of location and opportunities of seeing or serving people noted for position, power, or learning. The ecclesiastical relation of the business was partly the reason, which relation was symbolised by its being the only closed shop on Christmas and Good Friday in Princes Street, and perhaps in the whole town, and one of the few places where "Christmas presents" in contradistinction to "New Year gifts" were much heard of. But times have changed, and there is hardly a store or a railway station that does not—for a week at least ahead—herald the coming reign of Christmas, while hot-cross buns are displayed and swallowed as readily as the younger generation take to hymns and choral services, Episcopal, Presbyterian, or Congregational: not to marvel at Presbyterian Easter holidays, sermons, services, and Communion Sundays and Christmas carols.

The shop proper, in 82, was the upper one, the lower one being the "warehouse," for sheet-stock and packing purposes, the big key of which hung handy upstairs. Behind it was a large open space, which might be respectfully called a green, either in the light or in the dark.

In hours of business in 1848 the "green" was "without bounds," and I think I only once bounded up the steps and to the top to explore the ground and survey the uniform back elevations of the tenements, with their world of linen drapery and clothes-poles. It was not available for a walk, far less a frolic, and the establishment had no carpets to beat, the shop floor being of well-worn plain wood, unadorned save by worn nail heads, by the prominence of which might be calculated the age of the mansion, having regard to the literary soles that had passed over it, or shuffled about the shelves. All such back greens in Princes

Street are probably now built over, and I am told the only one left in George Street is that behind the Northern Lighthouse Board offices, No. 82.

With the Royal Scottish Academy across the way, and a garden gate opposite, the fair ones made R. Grant's a convenient point at which to meet their lady friends or members of the Club with whom they had an appointment. Court beauties or favourites and eminent authoresses or artistes would lend enchantment to the transactions or scenes of the day, not the least memorable in a later shop being the visit of a now much lamented royal princess on the occasion of one of her Majesty's visits to the city. Such celebrities may not be named, but the memories of them are ever fresh, and to have caught some of the rays of their benign presence is a joy to the last.

Edinburgh then had "A Season" as well as London, and lords and landed gentry could better afford to live on and entertain at their country seats their English friends of high estate. Many of them could also maintain a town residence, so that equipages of the county nobles were a part of Princes Street pleasures before the iron king carried the city to the suburbs of London and bolted the stable door against any drives to town.

As publishers to the Royal Society, the rooms of which were opposite, and stationers to the University, with an important *clièntele* among Principals and Professors of colleges, scientific men and bookhunters, and the judges and gentlemen of the Parliament House, who came down the Mound to the reading club or library—two separate collections on different

COUNCILLOR ROBERT GRANT
From a Painting

principles, one a fixed membership subscription with certain rights to nominate books and the other independent of members—it was my privilege and advantage to converse with many whose names are remembered and honoured—not a few eminent in literature, science, and art. In those days the city had more bookworms and fewer butterflies, and the worms had time more to mould their mind's enterprise for the country's benefit than to expend it in making their way in the world.

There are memories in the half-century vista; reminiscences of groups variously disposed in the inner room or library, where furthest back in one's thoughts the senior partner, a town councillor of aldermanic presence, would continue or pause in his posting as the coterie's conversation or discussion suggested. The party might be municipal, political, or ecclesiastical; literary, musical, or æsthetic, agricultural or histrionic, and might embrace Lord Provost or Bailie; Bishop, Dean, or Deacon, Judge or Sheriff, Principal or Professor; painter, poet, or actor. The visit of a duke, pleasant and courtly throughout, would end with the purchase of something new on the recommendation of the firm, to be put down to his Grace's account and sent to some palace or into the New Club, an experience thinning with the age: or a parcel of nice new or lately published books, or some standard bound one, would precede to the carriage some elegant countess or lady of the upper ten whose conversation, manner, and nobility of mind would leave behind an uplifting influence.

The "Son" in the firm—Robert Grant, jun., of

necessity, and by inclination, the more active at that time—while attending the minutiæ of business, would occasionally form one of a group in earnest or lively converse; managing all the while to be busy about the shelves or among papers of some kind, and setting a healthy example of never being a moment idle, which probably accounted for his good health and his wonderful vigour surprising to everyone, even to an advanced age and until within a day of his death. While he was always a good listener when his attention could be gained, he could express his opinions calmly and to the point, and infuse a vein of humour which made his remarks palatable to any with whom his views might not coincide. Favoured as the firm ever was with the patronage of retired Indian military and Civil Service officers, he had a peculiar pleasure in chatting with them, although in my time the reason for that may have hardly appeared because of the sad fate which befell his brother, George Morison Grant, assistant-surgeon, H.E.I.C.S., who behaved bravely in one of the most momentous events in Anglo-Indian history, when Cabul was first lost to the British in 1841, through the treacherous outbreak that ended with a massacre of 16,000 soldiers and followers. Vincent Eyre narrates how Dr. Grant had rallied the men and secured a point round which the disabled Major Pottinger when he arrived was able to gather the native officers and many Sepoys to assert their fidelity. Besides attending to surgical operations, and dressing the wounds of another officer whose arm had to be amputated on the spot, he spiked all the guns with his own

ROBERT GRANT

hands, and brought out the main body in the advance made under the command of the wounded Major and the other wounded officer, after the junction of which with the rear he was not again seen, having suddenly disappeared, either by being at first taken prisoner or immediately killed by the mutinous Sepoys.

A glance at the Post Office Directory shows that there were, after various changes, still ninety publishers, booksellers, stationers, and librarians. Of the last there were about ten or twelve. Now the number of libraries is double, the booksellers in 1898 totalling 150, but those who could afford to add new books of general interest to their catalogues were formerly half-a-dozen, compared to the present three, who have to purchase supplies daily, not few and far between, but in increasing quantities to suit the intellectual, if somewhat confectionery, insatiable appetites, craving for delectable mixtures.

With decoy titles, as much a mortification to librarians who have to purchase the books as to the readers who expend time and temper over them, the circulating libraries and the public libraries are literary industries that would have astonished Sir Walter Scott and surprised Allan Ramsay. The average consumer, from the inconstant to the constant reader, tries, tastes, or wades through a hundred books at least per annum, with extra for field banks and garden arbours. The librarian is supposed to read through all he recommends or even lends, but he has an art and air that disarm anyone from thinking the contrary.

Only five principals of the ninety firms survive—the three eminent publishers, Sir Thomas Boyd, of Oliver & Boyd Almanac fame (a specially bound copy of which my firm has the honour of annually presenting to her Majesty); Sir Thomas Clark, Bart., whose house, having produced both law books of great importance, and much widely sold theological literature, has been said to have published the Law and the Gospel; and Mr. David Douglas, who, besides issuing works of the highest merit and of the most solid kind, gave to the world the much prized volumes of the *Diary of Sir Walter Scott.* He is the father of Edinburgh publishers still in business, the two before mentioned having lately retired; and but for his removal to Castle Street he would have been the literary merchant patriarch of Princes Street. Mr. Ritchie, now the head of William Ritchie & Son, the extensive wholesale stationers, is the survivor of Paton & Ritchie, of 81 Princes Street (1856 to 1863), formerly T. Paton (1831), W. Ritchie (1843), booksellers and stationers. Mr. Taylor, of Grant & Taylor, (1847), latterly of 31 Castle Street, retired from business in 1896. The present principals who were Edinburgh booksellers' assistants in 1848 are Mr. Robert Anderson of Messrs. Oliphant, Anderson & Ferrier, Mr. Andrew Elliot, Mr. James Thin, Mr. Andrew Stevenson of A. Stevenson & Co., and myself.

Of these former assistants I am the youngest, and in my collecting days I came daily into contact with the others. There was a close relationship between every bookseller and a spirit of fraternity which the present knows little of. There was also more intercourse between principals, with a readiness to oblige and accommodate one another upon fair and friendly principles that was praiseworthy and probably unique in trade, the law to do to others what one would like done to one's-self being respected by buyers and sellers.

According to the Directory and my own recollection, there were fifty-five of the ninety booksellers in the New Town. Of these ten were in Princes Street, with three printsellers, two musicsellers, and one wholesale stationer, a trade phalanx in the front rank of streets of sixteen, most of whom were also retail stationers in intercommunication with one another, and with all booksellers and stationers in the city. The stationer was really the beginning of the bookseller as well as the printer, who, after man began to make paper for others out of the reed papyrus down to the time when he began himself to read, might have appropriately been styled a paperer —plain, printed, or bound. The name originated with those who occupied a "station" at the markets to sell such novel requisites as paper, quills and ink, and *horn* books, after these were made of paper, and the younger generations were helped to get out their horns, long before School Boards required them to learn by law, and some became lawless by learning.

Among the wholesale stationers Sir John Cowan, papermaker, is the only principal left. The other very old established firm, James Dickson & Co. (1807), has for its head a grandson of the founder, who is ex-Colonel of the Queen's Rifle Volunteers. The founder joined one Berry in 1807, when the business was that of seedsmen and stationers, and as such became Dickson & Berry in 1809. After Berry retired in 1816 the business was confined to stationery. It was begun in Drummond Street about 1804, and removed to Nicolson Square about 1809, 221 High Street in 1814, to Milne Square in 1816, the Lawnmarket in 1820, Meuse Lane in 1837, and to the present premises in 1840. When the great fire already referred to occurred, the flames reached the firm's warehouse, then close to the Tron Church, to which the fire extended from the Parliament Square. As St. Giles' had been made a sanctuary for law and literature, the Tron Church walls afforded a refuge for the columns of unprinted paper, and down to a recent date the firm retained as a memento of the event one of the reams on which were the marks of the molten lead from the church roof, which had poured down on the paper when the spire was burnt away. If the roof had been slates these would have been "stationery."

G. Waterston & Sons represent by two great-grandsons the business of sealing-wax manufacturers, &c., founded in the High Street by William Waterston in 1752, which the half-century has greatly developed. Macniven & Cameron, who were established in 1770, are represented by a brother and grandson of Mr. Cameron. P. W. Macniven dates from 1840. Andrew Whyte & Son (1823) were originally Sommerville, Fullarton & Co.; then Sommerville, Whyte & Co.; Whyte & Fullerton; then Sommerville, Whyte & Co.; Tullis & Co., 1827 (*vide* p. 252).

Of later firms, George Stewart, of G. Stewart & Co., established in 1880, from the firm of Waterston, Stewart & Co., who began his apprenticeship in the bookselling as well as the stationery side some months before myself, and whom I esteem among my oldest friends and fellow-workers in youthful Christian effort, is the present head of the extensive stationery store in George Street, with a branch at London, established in 1888. He served his apprenticeship in Mr. Chalmers', Dundee, who claimed to be the inventor of the adhesive postage stamp. It was there, I think, that the new boy in his master's absence, being obliged to serve one wanting a wedding present, followed the example to show a bound book and one that was popular, and recommended Buchanan's *Comfort in Affliction*, with suitable sombre binding.

Among printing offices, Alexander and Patrick Neill Fraser, sons of Dr. Neill's partner, William Fraser, of the old established firm of Neill & Co. (1749), and Mr. Pillans, grandson of the founder of the business of Pillans & Wilson, established in 1780, are perhaps the only surviving principals. The other printing houses that have come down to us from older times are Ballantyne, now Ballantyne, Hanson & Co. (1796); T. & A. Constable (1834), *v.* page 299 (formerly Willison, established prior to 1793); Morrison & Gibb (1836); R. & R. Clark (1846); Blackwood & Sons (1846); W. & R. Chambers (1838); Nelson & Sons (1851); and Colston & Co. (1822); to whom Turnbull & Spears (1857) should be added.

Morrison & Gibb were originally Wm. Oliphant,

Jun., & Co. (1836), Murray & Gibb (1838), Morrison & Gibb (1864), and are now Morrison & Gibb, Limited, with which is incorporated Scott & Ferguson, lithographers (1850; J. Kirkwood & Sons, 1793), and Burness & Co., printers (1825).

Henderson & Bisset, the celebrated leather bookbinders to the Queen, for 66 years in 19 Hill Street (established in St. James' Square in 1823, and after in George Street 1828), have been located in Hanover Street since 1893; while Orrock & Son continue the business begun by Orrock & Romanes in the South Bridge in 1830, at 15 Victoria Street.

MAY MDCCCXCVIII.

On May morning, 1898, encouraged by the ease with which I had ascended and descended the Washington Monument in 1894, and emulating those mentioned at page 213, I rose to the occasion by five o'clock in celebration of this particular year, and ascended to the top of Arthur's Seat to obtain my *dew*, which was a mountain view of Auld Reekie—Modern Athens—Royal Edinburgh—the Queen City of the Kingdom — "Mine own romantic town." The sun too had risen to the occasion, so had also some three hundred sons and daughters of the human race—racy up but racier down—and half-a-dozen canine experts; my staff being my jubilee cane, for there wasn't an umbrella airing anywhere in the city that day.

After feasting eyes on the scene around and below, and absorbing much of the mountain air above, I retraced my steps by the heights over the village of

Duddingston as the parish church bell was ringing in the calmness of a Scottish Sabbath morn, and awaking around a thousand thoughts that made echoes in the soul. The curling smoke wandered slowly away, and as I gazed and listened and thought, I wondered in what little dwelling Prince Charlie had slept on the eve of Prestonpans, until a villager with pleasing gesture satisfied my longing desire. The lake reflected the scene of the morn, and mirrored as well the memories of many winter scenes, when the air was crisp and hills and plain were robed in snow, while the ice rang and rumbled with the activities of the city's gay and motley host of skaters, sliders, and curlers. I hastened step as I heard the convent bell by my house ringing the breakfast hour.

I thus came home well appetised for breakfast with primrose eggs, *à propos* of Arthurian rejuvenescence as prophetically determined by the sages of the hill. Then I went to church, after which I walked in the strength and grace of natural mountain dew to the Gentle Shepherd's statue, where I contemplated the changes of half-a-century's seasons since I cast about the "Word in Season" of a writer —now under the green turf—from opposite that spot, now the Life Association vestibule. The shops and occupants of earlier years had gone. The New Club—itself only a later new one—alone visibly represented the past, but how many nobles and gentry whom I had seen pass out and in had now passed away altogether, their sons perhaps at the other end of the world, one now and then returning pleased to find, as one did just the day before, some one who re-

membered their father. A new generation all round
was in possession for better or for worse. The cast-
down pillars and dug-up foundations of the Royal
Institution,* underneath which the piles laboriously
driven seventy years ago had rotted away, seemed to
suggest nature's insidious preparation for the coming
New Zealander. The row of flaming torches surmounting the Life Association symbolised the silent
lapse of life's interest in things under the sun, and
the New Club urns, conspicuous against the sky line,
correspondingly suggested repositories for the ashes
of the great, worthy of remembrance, and of occupying a high place in the mind's *repertorium*.

In my hour's early morning survey from the hill,
how insignificant from the altitude of an eagle's flight
did the whole city appear, yet how beautiful the
scene. It was a gem in mosaic of Modern Athens,
than which the promised land could not have been
more beautiful to Moses, wherein it seemed little
children or Lilliputians alone could be asleep in the
diminutive houses below, clustered round a tiny but
not tinsel castle, with a model of the Parthenon stuck
on a hillock. How sweetly in the sunlight did the
sea lap the near land, kiss the island, and carry our
sight across to the " Kingdom " on the further shore.
That ancient " Kingdom of Fife " once the most
cultivated, albeit the most warlike of the counties,
with Celtic and Roman remains still remaining, its
monastic, feudal, and palatial ruins sleeping with the
dust of St. Andrews, Dunfermline, Falkland, and

* Before going to press new foundations have been laid, and the pillars
re-erected.

Lindores, and its rivers, Tay and Forth and Leven, reflecting the past flowing memories of Perth, and the stirring scenes at Stirling, or telling anew of the unfortunate Queen Mary just 330 years ago, waiting in Loch Leven Castle to escape on the morrow—a kingdom 500 square miles with a succession of vales and hills filled with events, and a river Eden meandering for 20 miles in a goodly course.

Now when the sun had passed the noontide it cast the shadows to the east, and one's thoughts of the bright morning, alike of life as of day, sheltered in the shadows. But the sun spread only the light about the white marble statue of Allan Ramsay. Just as in the morning I had seen no shadow in the city, or on the sea, or on the further shore, so around it all was light. There stood, as much in reality to me as in marble, and on May Day's brightest meridian, the progenitor perhaps of half the statues in the avenue, and of the sixty-four statuettes that stud the Scott monument. How far may booksellers, librarians, and the public not have been indebted to his stores for what of his library was read with avidity by Sir Walter Scott. He has some claim to be associated with the great monument, and so with others, all in view range of the house he built for himself on the castle bank, straight opposite his statue.

MONUMENTS.

Perhaps all the monuments east of and on the line of Princes Street may be called literary. Beginning opposite the High School there is that of Burns, poet ;

on the Calton Hill, Dugald Stewart, Burns' friend and Professor of Moral Philosophy; and Professor Playfair; in the Calton, Hume, historian; in Princes Street, Wellington, whose despatches fill fifteen volumes; Livingstone, traveller, Christian pioneer, and writer; Black, Lord Provost, M.P., and publisher; Wilson (Christopher North), Professor of Moral Philosophy; Simpson, medical discoverer and writer; Dean Ramsay, pastor and writer. The statue of Chambers, Lord Provost, publisher, and writer, is in Chambers Street, where also is that of James Watt, of whom Sir Walter Scott (chairman of the first scheme for the monument) said that no man had done so much to bring London near Edinburgh, and who to-day would have said that he had moored the western continent to the eastern, and made coal and water the key to naval victory and the supremacy of nations. Excepting the Waterloo hero, all these are Scotsmen, men of thought, action, counsel, trade, steam, and esteem.

Allan Ramsay's was the first circulating library, and as it happens his statue faces the site where down to 1854 was what may be the oldest circulating library in Scotland. There, too, fifty years ago, were located more booksellers than in any other division, including the leading retail establishments. In 1848 there were six (from 1818 to 1840, William Tait was also there as already noted). Now there are none. The whole number in the street in 1848 was ten, with three printsellers, two musicsellers, and a wholesale stationer. In 1898 they have been reduced to four, with one musicseller, the three printsellers being closed, and the wholesale stationer having built premises elsewhere as already explained.

Andrew Elliot's business, No. 17, was in 1846 at 15 Princes Street, being Johnstone's (of Johnstone, Ballantine & Co.), from Hunter Square (where Mr. Elliot began his apprenticeship), then Johnstone & Hunter in 1850, and next Shepherd & Elliot in 1854, Mr. Elliot having in the interval been eighteen months in Hamilton, Adams & Co., London. In 1858 the firm's name was changed to its present by the retirement of Mr. Shepherd, who became a medical practitioner. It has an earlier history, however, the order of succession being Oliphant & Brown, 1807; Oliphant, Balfour & Brown, 1808; Oliphant & Balfour, 1809; Oliphant, Waugh & Innes, 1811-18; then Waugh & Innes, William Oliphant originating (in 1818) a separate business, at 22 South Bridge, afterwards Wm. Oliphant & Sons, at No. 7, now Oliphant, Anderson & Ferrier, publishers, St. Mary Street and Paternoster Row, London—Mr. Anderson having begun in that house as an apprentice. Waugh & Innes were publishers and printers to the Church of Scotland, also booksellers to the King from 1825 to 1834. Besides 2 Hunter Square, they occupied 41 Hanover Street, 1827-34. At 2 Hunter Square John Johnstone succeeded them in 1837, and the branch at Hanover Street (then No. 31) was continued by Wm. Innes, a son of the original Innes, Mr. Waugh going to Australia, where he lately died at a very advanced age. Mr. Waugh was a Magistrate of Edinburgh.

Macniven & Wallace, No. 138, established by themselves in 1879, eventually acquired Maclaren & Son's business in 1882, which was Elder & Ogilvy's, 1 Hope Street, 1830-36, and John Elder's, 1 Shandwick Place, 1835, from which he removed in 1846 to 139 Princes Street. In 1850 Mr. Elder sold his business to John Maclaren, from the above firm of Wm. Oliphant & Sons, and went out to Australia with his family, where he and his sons eventually attained to prominent positions in the Colony. The business was styled John Maclaren, 1850-73; Maclaren & Macniven, 1879; and John Maclaren & Sons, 1879-82. Both Mr. Macniven and Mr. Wallace were assistants with Mr. Maclaren.

Robert Grant & Son, No. 107, the longest in Princes Street (*vide* p. 227), acquired, in 1865, Thos. Lawrie's retail bookselling and stationery business, and thus added his circulating library to their own. The latter business was previously Laing & Forbes, No. 92, who succeeded Manners & Miller, that firm having removed, from the High Street in 1825, becoming Robert Miller in 1826, then Laing & Forbes—whose superscription on the door, " late Manners & Miller," I remember even before 1848—Charles Forbes in 1845, and then Forbes & Wilson, from 1851 to 1854; Thomas C. Jack, 1854 to 1862; and Thos. Lawrie, 1863 to 1865. R. Grant & Son may thus be considered the collateral representatives of the old firm of Manners & Miller, established rather earlier than their own a century ago (*v.* p. 293).

In 1863 they also bought the stationery business of Thomas Veitch, St. Andrew Square (1838-63), formerly Thomson & Co. (1804), Kerr & Co. (1836), and acquired other manufacturing stationery and binding relations. In 1860 the firm succeeded to the proprietorship of the County Directory of Scotland (first issued 1843); seven editions of which they have published, and successively enlarged. The work when first issued had only 310 pp.; the jubilee (1894) edition, 1048 pp., contained both postal and telegraph addresses. Scotland has now above 1800 post towns.

Douglas & Foulis, 9 Castle Street, though not actually in Princes Street, are practically so, both because of their long association with the street and their proximity to it. The present firm dates from 1877, when Mr. Edmonston acquired the right to continue as Edmonston & Co. (closed in 1880) in the original position in Princes Street of Edmonston & Douglas, and Mr. Douglas formed a new partnership with Mr. Foulis from the same firm. Eventually, on the retirement of Edmonston & Co. in 1880, Douglas & Foulis succeeded to or practically obtained their former relations. The old firm of Edmonston & Douglas succeeded Charles Smith, which business was established in 1823, as before stated.

John Menzies, 12 Hanover Street, the wholesale bookseller, of Scottish bookstall reputation, who came in 1834 to 61 Princes Street, as already mentioned, removed in 1859 to 2 Hanover Street, above what was once William Tait's shop at 78 Princes Street, and in 1870 to the present premises. As agent half-a-century ago for Dickens, Thackeray, Lever, and Jerrold's works, then issued in monthly shilling parts, and of all the popular publishers—Cassell, Routledge, Warne, Tegg, &c.—the wholesale department was from morning to night the busy rendezvous of the trade collectors, who were sure to meet one another there sometime in the day, and punctually for *Punch*, a pictorial attraction, at noon on Thursdays. In 1869 the firm became John Menzies & Co.

Richard Cameron, 1 St. David Street, adjoining Princes Street, was established at George IV. Bridge in 1870, and came to 63 Princes Street in 1872. He removed to 15 St. David Street in 1876, and to 18 George Street in 1880, and returned to St. David Street again in 1884.

William Brown, No. 26, opened in 1877 at No. 149 Princes Street, after having been several years in William Paterson's, No. 74, and also at No. 67. He removed to his present shop (No. 26) in 1883. Mr. Paterson gave up business in 74 Princes Street in 1885, and in 67 Princes Street in 1889.

Taking in the George Street and Hanover Street shops, booksellers numbered twenty-four in the three streets, compared with twelve in the present year. Roughly counted, twenty-five have closed within these years, after a longer or shorter life begun prior to or after 1848, the best known being Stillie, Stevenson, W. F. Watson, William Wilson, Whyte & Son, P. S. Fraser, W. P. Kennedy, Seton & Mackenzie, Braidwood, W. & C. Inglis, and Wm. Innes, who were all centres of influence and intelligence fifty years ago.

Not only have shops removed, changed, or closed, but time ravages in thought, literature, and habits have altered the whole aspect of the trade. Excepting the outstanding Athenian days of the early part of the century, perhaps the aristocratic, antiquarian, and ecclesiastical coteries were never more marked than after the Free Church disruption, including the early fifties. After that modern and multitudinous tastes developed, and the decadence of book shop resorts for information and talk began. Their places were gradually taken in political, ecclesiastical, and literary circles by the daily newspapers and serials without end, sectional reviews, party and parochial magazines, and political clubs; and now, with the increased value of knowledge, opportunities of learning, and thirst for reading, the habits of the multitude are more those of reading for amusement, in accord with the physical recreation of many who seek the open air continuously round the golf course or on the cycle, and the music of the home circle may be in danger, in the *rôle* of many who fly about the country fluttering on wheels, like fairies in revolving clouds.

Novels, no longer three volumes, sinful to print and sorrowful to buy, but standard at 6s., and yellow backs, their leaves once seared by sentiment right or wrong, and themselves kept behind backs, now fill the windows, not overspread with "Pick Me Up," or leave-me-lying, and crowd the front shelves once reserved for the instructive and entertaining work, the new religious book, or the latest biography. They have become, indeed, the saccharine media for airing views, solving problems, offering opinions, or spreading caustic criticism, the *sine qua non* being that *the old story* shall intertwine what of the infinite variety of the world's relations an author may discern, conceive, or invent surprising, sensational, breath-holding, or tear-suffusing. Suspected heresy and suspended heterodoxy, reserved in the recesses of stores, or high out of sight, have been brought forward and laid on a level with ordinary literature, their authors or editors among the hierarchy, or occupying pedestals in fields of scientific investigation.

In the forties and fifties, at the east end of Princes Street, Hugh Miller (editor of *The Witness*), and those still glowing embers of the Disruption, Dr. Chalmers, and the future Moderators of the Free General Assemblies of '48, '56, '59, '61, '62, and '65, Candlish, Cunningham, Guthrie, and Begg, Clason, and M'Crie, with presbyters and elders, might be seen in a shop discussing the pronouncements, activities, and missionary enterprise of the Church.

In the middle division, near the Mound, a daily retinue of carriages crowding each other on either side of the New Club would indicate the aristocratic relations of the two firms, and in one case the dominating Episcopal one, which constituted the firm the Rivingtons of Scotland, as well as the S.P.C.K. agents, from which the chief country booksellers obtained their supplies of "Episcopal literature," cheap Bibles, Prayer Books, and school books. Some shops upsteps and the down-steps ones, unfrequented by ladies, denoted the antiquarian lore to be found in those upper or lower stores. One at the west end had its Free Church character accentuated by the rich and well-to-do ladies that hovered there, and fostered one another's enthusiasm and sympathies. The Voluntary principle, then invigorated by the union of 1847, was ministered to by booksellers at the north end of the South Bridge, while the Established Church was well and dignifiedly taken care of by "Maga" in George Street, and locally by a less pretentious shop in St. David Street. Literary specialists and all faddists had their respective kinds of shops, which the booksellers' collectors learned to understand. Now the main division is that between old books and newly issued ones, the latter alongside of such articles as may attract the loves and graces to hover in the atmosphere of the shop, as Peter in his *Letters to his Kinsfolk* has it.

A writer in *The Nineteenth Century* for December, 1896, maintains that the existence of the bookseller is a necessity, and will always be so; that his shop, a part of the nation's educational machinery, should be in the future, as in the past, a centre of influence and intelligence, while he himself will have the satisfaction of having associated with the great men of his age as well as with a nation's literature. He wishes booksellers to console themselves by being classed with those who follow literature as a profession, and of whom Froude has said: "It happens to be the only occupation in which wages are not given in proportion to the goodness of the work done."

Edinburgh booksellers and their allies have been well represented by publishers who have served the city well, and become Lord Provosts and town councillors. Lately, those who have had the means have done generous acts. The restoration of St. Giles' Cathedral (Hay & Henderson, architects) in a manner worthy of the metropolitan city was due to William Chambers, and the splendid restoration of the Parliament Hall in the Castle (Hippolyte J. Blanc, R.S.A., architect) and the Argyll Tower was that of William Nelson, who also transformed St. Bernard's Well approach and grounds, while his brother Thomas left endowments for district free libraries.

Of sixteen Lord Provosts in office during the last fifty years, five have been publishers and one a paper maker—Adam Black, Sir William Johnston, William Chambers, James Cowan, Sir Thomas Clark, Bart., and Sir Thomas J. Boyd. Among the members of parliament for the city, booksellers and stationers have been honoured 'in the names of Adam Black, Charles and James Cowan. In the Town Council during the same period have been Robert Grant, William Wilson, Alexander Hill (printseller), David Dickson (treasurer), John Greig, sen. and jun., father and son (printers); Robert Anderson, Jas. Colston (printer), treasurer; John Maclaren, Adam Black, jun., John Murray, Robert Somerville, J. T. Paterson. Peter S. Fraser occupied the honourable position of Lord Dean of Guild, and the School Board has been well served by John S. Ferrier.

PRESBYTERIAN SCOTLAND.

I have alluded to the head centres of Presbyterian Scotland as visibly represented and viewed from Princes Street, and pointed out the spire beneath which the Establishment split in two, an event many are now gauging the meaning of with a view to re-forming. I have also indicated how under the crown of St. Giles' a spark of resentment ignited a ready to be excited people. I may now tell the towers of heart centres where—

"All people that on earth do dwell
Sing to the Lord with cheerful voice."

There are two hundred places of worship in extended Edinburgh, and 26 denominations, the congregations of which are all familiar with that "Old Hundredth." In 1848 their number was 100, and in 1843, before the Disruption, 75, when the denominations numbered 15. The effect of the Disruption was to add by division twenty congregations of a "Church of Scotland—Free," so to translate its principles and averments. From the heights, fifty or more of their spires or domes are seen, but Princes Street and George Street reveal only the more important or best known central edifices, which, added to St. Giles' and St. Andrew's and the Victoria Hall (the Tolbooth congregation), are the Tron, St. Cuthbert's, St. George's in Charlotte

Square, St. Stephen's (as seen from George Street), Free St. George's in Shandwick Place, and Barclay Church, as seen from the West End. Neither tower nor spire tells from Princes Street the whereabouts of a United Presbyterian Church, but the nearest and most important is Palmerston Place, one with two towers 100 feet high.

The simplicity of the early Free Church buildings, some built in brick, was a necessity when sites and funds had to be sought for a new church in nearly every parish in Scotland; but plainer United Presbyterian buildings were a matter of preference as much as anything else, although some of the finest ecclesiastical structures are now to be found among that denomination. Their names differ from those of the Free Church—which follows the Established almost parish for parish, saint for saint —saints' names being discarded, and the names of the respective streets being adopted; in which way those of royal, political, naval, and military personages find place on church plate and in the church papers.

In the Church of Scotland as by law established there are throughout the land 16 synods, each containing from 3 to 8 presbyteries, totalling 84, embracing 1755 congregations; the Free Church also having 16 synods, with from 1 to 9 presbyteries, totalling 75, and 1062 congregations. Instead of the General Assembly, the superior court of those bodies, the United Presbyterian Church has an annual Synod representing the Church corporate, in which every congregation has a clerical and lay representative, the presbyteries numbering 29, and the congregations therein 585. The Congregational Union has 181 churches similarly designated to those of the United Presbyterian, grouped into 9 districts. The Baptists have 129 congregations, the Methodists 47, while the Roman Catholics have 240. Of the Episcopal Church in Scotland I shall speak further on, parenthetically here noting that there exist four "English Episcopal Churches" in Scotland, not related to the Scottish Episcopal Church, and claiming only to be of the Church of England, served by clergy therein (their Episcopalness being their own).

In St. Cuthbert's, the perhaps too conspicuous West Church in the valley, once a rural kirk in a pleasant vale, with a sheet of water laving the Castle rock, affording aquatic pleasures to man and fowl and drinking water for cattle, as well as country strolls by the loch and about its braes, there is traditional association through past buildings back to the eighth century, when upon its exact site stood the Culdee Church of St. Cuthbert. Part of it at times was roofless, while the roofs it has had have been variously stone, thatch, and slate. Between Cromwell, who made it a barrack, and the fortress guns, it suffered disastrously. Gutted, pillaged, and cannon-shotted, the old church that for ages had been Catholic, then Presbyterian, and next Episcopalian, and again Presbyterian, was condemned to be taken down in 1772. The next structure dated from 1775, which, excepting the spire, has been replaced with a larger building with æsthetic interior, in accord with the ecclesiastical tastes of the times and signs of the Church for the twentieth century, including the observance of Christmas and Easter in many of the capital's Established churches.

The parish of St. Cuthbert was once the largest in Mid-Lothian. In 1767 a great portion was annexed to St. Giles' within the city, which became the modern parishes of St. Andrew, St. George, St. Mary, and St. Stephen. In 1834 the *quoad sacra* parishes of Buccleuch, St. Bernard, Newington, and Roxburgh were also formed out of it. In 1835 it had *quoad civilia* a greatest length of five miles, and greatest breadth of three and a half. In 1659 a parishioner was fined for "taking snuff in tyme of sermon," contrary to an Act of 1640 against breaches of "the Sabbath." Many male parishioners nowadays snuff *at* sermons, instead ot trying to get a pinch out of them, while fair ones refer the pinches to their friends.

THE NEW CHURCH OF ST. CUTHBERT'S.
Hippolyte J. Blanc, R.S.A., Architect.
(Block kindly lent by Mr J. G. Hitt, Publisher).

Parish Churches Ancient (Episcopalian), and Modern (Presbyterian), with Dates of foundation :—

St. Cuthbert's Chapel 690 ; re	1883
St. Giles' Cathedral 1150 ; re. 1829	83
Trinity College Church	1462
Old Greyfriars ,,	1412
Christ Church (Tron)	1437
Lady Yester's Church	1455
Canongate ,,	1484
New Greyfriars ,,	1721
Old Buccleuch Chapel	1757
Gaelic Chapel	1767
Lady Glenorchy's Chapel	1774
St. Andrew's Church	1781
St. George's ,,	1814
Newington ,,	1823
St. Bernard's ,,	1823
St. Mary's Church	1824
St. David's ,,	1827
St. Stephen's ,,	1828
Morningside ,,	1836
Dean ,,	1836
Greenside ,,	1838
St. John's ,,	1838
Victoria Hall (Tolbooth)	1842
West Coates Church	1849
Robertson Memorial	1871
Mayfield Church	1877
St. Michael's Church	1883
West St. Giles' ,,	1883
St. Matthew's ,,	1890

There are also the Abbey Church, Old Kirk, St. Aidan's, St. James', St. Leonard's, St. Luke's, St. Margaret's, St. Oswald's, and Tynecastle.

St. Cuthbert's Churchyard and that of Greyfriars' are the two most ancient and interesting in the city, containing the remains of distinguished men of three centuries. Greyfriars' was granted to the town by Queen Mary in 1562, in succession to St. Giles' Churchyard, abandoned about that time, and is the more interesting of the two. It is visited by a great number of Americans and other strangers. Among the graves are those of 37 Lord Provosts, 6 Lord Presidents, 23 Principals and Professors of the University, a Vice-Chancellor of England, many distinguished lawyers, and a host of others of genius, piety, and worth. I believe the first Episcopal funeral service at Greyfriars' since the Reformation was at the burial of a relative in 1862. The ground is seen off the Castle Esplanade to the south, in a line with and adjacent to George Heriot's Hospital.

In the pretty little cemetery and vaults of St. John's Church, next St. Cuthbert's, are buried many of the modern *literati* and distinguished men of the city; and prominently facing Princes Street is the memorial cross of Shap granite (26 feet high) erected by his countrymen to the memory of Dean Ramsay, one of whose works is *Reminiscences of Scottish Life and Character*. The Dean is interred in the Dormitory at the east end of St. John's.

ARCHBISHOPS VISIT THE GENERAL ASSEMBLY.

In the interval of an unavoidable delay in returning the last proofs for press caused by the time required for the verification of the data given at pages 225-263, an event, unique in the ecclesiastical firmament, has occurred—that of the visit of the Archbishop of Canterbury to the General Assembly of the Church of Scotland, as by law established, which was made on the 27th of May, in relation to the temperance cause. Last year, at the opening of the General Assembly, I saw his Grace the Archbishop of York (himself a Scotchman) leave Holyrood in the suite of her Majesty's Lord High Commissioner (Marquis of Tweeddale), enter St. Giles' Cathedral, and afterwards the Assembly Hall, to be given a place of honour in the throne gallery of the house. This year I saw the same place of honour beside his Grace the Commissioner (Earl of Leven and Melville) occupied on the above date by his Grace the Primate of All England; and, in course of the proceedings of the venerable house, his Grace of Canterbury received on the floor of the house with great honour and reverence, all upstanding—a scene to remain for ever deeply impressed on the minds of those privileged to witness it. The power of a Temple may yet out-distance in results the strong mind of Jenny Geddes and the arm of the State.

Amid the formal resolution to give official recognition to the event, Dr. Scott said his Grace's visit "might produce results far-reaching and beneficial, which none of them, the most clear-sighted, could predict or foresee"; while the Moderator, in presenting the formal thanks of the Assembly, said :—

"His Grace's presence that day was of great interest, apart from its connection with the cause of temperance. They must not venture to attribute to it more significance than courtesy allowed. But it was impossible for them to forget that the advocate of social reform to whom they had been listening was the greatest ecclesiastic in the kingdom. It was the first time that this Assembly had had the honour of receiving the head of the great Anglican Church. The memory of events, now remote, had kept the two communions more apart than need have been. Were these buried in oblivion, they should see more clearly how much they had been of one heart and one mind, notwithstanding difference in features. They knew how much they had learned from the saints and scholars of the Church of England. She, perhaps, had received something from them. They had the same holy faith to teach and defend, the same work to do for their respective peoples, with many difficulties and dangers in common, and the same foes abroad and at home. If they must meanwhile move on parallel lines, with the dividing space broader than they would wish, they could at least pray and hope that the force of spiritual attraction was bringing them nearer. The parting prayer, the declared intent of their Head in heaven, assured them that unity would come. When the relations between the two Churches had become other and closer than in these later centuries they had been, it might be that those who came after them might date one of the stages of approximation by the day on which the Primate of All England came to the General Assembly of the Church of Scotland, to give it the benefit of his experienced counsel, and was welcomed with the profound respect due to a father in God, a brother in Christ."

THE CHURCH HYMNARY, 1898.

Psalms and Paraphrases (1745-81) have been the heritage of Presbyterians. Among their leaves, however out of touch otherwise, all were under the same arbour, and there song notes, pitch-piped by the precentor, before harmoniums or organs voiced the way, blended in the open with remarkable earnestness—sentiment emboldening where skill was lacking. Long before *Hymns Ancient and Modern*, or the S.P.C.K. *Church Hymns*, or the *Hymnal Companion* appeared in England, the United Presbyterians had their *Hymn Book* (one section of the United at first disapproving). The wave of melody gradually overtook the Established and Free Churches, until both possessed their treasuries of sacred song—ancient and modern. The hymn book of the U.P.'s appeared in 1852 (the "Relief" congregations having had one from 1794, long before their union with others). The

Scottish Hymnal of the Church of Scotland had authority in 1870, and *Psalm-versions, Paraphrases and Hymns* were authorised by the Free Church in 1873. Now, after a quarter of a century, the demand for brighter services, when the world around is ringing with song, has eventuated in the compilation by a joint committee of the three Churches of a standard Hymn Book more ancient and more modern, with music as selected by a separate joint committee, the year being signalised by the Assemblies adopting, in conjunction with the Presbyterian Church in Ireland, "THE CHURCH HYMNARY," as printed at the Oxford University Press. (American Hymnals date from 1780.)

There have been harmonies and discords in both hymns and tunes committees, with marches and counter marches, from point to counterpoint, upon the floors of two or three years' Assemblies; but now the faithful of these Churches and their Irish brethren may all sing simultaneously with full authority "The Church's One Foundation," the *Magnificat, Benedictus, Nunc Dimittis, Gloria in Excelsis*, and the *Te Deum*; say with one voice the Lord's Prayer, recite the Apostles' Creed, and respond to the Ten Commandments and the Beatitudes. The *Hymnary* claims to be catholic and comprehensive, including hymns by authors of every branch of the Church from the second century, and the provision made for days and seasons and special occasions, and circumstances, indicate Presbyterian progression in the Christian year, Church order, and observances. The numbers run to 649, inclusive of fourteen doxologies and ancient hymns.

ONE IN SONG AND SORROW.

Again, after a half-a-century, the two General Assemblies have had mutual mourning, not as in 1847 for one who was a luminary in both, but for each other's loss of leaders. What parleying may not do, song and sorrow are effecting—unity in heart. That reached, a common war-cry against the power of evil may find them uniformed and in line. Scotsmen, however, proverbially united all the world over, are in these matters followers of the supporters of their country's arms, remember their coronal unicorns, and accentuate the motto of their land—
Nemo me impune lacessit.

VII.
IN ANGLICAN CHRISTENDOM.

THE ANGLICAN SCOTTISH CHURCH.

LOOKING westward along Princes Street the vision is interrupted by Shandwick Place, which bends to the left. At No. 6, before the translation of the houses into shops (about 1870), was the house Sir Walter Scott occupied in Edinburgh in 1828-30. The last visit he paid to the city was on January 31, 1831, when he stayed with his bookseller in Atholl Crescent just beyond, for the purpose of making his last will.

In the vista is the spire of St. Mary's Cathedral, which is in a straight line with the crown of Princes Street and overtops the streets between, as will also the site-less Usher Hall (*in nubibus*) if erected in Atholl Crescent.

The Cathedral was finished and consecrated in 1879, and is the largest ecclesiastical edifice erected either in England or Scotland since the

Reformation. It is said to be the finest of Sir Gilbert Scott's works, and is founded on the Early Pointed style of architecture. The spire is 275 feet high, and the building itself measures externally 278 feet from the west door to the east window, with a breadth of nave 98½ feet, the transepts being 35 feet from the north to south. Its erection has greatly increased the prestige of the Church in Edinburgh, if not also throughout Scotland, and has afforded a meeting place of worship to Presbyterians that find in it a freedom they did not feel they possessed to the same extent in the somewhat parochially arranged Episcopal churches in the city, the result being a large attendance of many non-Churchmen, particularly at the evening services. Its Cathedral relation has on one or two occasions given unique opportunities for public services. On the occasion of the Diamond Jubilee a public thanksgiving service took place, at which the Lord Provost, Magistrates, and Councillors attended in their civic robes of office, as well as members of the Court and University, and naval and military officers; the band of the Royal Scots regiment uniting with a special orchestra and an augmented choir.

The Cathedral cost upwards of £110,000, the Chapter House £5000. The latter was the legacy to the Church of Mr. H. J. Rollo, the late agent of the Church, who became the agent of

ST. MARY'S CATHEDRAL, EDINBURGH
The Western Spires not yet completed
Block kindly lent by Messrs. Adam & Charles Black, London

the trust estate out of which the Cathedral was built. The testators, the Misses Barbara and Mary Walker, were members of St. Paul's, York Place, long before the original date of their will in 1850, and thus in 1848 would be turning their thoughts to the Church's interest. The estate will, eventually—perhaps within ten or twelve years—have an income of about £8000. But the Church purposes to which it is to be applied are varied. Besides a certain endowment of the clergy, the erection of a chapel eventually styled the Church of St. Mary, and so made the Cathedral Church of St. Mary, was to be the primary duty of the trust. Until the Cathedral was opened several churches attracted strangers and tourists.

St. John's Chapel, Princes Street, and St. Paul's Chapel, York Place (as Episcopal churches were called, and by their vestries always designated in print and on their church books), were the leading places of worship of the Episcopal Church in Scotland, as styled by the present Code of Canons, 1890. Their members were "Chapel" people or folks, or "Chapel" men, or Episcopalians, and largely embraced the nobility and gentry, court and army officers, and a number in Government offices. We read that "on 9th August, 1850, the Queen's mother, her Royal Highness the Duchess of Kent, attended public worship at St. John's Episcopal

Chapel, going from Barry's Hotel, Queen Street, quietly on foot and returning in the same manner "; and when distinguished personages were in Edinburgh over Sunday it was assumed they were at St. John's. After morning service on fine days the upper walk in the West Gardens, now a part of the street, became a fashionable promenade, which ended immediately on the gardens becoming public grounds.

The advent of choral services which accompanied the Oxford movement had hardly touched Scotland in 1848, St. Columba's being the first church to introduce them in Edinburgh in 1847; and St. John's continued to attract, not only Churchpeople and strangers from England, but Presbyterians of æsthetic tastes (not a few of whom were grateful for the Liturgy). This occasionally made it difficult for seatholders to make their way in through the waiting crowd, every seat being let, and applicants waiting year after year. The choir, a mixed one, partly voluntary and partly professional, like those of other churches, occupied, according to common usage, the west gallery, and the anthem was listened to in a truly devotional atmosphere. The responses were audible, and I believe carried the spirit with them more than in most churches of the present day. The sermon was always preached in a black gown, the preacher entering the church so habited at the beginning of the service, or returning to the vestry to change the surplice if he had to read prayers. These remarks are also applicable to St. Paul's, York Place, and perhaps then to all others.

About that period the Communion Office which had been the use and wont of the Scottish congregations at the time of the consecration of Samuel Seabury for the Church in America at Aberdeen in 1784 (*vide* pp. 36, 37), and had been accorded a primary position in relation to the English Office, after the union of the English congregations with the Scottish in 1804, became an element of discord within the Church. Its existence was a reason to some without for denouncing the whole body, whether they understood the points in dispute or not; or were competent to do so even if they had patience to try. This was caused by two movements; one extending the knowledge of the Office among congregations then free to adopt it or leave it alone, others being free to disuse it, and by its adoption in new churches, which also began to drop the title "Chapel" and follow the Oxford revival; the other brought about by the religious circumambience, which postulated a freedom from rubrics by professing attachment to the Church of England as giving a liberty the Church in Scotland was supposed not to be equally able to do, if justifiable; and a reason for dissociating themselves from parties which time showed were

then as rampant and more powerful than any
few individuals in Scotland. The last movement commended itself to malcontents as a
technical justification of the separation, and ad-
duced evidence, as they contended, to Scotchmen and Englishmen that the Episcopal Church
in Scotland was not the same in doctrine as the
Church of England—a statement which, whatever be the merits of either Office, was ever untrue
in respect of the laity of those larger congregations, who as parishioners, so to speak, never
had any opportunity of using the office which
many clergy of the English party would have
preferred. Upon this Communion Office that of
the "Protestant Episcopal Church of America"
is based, and is declared by its presiding Bishop
to be a greater gift by Scotland to the American Church than that of the episcopate; because, while Bishops would have eventually
been given by the Church of England, that
body could never have transmitted any Scottish
Church Liturgy At the Aberdeen Synod of 1811,
it was two of the English clergy in Scotland, pre-
bendaries also of Salisbury and St. Asaph, who
proposed the Canon declaring the Scottish Communion Office to be "the authorised service," and
to be "used at all consecrations of Bishops," and
thus to be of primary authority, which it continued to be until the Canon of 1862, after
which the primary position was given to the

Office as contained in the Prayer Book of the Church of England, the canonically declared " duly authorised Service Book of this Church, according to the sealed books."

About 120 congregations or charges, mostly in the North, have authority to use the Scottish Office. Others, including St. Mary's Cathedral, St. John's, and St. Paul's, in Edinburgh, could only introduce it after such an event as a revision of the Canons by a Provincial Synod called by the Episcopal Synod whenever the circumstances of the Church may appear to the Bishops so assembled to require it. The Episcopal Synod constitutes the first chamber, and the second consists of the Deans, the Principal of the Theological College, the Pantonian Professor of Theology, and representative clergy, one for every ten presbyters or fraction of ten in each diocese.

Besides St. John's and St. Paul's, there were six other "Chapels" in 1848 in Edinburgh, with one in Leith, five in Glasgow, three in Aberdeen, one in Dundee, Perth, and Inverness; towns where more now exist, and number altogether, in place of those twenty, forty-eight churches and twenty missions. There were in all the then Edinburgh diocese sixteen, or including the area then attached to Glasgow, twenty churches. The total number in Scotland was 103; two incumbents of which are alive, Dr.

Walker and Canon Bruce, the rector of Culross, whose ordination jubilee has just been celebrated by his present and former parishioners. There are now 337 clergy, 171 churches, 167 missions, &c.

THE SCOTTISH SEES.

For the information of my American friends, whose dioceses have a total of 82 Bishops, 4776 clergy, 5339 parishes, 993 missions, I may say that anciently there were two Archbishops and twelve Bishops in Scotland, with a corresponding number of sees. Scarcity of people, limitation of land, and lack of intercommunication with some parts would leave to us no room in the present day for the multiplication of parishes, mission territories, and sees, as the American Church is able to do by a kind of electric power, so that in the Church's disestablished condition*—their gain in 1784—there are but seven dioceses in the Scottish Church—the archiepiscopal sees of St. Andrews and Glasgow taking rank with the others—these being united, as Aberdeen, Caithness, and Orkney; Argyll and the Isles; Brechin; Edinburgh; Glasgow and Galloway; Moray and Ross; St. Andrews, Dunkeld, and Dunblane.

Iona was the seat of the Primacy of the Scottish Church till 849. It was then Dunkeld

* See Bp. of Edinburgh's Paper, Birmingham Congress.

and next St. Andrews, in 905, which see had its first Archbishop in 1466, its last in 1684-1704. After Bishop Rose, of Edinburgh (1708-20), the presiding Bishop was called *Primus*.

St. Andrews was the primatial see in 1471. Before that date it had some pre-eminence, and prelates a thousand years back. Half-a-thousand before that again, as the legend has it, Regulus, a Greek monk, brought so much of the relics of St. Andrew the Apostle from Patræ, a city of Achaia, the only one of the twelve of Achaia which still exists, where they were preserved.

The see of Edinburgh was erected in 1633 (the diocese being formed out of that of St. Andrews), within which the city and five counties adjoining were included. St. Giles' Church was the chief, and would have become the Cathedral (by which name it now generally goes), but for ecclesiastical changes and political complications with Church interests. It was probably originally built about the ninth century, while the present edifice dates from the twelfth. St. Andrew became the titular saint of Scotland, and St. Giles that of Edinburgh, the latter being a native of Ancient Athens.

I pass over the earlier history of Christianity in Scotland, from its supposed introduction in the second century—St. Ninian, St. Palladius, St. Serf, St. Ternan, St. Kentigern or Mungo,

St. Patrick, St. Columba, St. Aidan, and St. Cuthbert, with the *Candida Casa* and Iona—and avoid ground so marshy as to require skill to determine land from water, and ballast and balance to keep to the stepping stones of truthful narration.

The occupants of the seven sees in 1848 were Bishops William Skinner (cons. 1815, Primus 1841); Alexander Ewing (1847); Alexander Penrose Forbes (1847); Charles Hughes Terrot (1841, Primus 1857); Walter Trower (1848, Bishop of Gibraltar, 1859); David Low (1819); and Patrick Torry (1808). These are all long ago dead, and seven others their successors. Bishop Eden, Moray and Ross (1851), was Primus 1862-86. Five of the present seven prelates are third in succession within the half-century, and one the fourth, the Primus the next of Brechin, and second in the Primacy to Bishop Skinner, Bishop Terrot having preceded him in 1872—twenty in all. A similar tabulation might be made of deans and synod-clerks, all gone. Nor is there a single survivor of the whole Anglican Episcopate of the time when I first had to learn or handle their names.

The Scottish Episcopal chapels in Edinburgh were St. Paul's, York Place—Right Rev. Bishop Terrot, and Rev. Francis Garden (Sub-Dean of the Chapel Royal 1859); St. John's—Very Rev. Dean Ramsay and Rev.

Berkeley Addison ; St. George's—Rev. T. G. S. Suther (Bishop of Aberdeen 1857); St. James's, Broughton Place—Rev. J. W. Ferguson (Synod-Clerk); St. Paul's, Carrubber's Close—Rev. E. B. Field ; St. Peter's, Roxburgh Place—Rev. G. Coventry ; Trinity, Dean Bridge—Rev. Robert Payne Smith (Dean of Canterbury 1871); St. Columba's—Rev. John Alexander ; St. James's, Leith—Rev. James A. White ; Dio. Chaplain—Rev. Franklin Tonkin.

Edward Bannerman Ramsay, after serving as curate in St. George's (1824), incumbent of Old St. Paul's, Carrubber's Close (1826), and assistant in St. John's (1827), succeeded Bishop Sandford in the incumbency of St. John's in 1830, and became Dean in 1846. Until the day of his death, in December 1873, he was loved by his flock, his Church, and his country, and his name as a Scotchman is more or less known beyond his native land. In 1842, when the Queen visited Scotland, the Dean wrote: "This day, 4th September, I read prayers and preached before her Majesty, and also dined and sat near Prince Albert and the Queen. In the evening presented to the Queen and Prince Albert, and introduced to Sir Robert Peel." At the end of the same month the Bishop of London (Blomfield) was in Edinburgh, and the Dean accompanied him to Glenalmond, to see the proposed site for Trinity College.

The Canonical Representative Church Council of to-day is the successor of the Scottish Episcopal Church Society, formed in 1838, mainly by the efforts and influence of the good Dean. Its office-bearers in 1848 were the Duke of Buccleuch as Patron; the Duke of Roxburghe, Marquis of Queensberry, Earls of Morton, Airlie, Home, Rosebery; Viscount Strathallan, Lord Forbes, Lord Saltoun, Lord Douglas, as Vice-Patrons; the Primus as President; and as Vice-Presidents the other Bishops, The Warden of Trinity College (the late Bishop Wordsworth), fifteen peers, baronets, and gentry; with a general committee of clergy, and a body of leading laymen, reading the names of which makes the heart sad and sick and lonely, for it seems as if one would never look upon their like again. One only of the list, now that the Hon. B. F. Primrose and the Right Hon. William E. Gladstone, ex-Premier, have passed away, survives in the person of Mr. John Mackenzie, ex-treasurer of Bank of Scotland, who, along with Mr. G. A. Esson, held the treasurership, the general secretary and moving power and pleader being Dean Ramsay, and the assistant-treasurers R. Grant & Son.

The same names recur on other lists; the 34 on the Scotch Episcopal Friendly Society have long ago disappeared from ordinary ken; likewise those on the S.P.C.K. (except the depot, still at 107 Princes Street), and the Glasgow Committee with its depot of the past ; also the 36 names of the Missionary Association (for the S.P.G., C.M.S., and Jewish Mission).

Reference being made to Trinity College, and also to Mr. Gladstone, it should be stated that that eminent statesman and Mr. James R. Hope, barrister-at-law, were the two distinguished men who originated the idea of the College, and that both, of Scottish blood, were pupils at Christ Church, Oxford, of the distinguished scholar and first Warden at Glenalmond, Charles Wordsworth, afterwards Bishop of St. Andrews. One of the incumbents of St. Paul's, Edinburgh, is also noted to have become Sub-Dean of the Chapel Royal. That up to 1840 could not have been possible. In that year, however, an act was passed placing the Scottish Episcopal Churches in *legal* communion as well as in the formerly ecclesiastical communion, and now we not only have Scottish Bishops and presbyters in St. Paul's, Westminster Abbey, and other English cathedrals and churches, but this year the Bishop of St. Andrews preached in the Chapel Royal.

Trinity College, Glenalmond, was fully opened fifty years ago ; the public school department commenced the year before. The present Marquis of Lothian (lately Secretary of State for Scotland) was the first boy to arrive. Mr. W. E.

Gladstone* was the last of the original trustees and members of Council. Several Wardens are dead, and probably all the original staff, Bishops Barry and Browne being later.

INFLUENCES EXTERNAL AND INTERNAL.

The spiritual independence of the body ecclesiastic formulated by the Free Church roused interest in the constitution of the Episcopal Church, the natural effect of which was to lead many thoughtful persons to an intelligent study of Church history and the nature of Church Orders. The Episcopal Church thus received some adherents from the Presbyterians; and, had the present greater elasticity in the Anglican Communion then obtained, prejudices against many things which are now regarded seemly and in order would have disappeared. As time has gone on the Presbyterians have adapted their services to the growing desires of their own people in these very things. To many who regarded the non-elasticity of the Church then as a barrier to work, their sphere of Christian usefulness as it then lay before them was a sacred trust which they could not lightly leave, and the unseen heroism of those who had to wrestle with their conscience amid the researches

* The delay in passing the later proofs, accounted for at page 330, gives opportunity to refer to the death of this illustrious statesman on Ascension Day, May 19, and his public interment in Westminster Abbey on Whit-Sunday Eve. On the day of the funeral a special service, appropriate to the event, was held at St. Mary's Cathedral, and also at St. Giles' Cathedral.

of their intellect is not for others to understand. In those days Scottish youths lived in a religious atmosphere. Taught in school to read and reverence the Bible, they continued to know it at home and practise it in their lives. Bible axioms, not business ones, were the standard of thought, word, and deed. They tried to live the Sunday services, and endeavoured to serve society and superiors, to commend their ways to equals, and be examples to any inferiors. Their effort was to worship God as a Spirit in spirit and in truth, and to follow in all things the Great Exemplar. The golden rule, applied in all work, and by which business was conducted on Christian principles, was not subordinated to that which would promote even good with baits on business principles of self-advertisement and aggrandisement. A desire to do justice to all was equal to, if it did not excel, any determination to have justice done to themselves. "It is better to suffer wrong than to do it" (*Plato*).

The love of mercy prompted its growth at all corners of the character in consideration for the interests, necessities, and feelings of others, while humbleness of walk and conversation lent a sympathic bond. Non-church-goers were unheard of, or were, at least, "not respectable." The air, too, was charged with Scottish religious enthusiasm, which in the wisdom or worthiness of its cause might not commend itself to all alike, but was of a kind which alone could have inspired in those stirred to what they regarded as a sense of duty, the creation in 1843 of a whole Church, when 470 poured into the street to bear the responsibility of financing a new denomination throughout the land. When Lord Jeffrey heard of that he said that there was not another country on earth where such a deed could be done. There was heroism too on the unpopular side ; and even in the Episcopal Church had many to stand the false charge against the Church of Popery, papal aggression in those days being a stalking-horse on platform and in pulpit, as Romish practices are to-day, when history appears to be repeating itself.

TWO DEANS.

The late Dean Montgomery, who succeeded Dean Ramsay in the Deanery of Edinburgh in 1873, was fourteen years incumbent of St. Paul's Church, York Place, after his curacy there, which covered a period of twenty years. On the consecration of St. Mary's Cathedral in 1879, he became (*qua* Dean) the incumbent. In the breadth of their sympathies for whatever made for the spread of Christianity, in their freedom from party as far as their discretionary wisdom required or permitted, and in the width of the circle in which they were esteemed by those that are without as well as throughout their Church, the two Deans, were like minded and alike revered. But for advanced age or infirmity, both by universal desire would have adorned the Episcopal office—they were both indeed unmitred Bishops—but the names by which they are endeared to all are those of Dean Ramsay and Dean Montgomery.

With these names I draw to a close. The one Dean I constantly saw from the beginning of my business life, covering a period of twenty-four years; the other knew me and mine for forty years. As, home from school and fresh from a father's grave, closed on an Easter Eve, the ideal of life began with the estimate of one, so it seems now to be ebbing with the same ideal of the other.

In 1865 Dean Ramsay did me the honour of being one of the clerical speakers at the public breakfast of the first Y.M.C.A. British Conference held in Scotland, his presence being a token of appreciation of the object to which I had early lent myself; and the late Dean did me a similar service when he admitted me and those with me into the Brotherhood of St. Andrew, and so in that and many ways supported the Brotherhood idea, which under one name or another is but the altruistic endeavour, in organised form, more or less obligatory on all according to their opportunities, to spread Christ's kingdom here on earth by following Him after the manner of St. Andrew—discerning the light, and endeavouring through prayer, word, act, and example, to bring others to know it.

THE BROTHERHOOD OF ST. ANDREW.

The Brotherhood of St. Andrew supplies a thread of this *omnibus* booklet from title to colophon ; but, running through half-a-century, as a portion of the contents does, that period embraces two other movements into which in their earliest years I locally threw myself. It has not fallen within the scope of the little volume to allude in any way to these. In both, however, I experienced discouragement, if obloquy indeed were not cast upon my efforts. Forty years after, Isaac Pitman, the inventor of the one, and George Williams, the founder of the other, had received the honour of knighthood. I had faith in the future of their creations, and my expectations were exceeded. I was present as a delegate at the International Shorthand Congress to celebrate the jubilee of Pitman's invention and the ter-centenary of shorthand, opened by the Earl of Rosebery, and honoured by others ; and, *inter alia*, was one of the invited guests at the Mansion House luncheon given by the Lord Mayor of London. I was not able to be at the International Jubilee and Thirteenth

International Conference of the other, when the present Archbishop of Canterbury preached at the special service in Westminster Abbey, and the Bishop of Ripon at the thanksgiving service in St. Paul's Cathedral; when, also, the Castle and grounds of Windsor Castle were opened for the social celebration of the event. I need hardly advert to the strides both of these movements have made since those years of disfavour around one. One has invaded law, literature, and Parliament, and entered the army and every kind of office, school, and institution; the other has extended into more than twenty-five countries in Europe, Asia, Africa, and America; so that the associations, which in the year 1855, when I joined, numbered 322, with 27,860 members, had grown in 1894 to 5147, with a membership of half-a-million; 1410 of which were American, with a quarter million members, 291 buildings, and a property value of £3,200,000 ($16,000,000).

Into neither of these movements did I thrust myself, but in both I spent and was spent according to my local opportunities and capacity, because I regarded as a duty the obligation then presented to me to take an oar. They were both outside Church relations, though the latter was for the Church and Christian work as conceived by Churchmen, the founder being such, and the first secretary soon being ordained a clergyman of the Church of England. If the Church looked askance it was not the fault of that association. As a delegate to Church authority I know what was done. The signs and bearings of the times, and consequent unreadiness for the co-operation, now desiderated, in some quarters, explains but does not alter the circumstances.

When Churchmen moved in the name of the Church, under the highest ecclesiastical patronage, and in imitation of the Y.M.C.A., the London Diocesan Association for the Welfare of Youth included the Y.M.C.A., as well as the Y.M.F.S., as objects for their promotion alongside of the Church of England Y.M.S. To avoid confusion I will not further refer to these, except to say that when elected *nolens volens* into Y.M.F.S. activities, I naturally regarded my vocation then as a work given me for the Church. It was thus the instrument which bound me to do whatever in me lay to discover or formulate the Church's relation to young men, and to determine their sphere in the economy of the Church. In the fulfilment of that duty, having heard of the Brotherhood originated in Chicago by a President of the Y.M.C.A., then I think on its International Council, and five years ago, if not still, treasurer of the finest as it was the first Y.M.C.A., I told others of it. While conscious of my own unimportance, I tried office-bearers of the above named Church societies to have it introduced to England, through which I hoped Scotland also would benefit. As it happened, England rather received it through Scotland, though, like the American Church, which has now so far outdistanced its Scottish earliest Episcopal origin, the English Brotherhood has naturally outrun the Scottish humble beginnings, opportunities, and encouragements.

BASIS OF OPINION—EPISCOPAL AND ARCHI-EPISCOPAL, 1894-98.

On page 82 I tell what faith I recited to the founder. That my judgment was right, and the appropriation of the words justified, I was lately further convinced when comparing impressions with the Bishop of Newcastle—his lordship, after speaking of the two opportunities he had had of forming an opinion of lay work in the American Church, concluding by using the self-same words. Here I may say that I have received the best opinions of many Bishops of the Church of England. Especially would I emphasise the personally received words of confidence from the Archbishop of York, the Archbishop of Ontario, the oldest and senior Bishop in the British Empire, and the Archbishop of Sydney, severally representing their portions of the Anglican Communion. I recognise, too, the words in the Archbishop of Canterbury's letter read at the Buffalo International Convention as similar to those his Grace addressed to me in 1893. I have also to add the forward opinion the Archbishop of Jamaica has adopted, and his endorsement of my Norwich Congress paper by communicating it to the Jamaica press soon after it was delivered, as the first of a series of articles on the Order.

Surely, then, I must be right, seeing also that a Canon of Westminster—Canon Gore—as the result of his contact with the American Brotherhood in and out of Convention, has this year dedicated his work on the Epistle to the Ephesians to its founder and president, "because the society represented a brave attempt to realise some of the chief practical lessons which the Epistle was meant to enforce." In a note he sets forth the idea of the Order, and its need amongst us for the promotion of a deeper idea of the obligation of Church membership, calculated, as he thinks it is, to revive the true spirit of laymanship. In that note the Canon says, "The brethren are pervaded by a spirit of frank religious profession and devotion. There appears to be a general tone among them of reality and good sense." He further says, "the greatest care must be taken that it should develop as a properly lay movement," and "it has successfully avoided becoming either a party society or a society rent by factions."

The Bishop of Glasgow in his Convention sermon to the Scottish Brotherhood, drew attention to the late Archbishop of Canterbury's pulpit utterance on the Brotherhood Idea. In the last sermon preached by his Grace in St. Patrick's Cathedral, Armagh, the Archbishop said :—

"It cannot be for nothing that in America there has sprung up a wide association of men of every rank and kind of employment, each one of whom pledges himself to bring a brother to Christ."

In these words the Archbishop was alluding to the Brotherhood, the American delegates from which his Grace had so cordially received but a few weeks before; and this was his last sermon, but a few days before his beautiful death at Hawarden.

To such ecclesiastical witnesses there has been added the honour extended to the International delegates, who were received at the White House, by His Excellency the President of the United States, with the members of the Senate and Congress, at a grand function on the occasion of the Buffalo Convention.

In imitation of the Brotherhood of St. Andrew has been instituted the Brotherhood of Andrew and Philip, an inter-denominational society, and on its model has been organised the Daughters of the King, while in imitation thereof has followed the King's Daughters among the denominations. Further, its constitution and operations have been commended to "the Young Men's Guild of the Church of Scotland," in Conference assembled, by its founder and president, the Professor of Biblical Criticism and Antiquities in the Edinburgh University, Rev. Dr. Charteris, a former Moderator of the General Assembly. It is an Order, not a society, binding its members together by two rules—Prayer and Service—both concentrated on and radiating from the Church as a divine institution, whose material visibility is a tangible object to point to, but whose reality is to be manifested in the everyday lives and opportunities of the members.

THE DAUGHTERS OF THE KING.

My Brotherhood relations have naturally led to my acquaintance with the Order of the Daughters of the King, and I have thus had correspondence and converse with some of its officers, both in America and in England, and have communicated information respecting it to several in the south during the past two or three years. I have the honour of acquaintance with the President of the Order in England, inaugurated at the Church House, Westminster, last March, and have possessed since last October what I may call a mandate from her to aid its extension as much as I may in England. Thus may I fairly add a few words respecting it.

Its rules run parallel with the Brotherhood's, the distinctive features being that it is (1) a mission of women to women, who, without leaving their daily occupations, are engaged as missioners in purely spiritual and aggressive work; (2) the pledging of all members, at an admission office in church, to the rules of Prayer and Service; and (3) the ruling aim of the members is to give, not to get, and for each member to concentrate her efforts upon individuals until they be brought under the influence of the Church. There are said to be 12,000 members in America; these being distributed in 450 Chapters throughout the Church. The Hon. Rev. J. Adderley admitted eight members of the Alpha Chapter in England in March, and the Rev. C. J. Ridgeway six more in April.

The President of the Order in England is Mrs. E. H. Parnell, widow of the late Dean of Laramie, who, though at present in America, returns to inaugurate the work, and to fulfil the wish of her late husband here, the late Dean having been very closely identified with it. The idea has fired a lady of indomitable energy to become the honorary secretary (Miss Granger, a strong Churchwoman of considerable experience in organisation). *The Royal Cross* is the organ of the Order for Great Britain and Ireland, and is published quarterly (Church Printing Co. Ltd.). Advice from the highest authorities in England has been sought, with the result that the Archbishop of Canterbury has become Patron, the Bishop of London, Visitor, and the Archdeacon of Middlesex, Warden, while the Chaplain is the Rev. C. J. Ridgeway, late incumbent of St. Paul's, Edinburgh. Various English Bishops have signified their interest and approval.

The opinions of two of the most prominent Bishops in the United States are as follows; the first being the Presiding Bishop of the American Church. The Bishop of Connecticut wrote—

My Dear Friends,—The longer I have watched the work of your Association, the more convinced I am of its value to the Church, and that in many ways. I especially desire here and now to thank you most cordially for the help you have been to me personally and officially, and to express the hope that the coming year may find you accomplishing as much for the Church and her divine work as you have done in years past.— Affectionately your friend and Bishop,

To the Daughters of the King. J. WILLIAMS.
May 11, 1897.

And the Bishop of Delaware wrote—

April 23, 1897.

Being familiarly styled the Bishop of the Daughters of the King, it will not, I trust, be considered amiss if I comply with the request formally made that I should in some such way as this commend the Order to the notice and favour of our mother Church of England. It is not an order that is temporal, or financial, or even social. As to women, it is in the Church in America what the Brotherhood of St. Andrew is to men. Its constitution is simple, yet sufficient. Its plan of operation is free from distracting influences. Its Rule is that of prayer and service. In its membership are to be found some of the most devout, capable, and influential women in the American Church. It does not in any way conflict with that other admirable organisation for women—The Girls' Friendly Society, but is rather its helpful companion. In many dioceses and parishes it has already been found by the clergy to be a valuable aid in the development of the spiritual life of our people. As such I heartily commend it to the good-will and co-operation of all to whom the contents of this letter may be made known. LEIGHTON COLEMAN.

"THE BANNER OF ST. ANDREW."

The Banner of St. Andrew, called until lately *The Cross of St. Andrew*, is a monthly paper devoted to the interests of the Brotherhood in England, or more comprehensively in Great Britain and Ireland, as its heading formerly indicated. Special news relating to the Order in this country appear in its pages, and also such proceedings and utterances in England as bear on the idea and the relation of laymen to spiritual work. Mr. Henry Clark, its editor, has laboured enthusiastically for more than four years in the propagation of the organisation in Britain, the *Banner* or *Cross* having reached its fiftieth number this Easter. In the earlier years of the paper, when we were almost daily correspondents, I had the pleasure of being associated with him in its preparation and issue, Liverpool and Edinburgh being its nominal publication places. Towards its cost of production I contributed for a time, Mr. Clark taking the graver responsibility, as I had my own connected with other Brotherhood literature and the Handbook, the last issue of which is now a *vade mecum* for Scotland alone, until the two handbook committees have issued their manual in common.

It is an axiom of the Order that it follows the Church's organisation, and thus wherever there is a Central Council in any branch of the Church, the chapters within it fall into relationship therewith. In this way a stream severs me from the English brethren as it did not before their Central Council was fully and formally organised at the Church House, Westminster, in June 1896, when they in England and I in Scotland bade one another an official farewell in the presence of the American delegation, bearing letters commendatory of the Brotherhood from the Presiding and other Bishops of the American Church, as well as from Bishops of the Canadian addressed to the Archbishops in England and other Bishops in both countries.

The American Church has never forgotten in its growing greatness its earliest tie to the Scottish Church. May I hope that the English Brotherhood will remember its Scottish relative, and that the latter may receive a reflex share of the progressive prosperity in England, where there are now sixty chapters with five hundred members, the earliest of which received their provisional charters from the Scottish Council. It may not be known that the first English Chapter was originated by two leading Scottish missioners,* and that two others † were the direct work of two of the junior Scottish clergy resident for a time in England, one of which was the first to address a body of English clergy on the subject, the other the first to name it at a Church Congress (1893).

Easters and jubilees are seasons of hope and review. In this, but for these leaves, relatively a fallow year, I have been looking back over the land I live in and forward to the world that is to come. The pages speak of some in the one now passed to the other. Alone here, many are mine in the Home beyond. They relate to times when I foresaw the development of two ideas. In this to me Jubilee-Easter, I look back to the beginning of the Brotherhood, and confidently forward to its future ; for an Order

* Rev. W. M. Meredith, Crieff, and Rev. H. Erskine Hill, Maryhill.
† Rev. W. Magee Tuke, Huntly; Rev. J. B. Hill, St. Mary's Cathedral, Edinburgh. The Bishop of Glasgow was, in 1893, the first Bishop to preach the Brotherhood Sermon, and the first to admit members.

that seeks to maintain active followers of Christ in an individual capacity, and to bind them in heart and sympathy as Churchworkers throughout the world of Anglican Christendom and Communion, and as far as may be in co-operation with all working for the expansion of Christ's kingdom, must have a future.

As a member of the Brotherhood International Council, it is my bounden duty to pray for its peace and prosperity, and its propagation throughout every land, as well in India, Africa, and other colonies and countries from which inquiries have reached me, as at home. Its fruitage in England or in Scotland, or where in Ireland I had touched, I cannot expect to hear much of, or to know long. My turn is coming to be added to the convention roll of those who have "entered into rest," in hope of a place on the great Easter roll when they who have known one another here will know each other better, and Him they followed.

Eastertide  *MDCCCXCVIII.*

VIII.

AUTUMN LEAVES.

IT has required the opportunities of the summer to collect the data given in the forty pages of interscript mentioned at page 330; some friends having only suggested these after the completed "copy," as at Easter, was in proof. There have also been earlier and later interpolations, the result of the inquiring interest of others. The main authorities for the former have been a century's city directories turned inside out, and read forwards, backwards, and zigzagwards.

Originating in a jubilee presentation by employees, and outgrowing the idea of a Christmas brochure for these—old and new—and for friends—American and Athenian—an unpretentious desire has thus developed into a little volume, the earlier portion belonging to last autumn. Of this origin and progression its form bears evidence, and its composite character is therein accounted for. The diversity of its contents may be allowed, I hope, on the ground, that in these days the magazine has accustomed people to handle what may be of some interest to them alongside of much that is not. According to the Peter quoted at page 297, one cover may serve several interests at once. Containing something desired, it may offer something else that might not otherwise have been seen, but which may be acceptable because it is there asserting no claim. The grave may therefore allow the gayer parts, the gay the graver; the serious may consort with the literary and the social, while much that is personal may be forgiven in the more general. If friends in one hemisphere find nothing novel concerning their own, they may be induced to glance into a portion of the other, the first half being designed for those at home, and the last for western friends and junior Athenians.

For words spoken that framed my thoughts, friends are responsible. The opening line gives those of one followed by what they led to, and the preface explains how they ended in print. Those of another, apart from these, levelled the retrospect on Princes Street, while a third endorsed an opinion that I might find a theme in people I had met.

I have not attempted the last suggestion, but the men and women I have known were factors in my impression of the past and my estimate of the world around me; while half-a-century's outlook on Princes Street has furnished a fair picture of the city which I thus offer to others, dreaming, as my friend and fellow-burgess does, of the city's archaic yore and magnificent everness. The respective sections intertwine but an ordinary life affected by influences such as make up the volume of everyone's being. In it the memories of the past, tinged by Time's crisping hand, golden amidst the evening colours of the autumnal sun, are pleasant to look upon in the parterre of the heart, and are riches in the treasury of the soul.

It is again Autumn, and I am loitering where in the spring-time of life * I learned the joys of association and union with great-souled men, who "look not every man on his own things, but every man also on the things of others," on things distant as well as things near—telescopic and microscopic men. Again, also for the sixth time, I am in Congress † with the mother-

* By coincidence I found myself on the 28th September, after a lapse of forty years, in Leeds, and at the Y.M.C.A., on the anniversary of the first Y.M.C.A. Conference in Great Britain, when the then Bishop of Ripon preached the opening sermon in St. George's Church, and I acted as joint-secretary. My preliminary correspondence—Leeds, Liverpool, Chester, Edinburgh *versus* London—shows that the parent association opposed the idea to the last, notwithstanding which the founder, its powerful secretary, and public leaders came down. They were destined to be converted, and at the farewell meeting they offered a cordial invitation to another and greater Conference at London in the following year. The London parent Association was formed on 6th June, 1844, by twelve young men. The name was determined on the 4th July. The first International Conference in Great Britain was held at London in 1862. The first British Conference held in Scotland was that at Edinburgh in 1864.

† The first of the Church Congresses was held in 1861 at Cambridge, and 1862 at Oxford. This year is the thirty-eighth. They meet in large cities, and that for 1899 has been arranged for London, October 10-14, at the Royal Albert Hall and elsewhere, St. Paul's, Westminster, &c.

Church of Anglican Christendom; and yet, again, I am once more, as oft before and long ago, beside the Minster* of many centuries' existence, and of still more of association with the past—with the little wooden church or oratory of St. Peter's of the seventh century, in which the King of Northumbria, Eadwin or Edwin, was baptized on Easter Eve, April 11, 627, and around which the Cathedral arose.

In York, I am in the city which was the centre from which Christianity was dispersed throughout Northumbria, brought about by the coming of Ethelburga, given to King Edwin for Queen, that he might learn the gentle grace of Christ, transform the idols of man into dust, and proclaim throughout his kingdom the worship of God uncreate. She, who was the Christian-nurtured daughter of Ethelbert—first Christian King of Kent, baptized by Augustine, first Archbishop of Canterbury—who came to Edwin under the spiritual tuition of Paulinus, created Bishop for the occasion—first Archbishop of York.

Yorkshire, the capital county of Northumbria, at the time of its conversion, I am reminded by the Bishop of Bristol † at the Congress, and it is interesting at this time to reflect, claims the credit of the whole conversion of England; the first point being that they were fair-haired

* First visited in 1862. St. Paul's and Westminster I had seen in 1851.
† Formerly Theological Tutor, Trinity College, Glenalmond, Scotland.

YORK MINSTER

Reproduced from copyright photograph by G. W. Wilson & Co., Ltd., Aberdeen, by special arrangement.

Yorkshire boys' whom Gregory noticed in the slave market at Rome, who said they came from Deira, which was the southern part of Northumbria, Bernicia being the northern portion, of which York was the capital—Professor Collins showing that the missioners from Iona and from the Continent were both nursing mothers, and yet that the work of the sons and successors of Columba deserves the loftiest language; to the labour of those from Iona being largely due the strength, learning, and vigour that characterised Northumbria. By Canon Savage I learn in the same connection that later on there were wisdom and originality in Aidan and Oswald, respectively Bishop and King—the national Church receiving from the Columban rather than from the Gregorian Mission many of the most distinguished characteristics, common-sense methods, and generous elasticity, and the principle of "combination in diversity." King Oswald, I find, because of his virtues, commanded people of four languages—the Britons, Picts, Scotch, English; that he sent to Scotland, where, at Iona, he was brought up, for a godly preacher, and that so came Aidan in 635, from the western Scottish island, to found a second island Iona at Lindisfarne, he being made Bishop for the purpose—thus first Bishop of Durham. Aidan again, a man above the level of the age, of wonderful moderation, and not carried away with the nice and trivial points of theology, which more desperately affected those of later times, by easy doctrines, and yielding in things ceremonial, made more Christians by far, though fewer disputants. Speaking Scotch, or broken English at first, Aidan had the King for interpreter, who thus devotedly and in humility added authority to Aidan's words. His brotherhood was strengthened by recruits from the Irish and Scots. According to Bede many from the Scots came daily into Britain, and with great devotion preached the word of faith to those Angles over whom King Oswald reigned. It is said that, while Augustine was the Apostle of Kent, Aidan was the Apostle of England. He selected twelve Anglican boys to train. Among them was Eata, his successor; Cedd, Bishop of Mercia; and Chad, Bishop of York, afterwards of Mercia.

But in Northumbria I am still in my homeland, not as it now is, but as it was then, and as late as 956, when England, stretching to the shores of the Forth, included the Lothians; Candida Casa too being one of the four bishoprics of Northumbria, with York, Lindisfarne, and Hexham. Though in this part I am thus linked to the Royal Capital of the North, to which Section VI. is devoted, and to the huge castle that "there holds its state," for, following Maitland's *History of Edinburgh* and other authorities, the Fortress of the Hill of Agnes, at a later period styled *Castrum Puellarum*, became Edwin's northernmost fortress, and was that castle which thus received the name of Edinburgh or Edwinsburgh, according to the charter granted to Holyrood Abbey by David I. in 1128.*

And now these days, and the leaves that rustle near and through the Yorkshire abbeys, as they must have done here and throughout old Bernicia, and around Edwin's castle, so long ago, remind me of those bright October days in Washington, so near and yet so far, which form the first leaves of my loiterings westward. The Bishop of Rochester has declared that he will not all his life forget the Buffalo Convention, and surely I may ever remember the Washington one, where autumnal leaves rustled around and gathered about so much that was true and honest, pure, lovely, and of good report, to think on, learn, receive, and do during the days

---

* The Scottish Regalia, consisting of a jewelled crown, sceptre, and sword of State, dating probably from the reign of Robert Bruce, after strange adventures in Scotland during troublous times from 1651, first under the charge of the Earl Marischal, their custodian by birth-right, were deposited in a locked chest within a locked room in the Castle, the keys of neither of which were ever found. Thus concealed from 1707, unseen by three generations, and unknown to two, royal authority was at last obtained, chiefly through Sir Walter Scott's influence, to re-open the room, and have the King's smith force the locks of the oak chest. When the regalia was thus discovered in 1817 (with which was also found the Lord Treasurer's rod of office), the crown was examined for cleaning by Mr. Marshall, the founder of Messrs. W. Marshall & Co., and that jeweller tried hard to place it upon Sir Walter's head, but he watched him too much to allow its being done. Sir Walter Scott, however, has won an enduring crown in the hearts of all Scotland-loving people, and has created a kingdom all his own, and a Scot-land where he will reign as long as the English language and Scottish hills endure.

of one's life. Particularly may I recall it now, for not far from that beautiful city, just my quiet hour's distance retraced, the American Brotherhood is again in session at Baltimore— 1240 representative Brotherhood men of life and action, from all parts of the States, and with them several of the Bishops and public men of distinction. I follow them in fancy as they proceed through their programme of a Quiet Day and Holy Communion, discussion and spirit-stirring converse, and I am in touch and sympathy with all their thoughts, for I, too, am among three thousand fellow-Churchmen in English Congress with the archiepiscopal heads and many more Bishops and leaders of religious thought for the times. There I—perhaps the only layman that crosses the Tweed south or the Atlantic west for such gatherings—am listening to the Bishop of Glasgow on brotherly love, words which the revised version has translated into what was in my own heart when in invisible presence I sent them one afternoon across the dividing western waters, impotent to stem the science current of spiritual feeling— love of the brethren, enthusiasm for the Church's welfare in its Divine reality, not in a mechanical or merely conventional impersonation.

I turn to Dr. Stephen's *History of the Scottish Church*, founded on more than a hundred high authorities, and there I read—" The Iona brotherhood were not mere recluses seeking a shelter from the stress of life and the temptations of the world, but a Christian community *banded together for the extension of Christ's kingdom among the nations.* They were, in their own language, '*militia* of Christ,' pledged 'athletics,' vowed to a life's warfare against sin and ignorance . . . 'until the day dawned, and pagan shadows fled away."

To compare a modern order with an ancient, relating it to the present-day life and opportunities, with one a thousand years ago so related to the nations, is to suggest some similitude between them. Though far removed in time and distance, in devotedness the St. Andrew's has some resemblance to the Columban Order, when its members are faithful and earnest ; and in its lower plane may give service to the Church. There is a parallelism in their constitution. Compare with the above the constitution of the Brotherhood in America, Canada, England, Scotland, Australia, Jamaica, and outlying places of the Anglican Communion. It is a voluntary society of business men banded together for the extension of Christ's kingdom among young men, no less forming nations in the present day, near and around to each individual member, but as distant from Church porch, and perhaps from Christian grace, as tribes or races were from the island of Iona.

St. Columba was not a Bishop. He disclaimed episcopal rank. The St. Andrew's chapters consist of laymen who disclaim clerical functions. Like Bishops in the Columban Order, clergymen may be members of their chapter (which, so far, unlike the Ionan plan in respect to episcopal rule, must be subject to the clerical power of the parish). The only admission is by the formal act of a Bishop or clergyman (a form of service in church being arranged). Not in any national Brotherhood council is a chapter chartered unless so related, members being elected by the chapter.

Dr. Stephen writes—"The education of the young is the hope of preserving the Church. The permanent strength of any Church lies in a native ministry. Foreign hands may enkindle the fire." May I extend the idea to laymen's influence among laymen, and add with other meaning his other words, "but native hands and hearts are needed to renew and sustain it."

As Oswald turned his eyes to Iona, where he had himself learnt the Christian religion, for missionary help in the conversion of his people, I may be forgiven, in my affection for the American Church, my love of the Brotherhood there, and my effort to translate their words and ways to those around me ; and may naturally look to it for a native Brotherhood extension throughout England and Scotland.

There are two prayers supreme in Brotherhood circles—the Collect for St. Andrew's Day, and the Prayer for the Unity of the Church. The spirit of one is in *The Christian Year*, St. Andrew's Day :—

" First seek thy Saviour out, and dwell
  Beneath the shadow of His roof,
  Till thou hast scann'd His features well,
  And known Him for the Christ by proof.

" Then potent with the spell of heaven
  Go, and thine erring brother gain,
  Entice him home to be forgiven,
  Till he, too, see his Saviour plain.

" No fading frail memorial give
  To soothe his soul when thou art gone ;
  But wreaths of hope for aye to live,
  And thoughts of good together done.

" That so, before the judgment seat,
  Though changed and glorified each face,
  Not unremembered ye may meet,
  For endless ages to embrace."

In Keble's lines are carved the Brotherhood ideal which these leaves would unfold. In the spirit of the Prayer for Unity I have desired to write them, whether as a neighbour, citizen, or cosmopolitan—a merchant, or Christian ; for wherever the spiritually minded man in one Brotherhood touches his brother in the other, there is an underlying union that binds closer and closer. In this influence of the Brotherhood in the American Church, and that Church's in the nation, with its majority of the seven supreme judges, dwell, I am assured, hopes in the Anglo-American Alliance and in the reconciliation of Churches.

BROTHERHOOD and UNITY are words proclaimed around. One, but a few years ago, lay cloistered and corded and girdled, known only where the vesper bell was heard. It is now ringing out from pulpit and press, and in all assemblies—social, commercial, and religious. It is one that must be first laid in the foundations of any unity, mural or extra-mural; neighbourly, national, or world-wide; and it has to be understood here to be known hereafter.

During the half-century's survey in these pages, forces have been transformed from centrifugal to centripetal, the most significant being the gathering together of Churches, the federation of Colonies, the drawing near of the English-speaking nations, notably the Anglo-American Alliance, the Ocean Penny Postage, and the Peace Union of Thrones. These are towering witnesses to the Power Divine, and a justification for aspiration from local fraternal spheres to any sphere international seeking THE UNITY OF THE SPIRIT IN THE BOND OF PEACE.

www.ingramcontent.com/pod-product-compliance
Lightning Source LLC
Chambersburg PA
CBHW022136300426
44115CB00006B/212